KONIGUN NINJUTSU

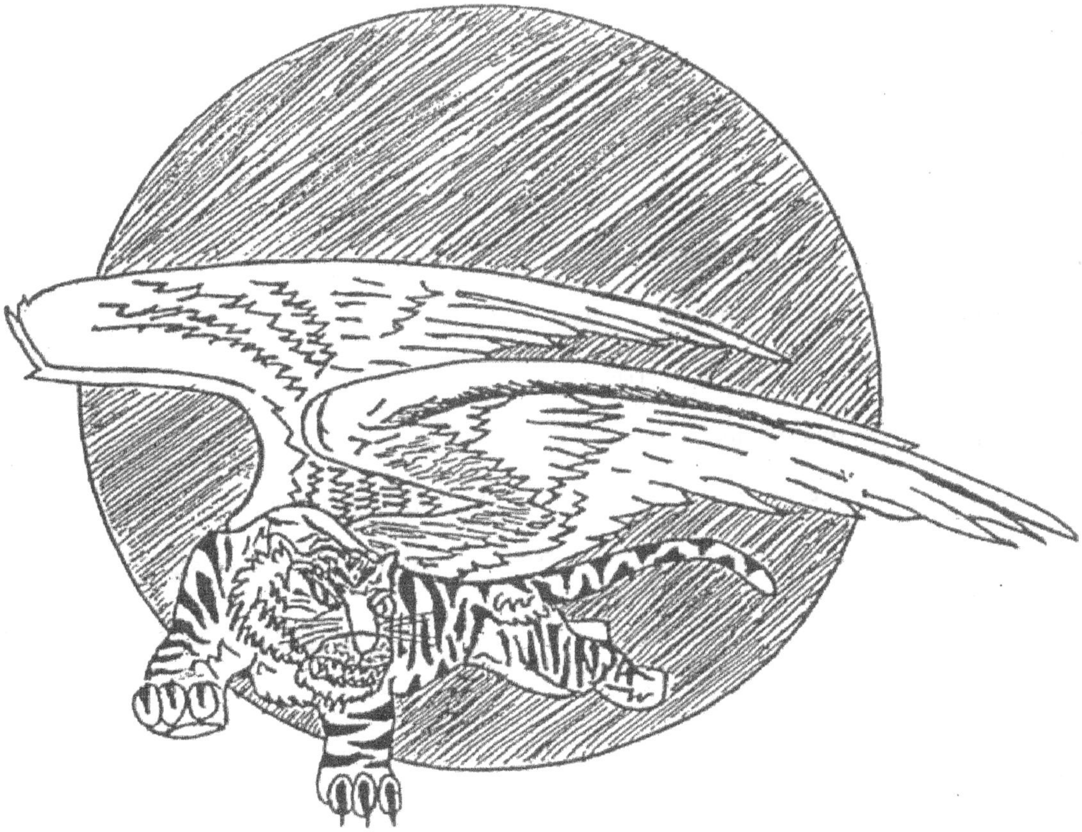

AUTHOR: SHIDOSHI BRYCE DALLAS

EDITING: JAY GREEN AND TRACY STEPHENS

MODEL: GENESE BUCKLER, ANTHONY OLBERDING, JEFF PERRY

ASSISTANT TYPEST: CHRIS GREENE, RICK LEMAK

SPECIAL THANKS TO: SAIJA SAN, SHIDOSHI FOR APPROVING PUBLIC RELEASE

KONIGUN NINJUTSU: THE TRAINING MANUEL VOLUME I; (STUDENT MANUAL)

PRINTED IN THE UNITED STATES OF AMERICA

FOR INFORMATION ADDRESS:

SEE OUR SITE AT **WWW.KONIGUNNINJUTSU.COM**

Preface

The following pages are written as a guide for the beginning martial artists as to what will be required of the student in the Konigun Ninjutsu Ryu. The martial arts school does not need to have each and ever piece of material covered in this book. Some schools may have similar or an entirely different form of organization. The key points for the beginning martial artists is to make sure that the school or system that they wish to join does display some key forms of organization. Examples of these organizational forms are rules and/or protocols; this allows you to see where your instructor stands on certain areas and helps maintain honesty. It is important that a style history exist. A history allows proof that the system is stable, tested, and will maintain the mindset of the organization. Some types of philosophy should exist because martial arts do not deal only with the body it should also strengthen the mind. In the 1900's many styles came into existence such as Isshinryu, Shotokan, Tang Soo Do, and other styles. A short lineage does not determine whether the system is good or bad. In the end, it is the practitioners that determine a style's worth.

This book was sixteen years in the making. The book was originally designed to assist the student's memory by outlining the art. This book is not designed to teach moves without a teacher.

Table of Contents

Greetings,

Through the years, my travels and travails in pursuit of my art, I have been asked many questions. One that sticks firmly in mind," Is life worth living? ". Yes, life is great and glorious. There is always that alternative between vertiginous summits and dreadful chasms. All is relative and there is no certainty. Realize this, and then you may live and make life worth living. We will teach you many things, and yet who can feel superior with so much to learn?

A person's example is more important than his teachings. Through living their teachings, a person raises his/her life to the level of prayer with his/her actions the request. This is ***KARMA.*** Nothing is high and nothing is low, my student, for the insect is just as important as a small man or a so-called great man. Reality is judged through the illusion of appearance, with light and dark interwoven so that any action may have the same aspect, (LOVE, NON INDULGENCE, KINDNESS, ETC.), and yet the most important thing, motive, may be different. So many people, who call themselves "spiritual," do not hesitate to judge others without truly knowing the motives responsible. Let us instead judge ourselves. We do know the motives of our actions, and this judging is very necessary and useful.

We have those, in life, who think so highly of themselves that they put their beliefs before the considerations of others. Even those, whose pursuit is the greater good, will in their fits of idealism tread on the worm while striving for the stars. All is relative with merely the passing and the eternal. What will be left of the bones of the greatest men in six thousand years time? Nothing may survive, perhaps, not even their memories. I am no greater than the bird in the sky or the worm in the ground once all that remains is my dust. The strongest force in nature is Love.

What about love? It's very simple. Love. Love more, and more intensely. And if your love is free from the poison of Ego-centrism, you will not feel superior, because you will have reached a deeper understanding and thereby be free from the dreadful pitfalls of spiritual arrogance. Assist the world as a signpost to those groping in darkness without understanding. Don't let the disparagement from others stop your enthusiastic loving and caring. Remain true and live in such a way that I shall never regret having helped you and taught you. Be a signpost for the style's family.

I did not write the hundreds of pages that make up our code, that tradition falls on those that came before, but like in the Bible's book of Job, "He knoweth the way that I take. When He hath tried me, I shall come forth as gold" (Chapter 23: 10). Here is a way to reach out and to touch people and help them better themselves in spirit, mind, and body, as well as how to protect themselves. We can reach out to the young and hopefully help them to not make our mistakes.

The style will not hold anyone accountable for acts protecting family or self, however, woe to him who brings shame while seeking glory or *gain.* Physical courage, which despises all danger, will make a man brave in one way, and moral courage, which despises all opinion, will *make him brave in another*. To constitute a great man, both are necessary. Welcome to our journey as we strive for greatness.

Shidoshi Bryce Dallas

SHIDOSHI NOTE

LET IT BE KNOWN BY ALL THAT I, BRYCE DALLAS, THE SHIDOSHI, OF THE KONIGUN NINJUTSU SECT IN THE YEAR OF OUR LORD 1997, HEREBY DECREE THIS MANUAL WILL BE THE MIND SET OF OUR KONIGUN NINJUTSU-RYU. I WILL PERSONALLY ENFORCE THE RULES IN EVERY LEGAL MANNER.

GETTING STARTED IN KONIGUN NINJUTSU

All students who enter class with us will begin with no sash and hold the rank of apprentice. These students will be drilled in basic dojo etiquette and safety. After a student learns the basic requirements, he/she will earn the most important sash in the entire system…

The White Sash.

The beginning rank of white sash can be considered the most important rank because it is at this level that the student will form certain habits of study and practice. The student will also begin the journey down the path of self-development and awareness that will have he/she discovering new heights of self-achievement through discipline and honor.

You are encouraged to work out any time the school is open as long as a class other than your own is not in progress. At any point in your training, if you have a question about a technique or need help in any way, get the attention of an instructor and they will be glad to help you.

Wear the rank of white sash with the same pride that you would wear any other rank because it shows others that you have a willingness to learn more about yourself and the world you live in. Remember, we all have been a white sash at some time.

Attendance

Your learning and development depends on you. You need to regularly attend class. In addition to regular class, you will be encouraged to attend workshops, seminars, clinics, special workouts, tournaments, and other functions designed to enrich your martial arts learning process. Attendance at as many of these events as possible will speed the learning curve and make the whole process better for you.

We encourage students who are going to miss class or be late, to let us know in advance when possible so that we can schedule make up classes if necessary. Also, this courtesy to us will help to ensure that we can meet their needs wherever possible.

Attentiveness

When you enter the dojo, you should adopt an attitude of seriousness. This means that you should be concentrating on the martial arts that you are there for, and that you are paying for.

Payment of Tuition

All training fees are expected to be paid on the 25th of each month, in advance, as payment for the following month. A late fee will be assessed after the fifth of the month. If a tuition payment becomes two months late, you will be suspended from active training until applicable fees are collected.

Uniform Requirements

Students will wear the black gi (student uniform).
Instructors will wear uniforms that are approved by the Chief Instructor.

Promotion procedures

In order to eliminate the idea that a student will get a sash for showing up for a certain length of time, we do not place a minimum or maximum time in grade for a student to be promoted to his/her next sash. The student will be given certain tasks that must be completed before he/she will be eligible for his/her next sash. Once a student is eligible for promotion, he/she will be tested both mentally and physically on the knowledge required for the next rank.
Tests for the kyu (below black sash) ranks are open, and though no two tests will be exactly alike. The student may watch others test if the instructor and the testing students do not object.

Testing for Warrior Ranks will be conducted secretly and without warning. The student will announce his readiness for testing by completing a thesis that will be pre-arranged with the instructor and by writing a formal letter requesting the testing. Once the instructor has received those materials the potential black sash should be prepared to test at any time. A sample formal test request will be given to the student when he/she reach the brown sash rank. As soon as the student reaches brown sash he should get his thesis information, research, and write the thesis and turn in his formal request for testing.

Code of Ethics

To conduct myself at all times as a person striving to my utmost ability.

To live up to the high principles of the martial arts, through fraternity, humility, truth, and honor.

To adhere to the high standards set forth by this school and system.

To promote in any way, and to cast a favorable impression on, my participation in the martial arts.

To respect others and their rights, to protect the innocent, to forgive the ignorant, and to temper judgment with compassion.

To respect all martial arts as to contributing to the development of the individual, to refrain from intimating that any one martial art is inferior to another, and to recognize that each has value to the individual studying the art.

Honor

There are three basic tenants of honor.

Obligation - Obligation is the root of honor, and it includes all types of obligation. In eastern society, they have a concept called Giri. Giri literally translates to "the right reason" and is a moral duty to fulfill one's obligations. Obligation must be backed by justice and courage to be honorable. Obligation for the sake of obligation can be ugly and dishonorable as is displayed by the Yakuza crime syndicates.

Justice- Justice is the heart of honor. Justice provides for three levels of righteousness. The lowest level being honorable for fear of punishment. The middle is being honorable out of shame of being dishonorable. The final level is being honorable for the sake of honorableness. Justice says, "that fulfilling an obligation to a dishonorable person may be worse than not meeting your obligation at all."

Courage- Courage is the fortitude to do what is right no matter what the personal cost. Courage is a crucial requirement of warrior honor. Fear is acceptable only if overcome.

In order to be honorable, a warrior must determine if an obligation exists; he must weigh the situation for justice, and he must have courage enough to act.

At all times, the warrior should practice:

Truthfulness
Courtesy
Restraint
Loyalty
Service

STUDENT GUIDELINES

To sustain a high level of training in class, you as a student are asked to do the following:

Always arrive a few minutes before class to insure promptness.

Keep talking to a minimum during practice, and/or never talk while receiving instruction from your sensei (teacher).

If you need to ask a question, remember to raise your hand and wait to be recognized before speaking.

Move rapidly when lining up for class, or whenever you are asked to.

Always jigi (salute) when:

- Stepping on or off the training floor
- Greeting a black belt or any instructor
- After receiving personal instruction
- At the beginning and end of each workout

The martial arts, if misused, has the potential to do great harm or damage.

Never boast or show off in public, but rather display yourself and always have respect for others.

Avoid all unnecessary disagreements to escape trouble.

Never use profanity to express yourself; for this is only a strong way to express a weak mind.

Never enter the dojo intoxicated or even with alcohol on your breath. In the martial arts, we strive to keep a clear head and tell the truth at all times. Being intoxicated causes truth and understanding to become distorted and vague.

Always be patient, for the process is long in acquiring the powerful knowledge of the Martial Arts. Persevere in your training; you will become strong physically, mentally, and spiritually.

WORDS TO REMEMBER

Just because you do not understand something does not mean it is wrong. Try it and you might benefit from the results.

Your goal is to become proficient at everything you learn. Your instructor's goal is not to make you as good, but better than he/she is.

Always remember... even if you surpass your instructor in skill, he/she will always have knowledge to share with you.

Always have an open mind for it never fills and always has room for wisdom.

A man may hold more knowledge than any one book, but any one book may hold knowledge that he/she does not know.

To say "I can't" means you never will. To say, "I'll try," means you will eventually.

Give everything your full effort or nothing at all.

Do not try to rush through everything. Take your time to learn to do it right.

Learn technique first, and speed and strength second and third.

Always learn from your mistakes; do not become discouraged by them. Life is a learning process of trial and error.

Fighting is a last resort, and death is not an option.

Have honor in your style. Dishonoring other systems only disrespects your own.

The uniform you wear is a symbol of honor and should be taken care of and properly worn.

Respect is a must. Even other black belts honor their higher ranks and equals as well as their students. This is part of being humble.

When you wear any ryu symbol in public, you should conduct yourself in the same manner as though you were in class.

CLEANLINESS

This means yourself and your dojo are to be presentable. If you see a piece of paper or other hazard on the floor, pick it up! Dispose of it properly. Keep your fingernails and toe nails at a safe length. Tie back long hair and remove all jewelry.

EQUIPMENT REQUIREMENTS BY RANK

RANK	EQUIPMENT
White Sash	white sash, black gi, handbook
Gold Sash	gold sash, sparring equipment
Green Sash	green sash, 6' bo
Blue Sash	blue sash, tonfa, han-bo, white karate belt, kama
Brown Sash	brown sash, mamba, yari
First Degree	black sash, nun-chaku, san-setsu-kan, diato
Second Degree	same black sash, diato
Third Degree	same black sash, grappling hook, shaken, shinbo/shabo, sai
Fourth Degree	same black sash, shurikens, caltrops, manriki-qusari, blowgun, shoge, ninja-to, 2 wakazashi
Fifth Degree	Private Information

PHYSICAL REQUIREMENTS BY RANK

In order to progress further in your rank you must perfect your technique at your current rank. The kick grid is used to build stronger and faster kicking technique.

The kick grid is to be done with both the right and left legs and it will use each of the 12 basic kicks.

Kick Grid (Students need to complete according to their rank.)

- Gold- 1 grid per leg
- Green- 1 grid per leg
- Blue- 1 grid per leg
- Brown- 2 grids per leg

Physical Training

- Run 5 miles in 42 minute
- 100 push-ups
- 60 sit-ups
- 20 pull-ups
- 12 mile 45 pound ruck in 3 hours

The physical training is required each time you test for a black sash degree.

OVERVIEW

In the Konigun way of Ninjutsu, we teach a self-development program based on sound martial arts theory and training. We stress the mental and physical lessons of martial arts. Included in our training are:

Empty Hand Techniques - The hard and soft style fundamental body movements for self-confidence and self-protection are studied in depth.

Weapons - The student is familiarized in both ancient and modern weapons. This familiarization is used to sharpen the empty hand technique, teach the student to deal with an armed aggressor and to develop coordination and reflexes.

Sparring - New to the art of Ninjutsu is the concept of sparring. Students will be trained to apply their skills in both practical contact sparring and kumite. Students who wish to compete in tournaments will be fully trained and encouraged to compete, but those who do not wish to compete will not be faulted in any way.

Mental Development - Students will be taught meditation techniques that can be used to enhance their physical, emotional, and energetic considerations of self-protection and combat. Additionally, meditation is an excellent way to relieve stress. Students will be taught to recognize the various moods and emotions that emerge under pressure of conflict or confrontation. By recognizing these moods and emotions, the student can learn to control himself and his moods/emotions.

Wilderness Survival
Also covered in this course are special classes in:
Stealth, camouflage and concealment, anatomy, and first aid

The student is encouraged to keep an open mind and a positive attitude. The students are encouraged to work together in a family oriented atmosphere because we have found that encouragement and support from each other drives us to achieve goals set forth in the form of day to day challenges. Overcoming these obstacles and striving for success will reflect in every aspect of your life.

CLASS PRAYER

DEAR LORD, BLESS US WITH PEACE, ENLIGHTEN US WITH THE KNOWLEDGE OF WHEN TO FIGHT AND WHEN NOT TO FIGHT. KEEP US FROM HARM AND DANGER; GIVE US THE STRENGTH TO STAY AWAY FROM TROUBLE. LET US BE THAT WHICH IS COMFORTABLE TO OTHERS. LORD, WE ASK THAT YOU HELP US JUDGE WITH OUR HEARTS AND NOT OUR DESIRES.

IN THE LORDS NAME WE PRAY,

AMEN

HININ

CATEGORY ONE (YOSU ICHI): MUSUBU OBI (TIE SASH)

Tips about a sash and on tying a sash:

A. The sash should be rolled at all time and ready to wear.
B. The sash is either rolled or hung never folded.
C. The sash should wrap around the waist in a front to back right side pattern.
D. The right hand should work with the underside end of the sash and do all the work in tying the sash.
E. When tying the knot the underside end of the waist wrap should wrap over both layers of the sash when tying the sash.
F. For a student knot the tying end goes around the other end then between the horizontal layers and the vertical end and pulls straight up, as if tying the first part of a bow. Return the same tying end back through the knot to create a loop at the top of the horizontal layers. The knot is then pulled to the right side of the body.
G. For a warrior's knot all the steps are the same except when making the knot the tying end will go behind the horizontal layers then fall back through the loop of the tying end to form a non-slipping knot.
H. The karate belt did not come into existence until 1888 when it was adapted by the judo systems.

CATEGORY TWO (YOSU NI): DESHI CHIKAI (STUDENT OATH)

1. SCHOOL STUDENT OATH (DOJO KUN)

2. The oath: "I AN UCHIDESHI (APPRENTICE) OF THE KONIGUN-RYU OF THE KAGEBUSHI SHIDARA, FROM THE SAIJA FAMILY WILL UPHOLD MY RANK AT ALL TIMES IN EVERY WAY AND OBEY MY SUPERIORS; OF THIS I,

(YOUR NAME)

____

GIVE MY WORD OF HONOR FOR ALL TIME.

3. This oath is a student's promise not to abuse his/her skills and for him/her to conduct himself/herself properly.

4. What is meant by, "up hold my rank at all times" is that the student will obey the rules set forth in the manual, to keep his/her skills up to standards, and conduct him or herself as a gentleman or as a lady.

5. What is meant by, "obey my superiors" is that the student will follow any higher sash's instruction while in a training area. The student will follow any black sash's instructions at all times, and at any location. This is to secure orderly running, safety, manners, and understanding at all functions, as well as, good public relations.

6. This oath should be given and received seriously by all parties. Only a black sash may give the oath. The black sash must be in good standing with the Konigun Ninjutsu.

**** OATH MUST BE MEMORIZED.**

CATEGORY THREE (YOSU SAN): THE KONIGUN SASH (KONIGUN OBI)

1. The Konigun sash is 4 inches wide. When tied it will not hang below the student's knees and the ends will be within 3 inches of each other.

CATEGORY FOUR (YOSU SHI): THE KONIGUN SASH KNOT (KONIGUN OBI MUSUBIME)

1. Konigun ninjutsu has a very special knot that has been handed down through out generations. We are not the only style with this knot. There are other publicly known styles in the united states that use this same knot. The purpose of this knot is to show *grace, honor, and respect.* The sash knot is tied in this special manner to prevent it from sticking out from the body where it would be in the way of working weapons. This type of knot also allows the person to lie flat on his/her stomach and to perform acrobatics. The karate square knots represent respect. But it sticks out from the body, often ending up in the way of close sword rotations. The karate knot also acts as a "hard ball" pushing in on your stomach when you lie face down. All ninja sects that use the akai-shrine belt knot are from an akai-ninjutsu sect. The akai-ninjutsu sect is better known as a red Ninjutsu sect. A red ninjutsu style is "good" and not evil.

CATEGORY FIVE (YOSU GO): NUMBERS (BANGO)
****MANDATORY LANGUAGE FOR 1-10****

**1.	ICHI
**2.	NI
**3.	SAN
**4.	SHI
**5.	GO
**6.	ROKU
**7.	SHICHI
**8.	HACHI
**9.	KU
**10.	JU
11.	JU-ICHI
19.	JU-KU
20.	NI-JU
100.	HYAKU
500.	GOHYAKU
1000.	ICHIMAN/SEN
5000.	GOSEN
10000.	JUMAN
100000.	HYAKUMAN

Native Japanese Numbers

Number	**Word**	**Pronunciation**
1	Kitotsu	(HE-TOTE-SUE)
2	Futatsu	(FUU-TOT-SUE)
3	Mittsu	(MEET-SUE)
4	Yotsu	(YOTE-SUE)
5	Itsutsu	(EET-SOOT-SUE)
6	Muttsu	(MOOT-SUE)
7	Nanatsu	(NAH-NOT-SUE)
8	Yattsu	(YAHT-SUE)
9	Kokanotsu	(KOE-KOE-NOTE-SUE)
10	To	(TOE)

CATEGORY SIX (YOSU ROKU): COLLOQUIALISMS (ZOGU GO)

1. RECOVER TO LAST STANCE (TAI-HI) **(MANDATORY LANGUAGE)**

2. NINJUTSU STANCE (HA-SHI)

   A. Spring up and place feet shoulder width apart.
   B. Place hands, in fist position, at the top of the hip joints on the side of the body.

3. NINJUTSU SEAT (KA-SHIA)

   A. Sit down with your feet underneath your buttocks by kneeling with the right leg first.
   B. Overlap one foot over the other.
   C. Place the hands on top of the hip joints.

CATEGORY SEVEN (YOSU SHICHI): EXERCISE (UNDO)

1. 10 COUNT PUSH UP (OSU KAMI JU KAZOERU)
   (Order of hand positions for the 10-count push-up is: start out palms flat on the ground then bridge up to fingertips, roll forward to thumb and 1st joint of all fingers, roll forward to fist with thumbs pointing inward, turn fists so thumbs point away from the body, then roll fists back to palm hands.)
2. 06 COUNT SIT UP (SUWARU KAMI ROKU KAZOERU)
3. 10 COUNT JUMP HOP (HANERU ODERU JU KAZOERU)
4. RIGHT/LEFT SCISSORS (MIGI/HADARI HASAMI)
5. SIDE SPLITS (YOKO WARU)
6. WALL SCISSORS (KABE HASAMI)
7. FLOOR SCISSORS (YUKA HASAMI)
8. WALL SIDE SPLITS (KABE YOKO WARU)
9. FLOOR SIDE SPLITS (YUKA YOKO WARU)

TIPS: Remember that when doing partner stretching, the person on the ground will tell the person stretching him/her when to stop and hold. The person holding will then stop, count to five, and then the person stretching will tell the person lying down to push against you causing resistance. The person standing will then count to five again and say release.

When performing push-ups be sure to always cross the right foot over the left, the arms are slightly wider than the shoulders, the back is straight, look up at a 45-degree angle so that you are glancing straight out from the body, on the downward motion the arms must break the shoulder plain, and if a break/ breather is needed then the hands do not leave the ground and the knees can not touch the ground. A tip to help perform more push-ups is to grab the ground with the fingers. This tightens the arms and keeps them from shaking thus allowing you to push up and down in a faster controlled manner. To aid in strengthening the wrist you can curl the fingers toward the forearms and perform push-ups on the tops/ backs of the wrists.

When performing sit-ups the knees are always bent, the individual aiding the performer always sits on the performer's feet and grabs at the knee joints. Remember; do not push the knees together. Touch the right elbow to the left knee and the left elbow to the right knee as you alternate lifting each shoulder off the ground.

Crunches will aid in getting the stomach muscles in shape faster. To perform a crunch lay on your back and lift the feet off the ground so that the thighs are perpendicular to the body. Extend the hands out in front of the body so that they are parallel to the thighs. Touch the right hand to the left knee and the left hand to the right knee as you alternate lifting each shoulder off the ground approximately 2-3 inches.

SHIROTO

CATEGORY ONE (YOSU ICHI): JIGI (SALUTE)

The right foot/leg will always move first.

1. SECT SALUTE (RYU JIGI)

   A. Place feet together by bringing the right foot to the left foot.
   B. Put the hands together in the center of the body.
   C. Place the hands 6-8 inches out from the body.
   D. Fold the index fingers back so that they touch the thumbs.
   E. Line up the knuckles on the hands.
   F. When you salute bend at the knees, do not bend the back, keep the hands level and do not lean forward.

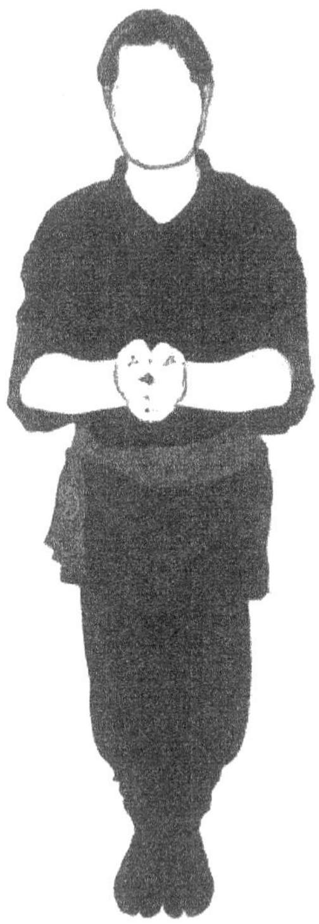

2. SECT SEATED SALUTE (RYU ZA JIGI)

   A. Sit down with your feet underneath your buttocks by kneeling with the right knee first.
   B. Overlap right foot over the other.
   C. Put the hands together in the center of your body.
   D. Place the hands 6-8 inches out from the center front of body.
   E. Fold the index fingers back so that they touch the thumbs.
   F. Line up the knuckles on the hands.
   G. When you salute, bend the back and lower your whole torso.

3. COMMON KARATE SALUTE (BUDO JIGI)

A. Place the feet together by bringing the right foot to the left foot.
B. Place the hands on the side of the body.
C. Salute by bending forward at the waist.

4. COMMON SEATED SALUTE (BUDO ZA JIGI)

A. Sit down with your feet underneath your buttocks by kneeling with the right leg first.
B. Overlap right foot over the other.
C. Place the hands down the side of the body.
D. Salute by bending the back and lowering the torso forward.

5. WARRIOR SALUTE (BUSHI JIGI)

A. Place feet together by bringing the right foot to the left foot.
B. Make a fist with the left hand.
C. Place it in the right hand and close the fingers down over top the right hand. The Japanese styles are right over left, but other styles maybe left over right.
D. Place the hands 6-8 inches out in front of the body.
E. Salute by lowering the head, and pushing the hands out.

6. WARRIOR SEATED SALUTE (BUSHI ZA JIGI)

A. Sit down with your feet underneath your buttocks by kneeling with the right leg first.
B. Overlap right foot over the other.
C. Place it in the right hand and close the fingers down over top the right hand. The Japanese styles are right over left, but other styles maybe left over right.
D. Place the hands 6-8 inches out in front of the body.
E. Salute by lowering the head, and pushing the hands out.

7. <u>WARRIOR SALUTE FOR PUPIL (BUSHI JIGI NO SHOSEI)</u>

A. Place feet together by bringing the right foot to the left foot.
B. Make a fist with the left hand.
C. Make a shuto hand with the right hand.
D. Place the left fist in the right shuto hand. The Japanese styles are right over left, but other styles maybe left over right.
E. Place the hands 6-8 inches out in front of the body. Salute by lowering the head, and pushing the hands out.

8. <u>FORM SALUTE (KATA JIGI)</u>

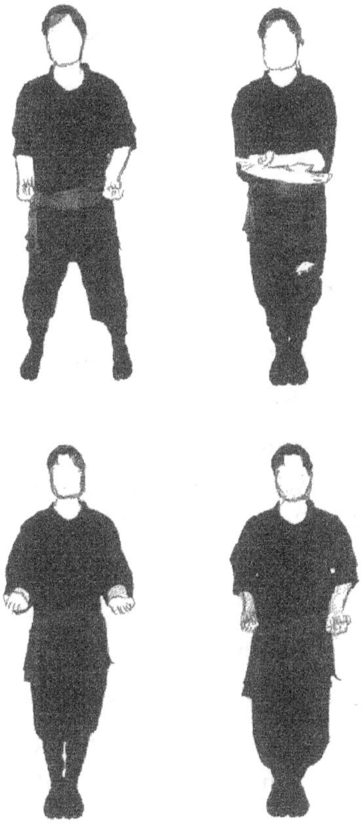

A. Get into jusha kamae.
B. Bring the right foot to the left foot.
C. Simultaneous with the placing of the feet bring two shuto hands out in front of the body and cross them.
D. As the hands return to fists at the side of the body, place the feet back into jusha kamae by moving the right foot out.

9. CEREMONY SALUTE (REISHIKI JIGI)

B. Get into ka-shia.
C. Place the right hand on the ground first followed by the left.
D. Place your forehead between the hands on the ground.
E. Rise up and return the hands back to ka-shia in reverse order.

****SALUTE FUNCTION (HATARAKI JIGI)**

A. ENTRANCE (IRU)

1. Perform a sect salute.
2. Step forward with the right foot and do not break the salute until you move the left foot.

B. EXIT (DE-GUCHI)

1. Perform a sect salute.
2. Put the right foot behind the left foot and spin around facing in the opposite direction.
3. Step forward with the left foot and do not break the salute until you move the right foot.

C. STAY (YAMU)

1. Get in jusha kamae.
2. Perform a sect salute. Remember to step with the right foot.
3. Return to jusha kamae by only moving the right foot.

NOTES:

1. Salute when passing within four feet from the front of a higher sash and await the return of the salute before continuing travel. Use ryu jigi.
2. Salute when passing through a line of viewing and / or conversation of a higher sash, then wait for the higher sash to return salute. Use ryu jigi.
3. Salute when a higher rank has finished giving direction or orders and await his return salute to signify that he is finished. When receiving orders always stand in front of the higher rank it is disrespectful to stand anywhere else.
4. Salute when entering or exiting the training areas, no return salute required.
5. When entering or exiting exterior doors of the martial art building, where the training area is not directly within the door, no salute is required.
6. When entering or exiting the test, the ryu jigi will be used.

7. When entering and exiting the kumite, the ryu jigi will be used. If weapons are used in the kumite, then use weapon's jigi.
8. When entering the ring of kumite for the first time in a series of kumite to be had, the competitors and official will salute the spectators, and then the competitors will salute the official (if any other than the center judge), then the center judge, and last, each other. At all times ryu jigi will be used. The aforesaid will occur only at the beginning and then again at the last match, with the salute order being in reverse of the beginning salute order. All matches in between the beginning and ending matches will use what is known as half-ceremonial salutes, where the spectators are not saluted.
9. The ryu jigi will be used when entering or exiting the formation placement.
10. The ryu jigi will be used when entering or exiting a training group.
11. The kata will always use the kata jigi.
12. The office room is considered a training area and the ryu jigi will be used.
13. The weight rooms will not use a jigi unless being used to train martial arts.

***** SPECIAL NOTE: THE SALUTES ARE USED FOR SAFETY AS WELL AS FOR RESPECT. THE USE OF SALUTES WHEN ACKNOWLEDGED BY THE INSTRUCTOR WILL MAKE STUDENT PRESENCE KNOWN TO THE INSTRUCTOR.**

NOTE: SALUTING

It is common for people to ask about the practice of saluting. In particular, many people are concerned that saluting may have some religious significance. It does not. In western culture, it is considered proper to shake hands when greeting someone for the first time, to say "please" when making a request, and to say "thank you" to express gratitude. In Japanese culture, saluting (at least partly) may fulfill all these functions.

Incorporating this particular aspect of Japanese culture into our practice serves several purposes: it inculcates a familiarity with an important aspect of Japanese culture in practice. This is especially important for anyone who may wish, at some time, to travel to Japan to practice. There is also a case to be made for simply broadening one's cultural horizons.

Saluting may be an expression of respect. As such, it expresses open mindedness and a willingness to learn from one's teachers and fellow students.

Saluting to a partner may serve to remind you that your partner is a person-not a practice dummy. Always train within the limits of your partner's abilities.

The initial salute, which signifies the beginning of formal practice, is much like a "ready, begin," uttered at the beginning of an examination. So long as class is in session, you should behave in accordance with certain standards of deportment. Class should be somewhat like a world unto itself. While in this "world," your attention should be focused on the practice.

Saluting out is like signaling a return to the "ordinary" world.

CATEGORY TWO (YOSU NI): STANCES (KAMAE)

1. SEAT (ZA)

   A. Sit down anyway you want to.

2. STAND (DAI)

   A. Stand anyway you want to.

3. SIT AT EASE (ZA ORUKA NA)

   A. Sit with the feet in cross leg style. Right leg in front.
   B. Place the hands on top of the knees in a fist position with palm side up.

Note: If you are already in a kashia and told to go to a za oruka na then lean to the left and roll the feet out to the right.

4. <u>STAND AT EASE (DAI ORUKA NA)</u>

   A. Place feet shoulder width apart
   B. Put the left wrist in the right hand
   C. Pull shoulder back and stand without moving.

5. <u>ATTENDANT STANCE (JUSHA KAMAE)</u>

   A. Place feet shoulder width apart with feet forward
   B. Place hands on the waist in fist position at top of hipbone.
   C. Push chest out and pull stomach in.
   D. Rise up slightly on the balls of the feet and gently tense all the muscles in the body.

6. COMMON MARTIAL ARTS STANCE (BUDO KAMAE)

A. Stand with feet pointing forward at shoulder width.
B. For a right side stance the right foot will drop back and out. Make sure that the feet are a little more than shoulder width apart.
C. The front foot always stays pointed at the
the
opponent.
D. The back foot is always perpendicular to the front foot.
E. Bend the knees and rise upon the balls of the feet. Do this while making sure that your feet are not in line with each other. If the feet are in line then there will be no balance in the stance.
F. Shoulders should be at a 45-degree angle with the feet, and the head should always be pointed forward.
G. The backhand or right hand will be in a fist, and it will rest on the hip.
H. The front hand or left hand will be in a knife hand. The hand will extent out in front of the body at an angle greater than 90-degrees, and the knife hand will rest in the center of the chest.

FOOT PATTERNS FOR THE BASIC STANCE

A. NON-AGGRESSIVE

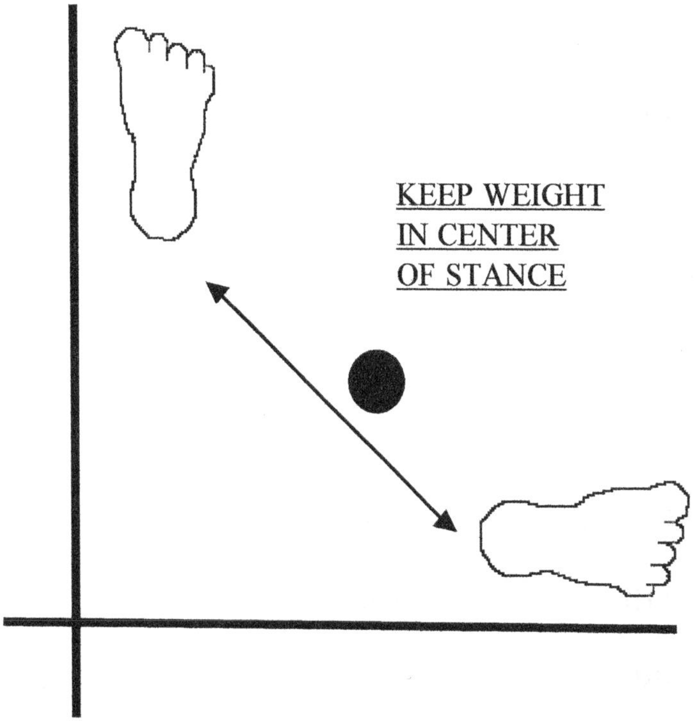

B. AGGRESSIVE

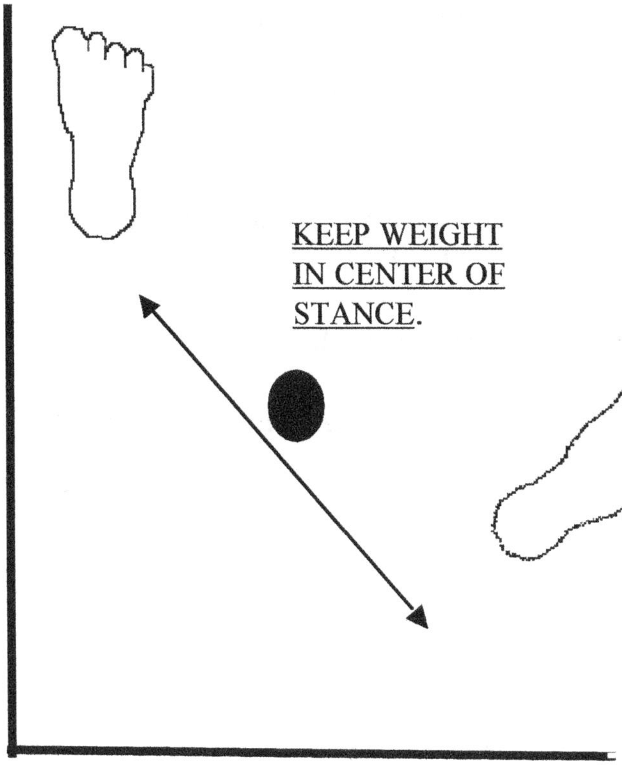

CATEGORY THREE (YOSU SAN): RANK (KURAI) *{JAPANESE COLOR NOT MANDATORY}*

TITLE: (GEDAI)	SASH: (OBI)	TRANSLATION: (NAOSU)
1. HININ	WHITE (SHIROI)	COMMON PERSON
2. SHIROTO	GOLD (KOGANE)	AMATEUR
3. DESHI	GREEN (NAMA)	PUPIL
4. MONJIN	BLUE (AI)	ADVANCE PUPIL
5. SENPAI	BROWN (KURI-IRO)	SENIOR PUPIL
6. BUSHI	BLACK (KURO)	WARRIOR
7. SAMURAI	KURO	DIVINE WARRIOR
8. YOSHI	KURO	DISTINGUISH WARRIOR
9. TAIBUSHI	KURO	GRAND WARRIOR
10. KAGEBUSHI	KURO (GOLD TORA)	SHADOW WARRIOR
*** KUNICHI	KURO (BLUE TORA)	FEMALE SHADOW WARRIOR
*** YAMABUSHI	KURO (GREEN)	DISTINGUISH NINJA "MOUNTAIN WARRIOR"
11. MEIJIN	KURO (RED TORA)	MALE MASTER
*** MIKO	KURO (PURPLE TORA)	FEMALE MASTER
12. TAISHU	KURO (BROWN TORA)	GRANDMASTER
13. SHIDOSHI	KURO (SILVER TORA)	DIRECTOR

MEIYO- is a prefix for spouses of a black sash.

FUNCTION CHAIN OF COMMAND

1. Shunin Coordinator
2. Chunin Advisor
3. Jonin Technician

NOTE: this chain of command is developed for running cam| other functions.

CATEGORY FOUR (YOSU SHI): BLOCKS (KIRE)

1. SIDE (YOKO)

A. Common stance.
B. Arm is directly out in front of the body. The arm is no more than shoulder width and the angle between the fist and the biceps is greater than 90-degrees.

2. KIDNEY (MURADO)

A. Common stance
B. Blocking arm is out from the side of the body and covering the kidneys.
C. The forearm is angled at a 45-degrees so that the wrist is lower than the elbow. This is done in order to make sure that the strike will glide off the block and not make a direct connection.
D. The inside angle between the forearm and the biceps is greater than 90-degrees. This strengthens the block and keeps it from collapsing.
E. Always make sure that the wrist is not bent. The wrist should always be inline with the forearm. This will make the block stronger and keep the wrist from being broken.
F. The wrist is slightly turned forward toward the opponent in order to make sure that the meat of the arm is used in the block.
G. Do not let the forearms get to close to the body. Never let them rest on the body.

3. NECK AND HEAD (KUBI)

A. Common stance
B. Blocking arm is out from the side of the body and covering the side of the neck and head.
C. The blocking arm covers half the face and angles down at a 45-degree angle toward the shoulder. This is done to assure that the strike will glide off the block and not make a direct connection.
D. The inside angle between the forearm and the biceps is greater than 90-degrees. This strengthens the block and keeps it from collapsing.
E. Always make sure that the wrist is not bent. The wrist should always be inline with the forearm. This will make the block stronger and keep the wrist from being broken.
F. The wrist is slightly turned forward toward the opponent in order to make sure that the meat of the arm is used in the block.
G. Never let the block rest on the head.

4. <u>OVERHEAD (NOKORU)</u>

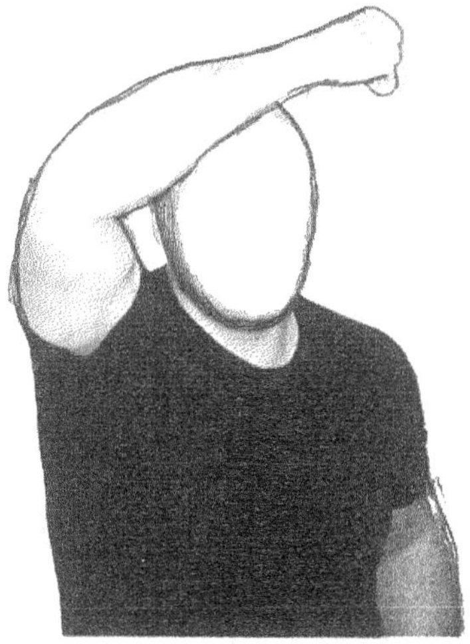

A. Common stance.
B. Blocking arm is raised above the head.
C. Make sure that the inside angle between the forearm and the biceps is greater than 90- degrees. This strengthens the block and keeps it from collapsing.
D. The forearm and wrist are slightly angled so that the wrist is higher than the elbow. This allows for the strike to slide off the block instead of making a direct connection.
E. Always make sure that the wrist is not bent. The wrist should always be inline with the forearm. This will keep the wrist from being broken and make the block stronger.
F. The wrist is slightly turned forward toward the opponent in order to make sure that the meat of the arm is used in the block.
G. Never let the block rest on the head.
H. Never lean sideways to assist the block.
I. Never lean the head. Always keep the neck straight.

5. <u>CATCH (TORU)</u>

A. Common stance.
B. Get in left neck block position.
C. Do a left face block and stop the face block in its finished position (on the right side of the body).
D. Make a knife hand with your right hand and bring it up to the inside of the elbow joint on the left face block. From here slide the right hand out and the left arm down at the same time while keeping the right hand in a knife hand.
E. As the knife hand slides rotate the hand so that the palm of the hand is facing outwards.
F. At the same time the palm is rotating outwards bring the thumb down so the right hand is in the shape of a "C", or catch position.
G. Drop the left arm down to your side so you are ready for future strikes or blocks.

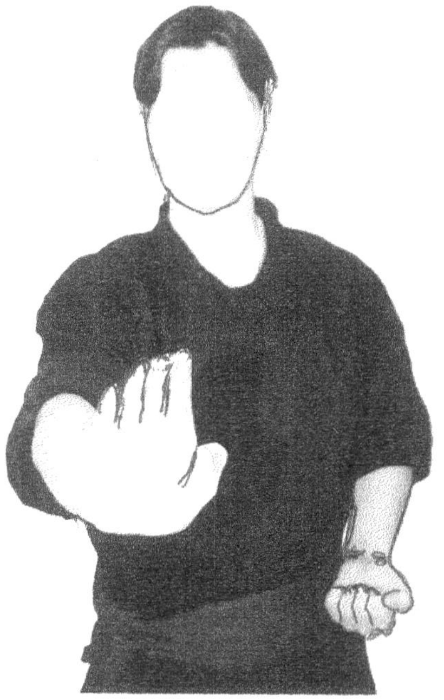

6. <u>FACE (KAO)</u>

A. Common stance.
B. Bring arm up into neck block.
C. Drop the elbow down and across the face.
D. While the elbow is dropping, rotate the forearm so that the meat of the arm is used in the block. This is done by twisting the fist, so that the palm points toward the face.
E. The forearm will swing directly in front of the face and carry the strike away from the target area.
F. If opponent punches with a right punch and you perform a left face block this will bring the opponent's punch across the face and out away from the body. The opponent's backside will be left exposed. If the opponent punches with a right hand and you perform a right face block the opponent's right side of the face and neck will be exposed as well as his front section, but your right side will be exposed to the attacker.
G. This block is used to grapple and as a second defense.

7. UPPER CROSS (AGERU JIRERU)

A. Common stance.
B. Make an "X" block with the forearms.
C. The "X" block should extend above the head, and the backs of the hands should be facing each other.
D. Be sure to squat with the legs when using this block against a strike. The squatting allows you to absorb some of the force from the strike.
E. The flats of your arms (back of hand side) should be on the outside or impact area.
F. Since objects will impact on an up or down motion: the forward 45-degree angle impact zone should be turned to meet the impact.

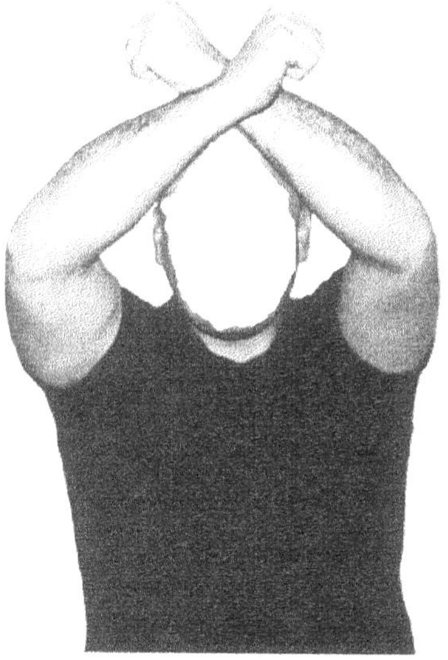

8. MIDDLE CROSS (NAKABA JIRERU)

A. Common stance.
B. Make an "X" block with the forearms.
C. The "X" lock should be positioned in the center of the chest, and the thumb side of the fists should be facing each other.
D. Be sure to have an angle of 90-degrees or better between the chest and the block. This will allow you to absorb some of the force from the strike.
E. Never allow the cross block to rest on the body.
F. It does not matter which arm is in front on the cross; unless you are in a forward stance, then the leg that is forward should have the same arm in front on the block.

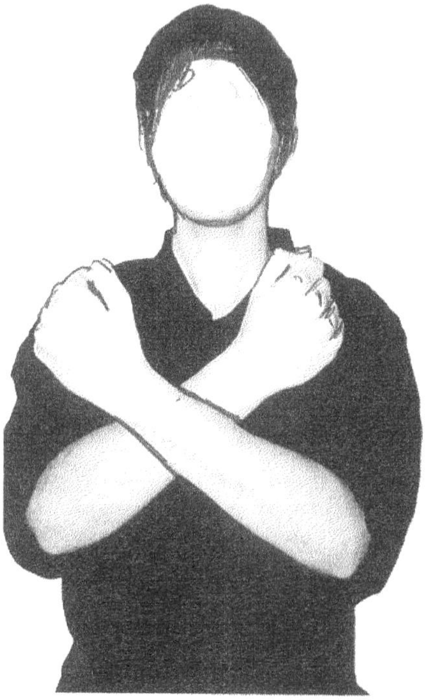

9. LOWER CROSS (SHITA NO JIRERU)

A. Common stance.
B. Make an "X" block with the forearms.
C. The "X" block should be positioned beside the front leg in the stance, and the backside of the fists will be facing each other.
D. In order to get the block lower, do not bend the back. Always squat with the legs, and always keep the back straight.
E. Make sure you squat low so that you can rise up when blocking a strike. This will allow you to absorb some of the force from the strike.
F. If you lean over the block and miss the strike, then the strike will hit you. Always squat and never lean.

10. <u>ROLL (KOROGARU)</u>

A. Common stance.
B. Make a ridge hand or knife hand with the hand that you intend to block with and bring the blocking arm in a circular motion across the front of the body.
C. Strike the wrist of the opponent with the ridge hand or knife hand and roll your hand around so that you can grab the opponent's wrist.
D. Depending on where you want the opponent to be depends on which roll catch is used. If opponent punches with right hand and you perform a right hand roll catch, then the opponent's backside will be exposed. If opponent punches with a right hand and you perform a left-handed roll catch, then the opponent's front (face, chest, etc.) will be exposed, and so will your right side so make sure that the right hand is ready to block.

11. <u>PARALLEL (SOROTE ORU)</u>

A. Common stance.
B. Make two side blocks, and keep them shoulder's width apart.
C. This block is used for a lot of kappo moves.
D. Elbows should be more than 90-degrees.
E. Back of fists should point outward.
F. Do not let the backs of the arms rest on your sides.

12. <u>HORIZONTAL (TAIRAKA NA)</u>

A. Common stance.
B. Make two forearm blocks extending across the front of the body.
C. Turn the forearms so that the thickest area of the arms are facing out, and thumbs are face up.
D. Make sure the angles between the forearm and the chest are 90-degrees or better.
E. Forearms should be a hands length apart according to the person who is using the block.

NOTES:

1. To say side block, use the words "yoko kire" as the diagram above details.
2. Be sure the elbow is kept bent at an angle between 90 and 110 -degree when blocking.
3. Use meat to block with, never bone. (Meat bruises, bones break.)
4. Try to carry all strikes to the outside of the body. However, some strike may force a cross-body defense. Try to turn the body away to the side the block is coming from to assist the effort.
5. Remember to deflect or redirect the strike instead of attempting to stop the strike.

CATEGORY FIVE (YOSU GO): HANDS (TE)

1. <u>WAR FIST (KOBUSHI)</u>

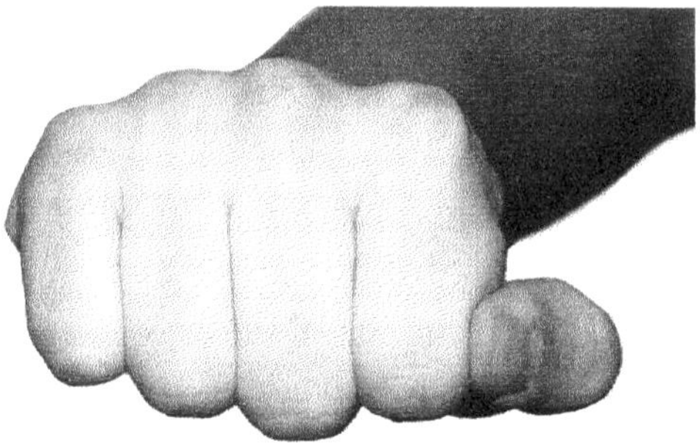

A. Open the hand.
B. Roll the fingers toward the center of the palm while keeping the roll tight.
C. Once the fingers are roll to the center of the palm place the thumb in the crease of the index finger.
<u>D. Do not wrap the thumb under the fist!</u>

2. <u>BACK FIST (URA-KEN)</u>

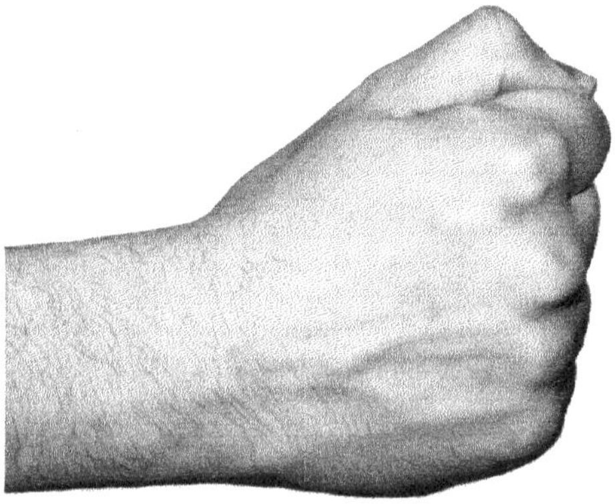

A. Make a fist.
B. The strike from this hand will be the backside of the fist.

3. <u>HAMMER FIST (KANAD'ZUSHI-TE)</u>

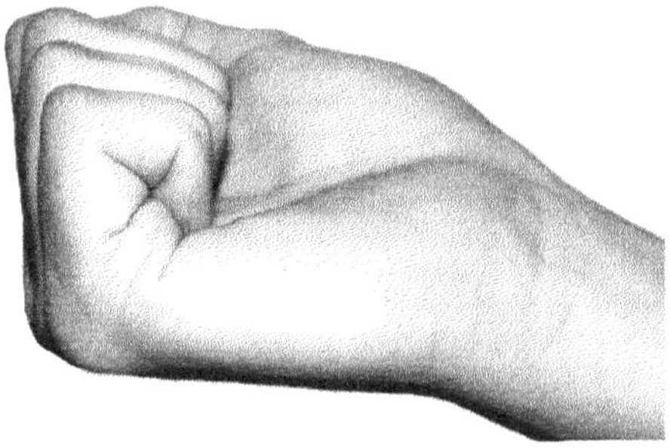

A. Make a fist.
B. This strike from this hand will come from the "little finger" side of the fist.

4. <u>CLUTCH FIST (NIGIRU)</u>

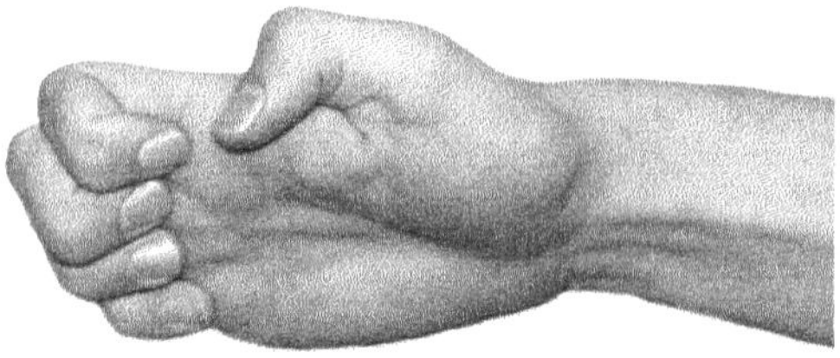

A. Make a fist.
B. Slowly open the fist until the fingernails are directly opposite the palm.
C. Place the thumb along the side of the hand so that it lays flat against the hand.
D. The strike from this hand will come from the four knuckles.

5. SWORD HAND (SHUTO)

A. Make a clutch fist.
B. Roll the fingers on out so that the fingers are pointing forward with a slight curve in them.
C. Place the thumb along the side of the index finger so that all the fingers on the hand point in the same direction.
D. Strikes from this hand will come from the "little finger" side of the hand in a knife or sword style movement.

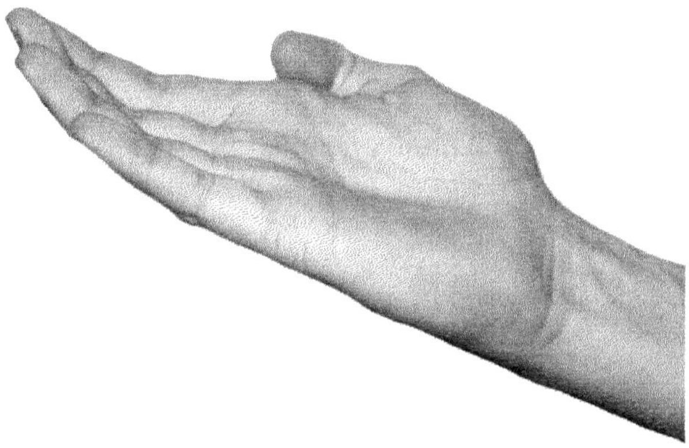

6. SPEAR HAND (YARI-TE)

A. Make a shuto hand.
B. The strikes from this hand comes from the fingertips in a spear like motion.
C. Slightly bend all the fingers to make for a tighter hand.

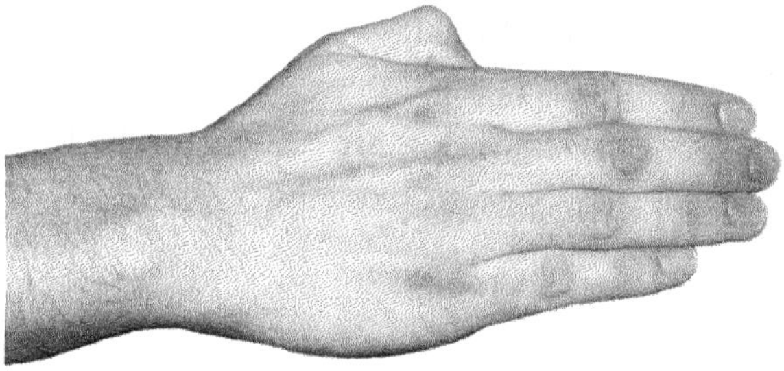

7. RIDGE HAND (MINE-TE)

A. Make a knife hand.
B. Place the thumb to the center of the hand so that the hand has a flat surface from the index finger to the wrist.
C. Strikes are made with the area between the thumb and index knuckles.
D. Slightly bend all the fingers to make for a tighter hand

8. <u>WHIP HAND (MUCHI-TE)</u>

A. Make a shuto hand.
B. Strike with the backside of the hand and not the fingers.
C. Slightly bend all the fingers to make for a tighter hand.

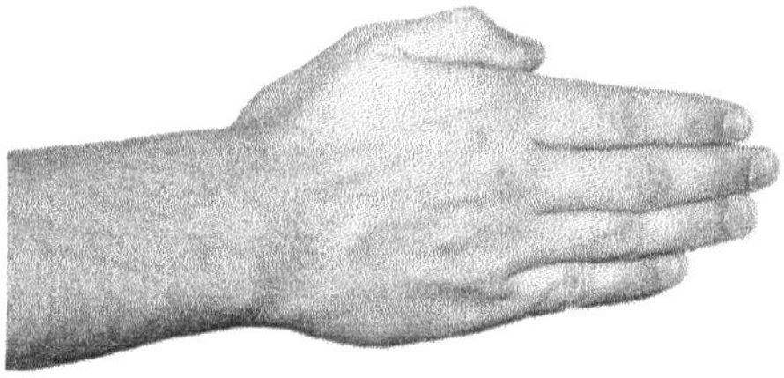

9. <u>TIGER'S EYE (TORA-ME)</u>

A. Make a shuto hand.
B. Spread the fingers so that the hand forms a "v" shape.
C. Slightly bend all the fingers to make for a tighter hand.
D. Strikes are made with the fingers in a spear like motion.

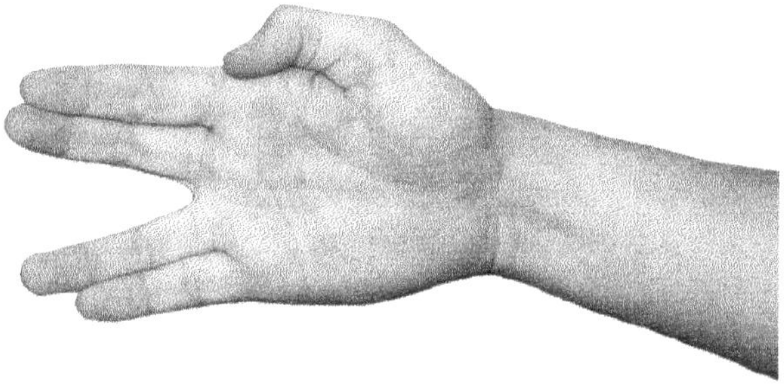

10. <u>CLUTCH PALM (NIGIRU-TANAGOKORO)</u>

A. Make a clutch fist.
B. The strike is made by the flattened area at the base of the palm.

CATEGORY SIX (YOSU ROKU): MOTION BLOCKS (UNDO KIRE)

FORE NOTES: **A.** Set up in jusha kamae.
B. Start in a saddle stance with only the right arm in side.
C. Block position with the left hand in a fist position at the side.

1. LEFT SIDE	(HADARI YOKO)
2. RIGHT SIDE	(MIGI YOKO)
3. [L] NECK & [R] KIDNEY	(MIGI KUBI & HADARI MURADO)
4. [R] NECK & [L] KIDNEY	(HADARI KUBI & MIGI MURADO)
5. LEFT OVERHEAD	(MIGI NOKORU)
6. RIGHT OVERHEAD	(HADARI NOKORU)
7. RIGHT FACE	(HADARI KAO)
8. LEFT FACE	(MIGI KAO)
9. RIGHT CATCH	(HADARI TORU)
10. LEFT CATCH	(MIGI TORU)

D. END BY STANDING IN JUSHA KAMAE

CATEGORY SEVEN (YOSU SHICHI): KICKS (KERU)

FORE NOTE: If the kicking leg is placed in front in a forward motion, then the kick called an aggressive kick. If the kicking leg is placed back in its starting position, then it is called a non- aggressive kick.

1. <u>FRONT SNAP KICK (MAE ORU KERU)</u>

A. Migi budo kamae
B. Chamber the kicking leg. This will be the back right leg.
C. Raise the foot straight up until the knee is above the waist.
D. Curl the toes back so that the ball of the foot is exposed.
E. Fire the kick out. The strike from this kick will be made with the ball of the foot.
F. Return the kicking leg to the chamber position.
G. Replace the kicking leg back into the stance.
H. Remember when performing a front snap, there should always be two side blocks brought up with the kick. This will help insure the opponent's kick or strike is blocked or deflected. The blocks also help with balance.

2. PIVOTING SIDE SNAP KICK (MAWASU YOKO ORU KERU)

A. Migi budo kamae
B. Bring back knee up above waist (this will be the right knee). This is called chambering the kick.
C. Pivot on the ball of the front foot, left foot, and hold the knee in its chambered position.
D. Turn the foot so that the blade of the foot points down.
E. Simultaneous with the positioning of the foot curl the toes back. This will tighten the blade of the foot and help keep the toes from snagging and being broke.
F. Fire the kick outwards from the chamber position, and bring the kick straight back to the chamber position. The strike from this kick will come from the blade of the foot.
G. Pivot the hips back and replace the kicking leg into the stance.
H. When performing a side snap the under side arm, or left arm if a right kick, should be in a kidney block, and the top hand, or right arm should be extended out over the kicking leg to prevent a strike to the knee. The position of the top arm is important in helping to maintaining balance.

3. WHIP KICK (MUCHI KERU)

A. Migi budo kamae.
B. Chamber the kicking leg by bringing the back knee up to waist level.
C. While pivoting the ball of the front foot fire the kick out at the target. Be sure to "cock" the hips. Make sure you chamber the kick. This will help cut down on telegraphing your kick.
D. The strike will come from the top of the foot.
E. Re-chamber the leg while pivoting back.
F. Replace the kicking leg back into the stance.
G. The whip kick will use the same blocks as the side snap.

4. HOOK KICK (KAGI KERU)

A. Migi budo kamae.
B. Chamber the kicking leg by bringing the back knee up to waist level.
C. Pivot on the ball of the front foot.
D. Kick across the front and down the side of your target. This will set up the hook kick. You will pivot on the ball of your front, left, foot; while bringing your hips into a roll as the knee rises.
E. Jerk the heel of you foot back toward your target. The strike from this kick will come from the heel of the foot.
F. Return the kicking leg to its chambered position.
G. Replace the leg back into a good stance.
H. Use the same type of blocks for this kick that you used for the whip kick.

5. INNER ROUND KICK (NAKA NARU KERU)

A. Migi budo kamae.
B. Chamber the kicking leg.
C. The kick will come up in a circular motion from the chambered position.
D. The kick will move from the inside or left side of the body and strike out toward the outside or right side of the body. Keep your shoulders square.
E. Re-chamber the kicking leg, and replace it back into the stance.
F. Use parallel blocks with this kick.
G. The strike from this kick will come from the blade of the foot.

6. OUTER ROUND KICK (UWA NARU KERU)

A. Migi budo kamae.
B. Chamber the kicking leg.
C. The kick will come in a circular motion from the chambered position.
D. The kick will move from the outside or right side of the body and strike to the inside or left side of the body. Keep the shoulders square.
E. Re-chamder the kicking leg, and replace it back into the stance.
F. Use parallel blocks with this kick.
G. The strike from this kick will come from the instep of the foot.

7. BACK SNAP KICK (URA ORU KERU)

A. Migi budo kamae.
B. Turn head and look behind you. You will look over the shoulder of the leg that the kick is coming from.
C. Pick up front foot, left foot, and pivot on the back foot, right foot.
D. Simultaneous with the pivoting of the back foot, chamber the left leg. (This will place you in a side snap position with leg up).
E. As the left leg is chambered turn the blade of the foot toward the ground and curl the toes back.
F. Fire the kick out and return it back to the chambered position.
G. Reposition the chambered leg back into the stance.
H. The blocks used with this kick are the same as those used with the side snap.

8. BACK HOOK KICK (URA KAGI KERU)

A. Migi budo kamae.
B. Turn head and look behind you. You will look over the shoulder of the leg that you are going to kick with.
C. Pick up the front foot and chamber the leg with the simultaneous pivoting of the body on the ball of the back leg.
D. Fire the kick down the side of the target.
E. Strike the target by jerking the heel of your kick into the target area.
F. The strike from this kick will come from the heel of the kicking foot.
G. Re-chamber the leg and place the leg back into the stance.
H. Blocks for this kick are the same as those used on the back snap.

9. BACK ROUND KICK (URA NARU KERU)

A. Migi budo kamae
B. Turn head and look behind you. You will look over the shoulder of the leg that the kick is coming from.
C. Pick up front foot, left foot, and pivot on the back foot, right foot.
D. Simultaneous with the pivoting of the back foot, chamber the left leg.
E. As the left leg is chambered curl the toes back.
F. Fire the kick out. The kick will move in a circular motion from the outside or left side toward the opposite side or the right side.
G. Re-chamber the leg.
H. Reposition the chambered leg back into the stance.
I. The strike will come from the blade of the foot.
J. Parallel blocks are used in defending with this kick.

10. DOUBLE WHIP KICK (NISOBAI MUCHI KERU)

A. Performed the same as a single whip kick but the targets are the ankles and knees, knee and ribs, or the ribs and neck.

11. JUMPING DOUBLE FRONT SNAP KICK (TOBU NISOBAI MAE ORU KERU)

A. Performed the same as a single front snap.
B. The first front snap strikes the stomach area, and this will buckle the opponent over.
C. The second front snap will strike the opponent in the throat area.
D. The second kick will already be off the ground the same time the first kick strikes its target.
E. Use parallel blocks to block with on this kick.

12. FOUR WAY KICK (SHI-DO KERU)

A. Migi budo kamae.
B. Front snap kick (right leg).
C. Back snap kick (right leg).
D. Side snap kick (right leg).
E. Front snap kick (left leg).
F. This kick is used against multiple attackers and to practice balance.

13. NO PIVOTING SIDE SNAP KICK (IIA MAWASU YOKO ORU KERU)

A. This kick is made in the same manner as the pivoting side snap except the kick comes straight out to the side. The hips do not pivot in this kick.

CATEGORY EIGHT (YOSU HACHI): WAR FIST STRIKES (KOBUSHI UTSU)

1. 50 WARFIST IN 1/3 MIN (50 KOBUSHI NI 1/3 FUN)

CATEGORY NINE (YOSU KU): BREATHING (KOKU)

1. IN NOSE (UCHI HANA)

   OUT MOUTH (SOTO KUCHI)

2. TIMING AND CONTROL OF BREATH (WAZA-NO-KANKYU)

   A. Breathe out on power strikes.
   B. Breathe out when getting hit.
   C. Breathe shallowly through the nose and mouth on long attacks.

CATEGORY TEN (YOSU JU): STRIKES (TE UTSU)

Practice the strikes with an aggressive step and never reverse or offset strike. Reverse or offset strike refers to a right strike with a left step of vice versa.

1. INSIDE KNIFE (NAKA SHUTO)

   A. Make a knife hand.
   B. The strike comes from the opposite or inside shoulder and moves across the body.

2. OUTSIDE KNIFE (HOKA SHUTO)

   A. Make a knife hand.
   B. The strike comes from the outside or same shoulder and moves across the body.

3. INSIDE RIDGE (NAKA MINE)

   A. Make a ridge hand.
   B. The strike comes out and up in a circular motion from the opposite or inside shoulder.

4. FORWARD PUNCH (MAE KOBUSHI)

   A. Make a war-fist.
   B. The strike comes straight out from the side and strikes the center of the target. Remember to keep the elbow bent at all times.

5. SIDE HAMMERFIST (YOKO KANAD'ZUSHI)

A. Make a hammer-fist
B. The strike comes from the outside or same shoulder and moves across the body.

6. DOWNWARD HAMMERFIST (SHIMO KANAD'ZUSHI)

A. Make a hammer-fist
B. The strike will move in a circular motion starting at shoulder level and move down toward the groin area.

7. UPPER HAMMERFIST (AGERU KANAD'ZUSHI)

A. Make a hammer-fist.
B. The strike will move in a circular motion starting at the waist level and move up toward the shoulders or face.

8. SIDE BACKFIST (YOKO URA-KEN)

A. Make a back-fist.
B. The strike will move from the opposite or inside shoulder and move across the body.

9. UPPER BACKFIST (AGERU URA-KEN)

A. Make a back-fist.
B. The strike will move in a circular motion starting at the waist area and move up toward the shoulders.

10. DOWNWARD BACKFIST (SHIMO URA-KEN)

A. Make a back-fist.
B. The strike will move in a circular motion starting at the shoulders and move down toward the groin area.

11. CLUTCH PALM (NIGIRU-TANAGOKORO)

A. Make a clutch palm.
B. The strike will come straight out from the body and strike the center of the target area.

12. CLUTCH FIST (NIGIRU-KOBUSHI)

A. Make a clutch palm.
B. The strike will come straight out from the body and strike the center of the target area.

13. WHIP (MUCHI)

A. Make a whip hand.
B. The strike will come from the opposite or inside shoulder and move across the body.

14. <u>SPEAR (YARI-TE)</u>

A. Make a spear hand.
B. The strike will come straight out from the body and strike the center of the target area.

15. <u>TIGER'S EYE (TORA ME)</u>

A. Make a tiger's eyes hand.
B. The strike will come straight out from the body and strike the opponent in the eyes.

CATEGORY ELEVEN (YOSU JU-ICHI): TOOLS OF THE FOOT (ASHI DOGO)

1. KEN (BLADE)
2. ASHI NO KO (INSTEP)
3. KAGATO (HEEL)
4. ZETCHO (HIGHEST PART BY THE JOINT ON TOP)
5. MARI (BALL)

CATEGORY TWELVE (YOSU JU-NI): TOOLS OF THE BLOCK (KIRE DOGU)

1. MEAT (NIKU)

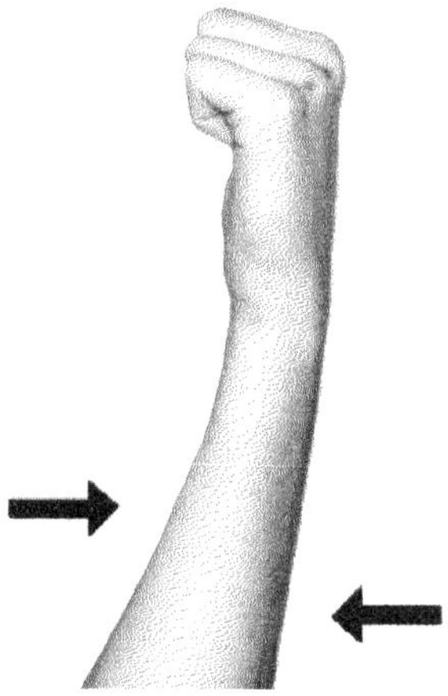

A. The meat is the widest part of the arm.

2. BONE (HONE)

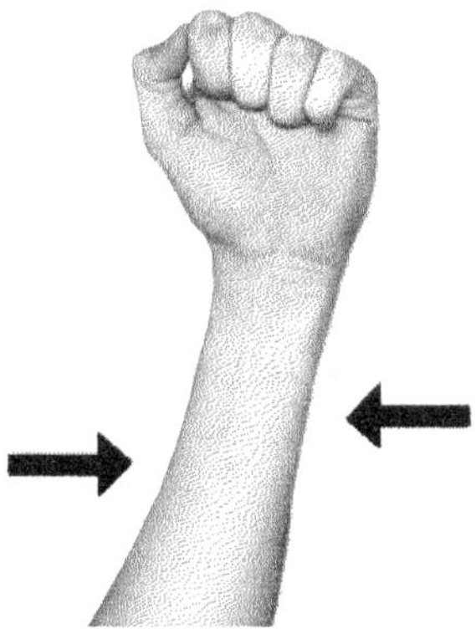

A. The bone is the thinnest part of the arm.

CATEGORY THIRTEEN (YOSU JU-SAN): TOOLS OF THE KICK (KERU DOGU)

1. MAE ORU KERU	BALL (MARI)
2. YOKO ORU KERU	BLADE (KEN)
3. MUCHI KERU	TOP OF FOOT (ZETCHO)
4. KAGI KERU	HEEL (KAGATO)
5. NAKA NARU KERU	BLADE (KEN)
6. UWA NARU KERU	INSTEP (ASHI NO KO)
7. URA ORU KERU	BLADE (KEN)
8. URA KAGI KERU	HEEL (KAGATO)
9. URA NARU KERU	BLADE (KEN)
10. NISOBAI MAE ORU KERU	BALL (MARI)
11. NISOBAI MUCHI KERU	TOP OF FOOT (ZETCHO)
12. SHI-DO KERU	BALL/BLADE/BLADE/BALL (MARI/KEN/KEN/MARI)

CATEGORY FOURTEEN (YOSU JU-SHI): ROLLS (KOROGARU)

1. HALF SHOULDER ROLL	(HAN KA'TA KOROGARU)
2. FULL SHOULDER ROLL	(AKU KA'TA KOROGARU)
3. CARTWHEEL	(NI NIN NO NI-GURUMA KURUMA)
4. REVERSE ROLL	(URA KOROGARU)
5. SIDE ROLL	(YOKO KOROGARU)

CATEGORY FIFTEEN (YOSU JU-GO): LEXICON (JIKIBI)

1. **TYPE** (SHIDARA): NINJUTSU
   SYMBOL (HANJIMONO): MEDALLION
   TRANSLATION (NAOSU): STUDY OF RESPONSIBILITY, TASK, AND DUTY.
   COLLOQUIALISM (ZOKU-GO): STUDY OF NATURE
2. **STYLE** (RYU): KONIGUN:
   SYMBOL (HANJINOMO): TOBU TORA
   TRANSLATION (NAOSU): FRIENDLY FORCE
   COLLOQUIALISM (ZOKU-GO): ETERNAL SUN
3. **FAMILY** (SHURUI): EACH NINJUTSU-RYU WILL HAVE DIFFERENT FAMILIES FROM EACH NINJA MASTER IN THAT RYU, SUCH AS THE SAIJA FAMILY (THE IMPERIAL FAMILY OR HEAD FAMILY OF KONIGUN).
   EACH FAMILY WILL IN MOST CASES BE IN CHARGE OF A GIVEN AREA ALLOTTED BY THE SHIDOSHI.
   FAMILY: SAIJA
   SYMBOL: SAI ENGRACED WITH WINGS
   TRANSLATION: THE KNOWING ONE
   COLLOQUIALISM: IMPERIAL OR SENIOR FAMILY

****** KONIGUN NINJUTSU WAS FOUNDED IN WHAT IS KNOWN AS JULY, 1196 BY THE GREGORIAN CALENDAR. THE TOWN OF ORIGINATION IS KAGOSHIMA, JAPAN, ON THE ISLAND OF KYUSHU. THE STYLE'S FIRST SHIDOSHI WAS SHIDOSHI SAIJA. SHIDOSHI BRYCE DALLAS INTRODUCED KONIGUN NINJUTSU TO AMERICA. THIS ART IS A "RED ART". THE TERM RED ART MEANS THAT THE "NINJA (S)" OF KONIGUN NINJUTSU ARE STRICTLY FORBIDDEN TO BE EMPLOYED AS ANY TYPE OF ASSASSIN (S).**

CATEGORY SIXTEEN (YOSU JU-ROKU): SHIN KATA

1. ENTRANCE FORM SALUTE (IRU KATA JIGI)

2. RIGHT BASIC STANCE (MIGI BUDO KAMAE)

3. RIGHT WAR FIST STRIKE (MIGI KOBUSHI UTSU)
   [RIGHT STEP]

4. LEFT WAR FIST STRIKE (HADARI KOBUSHI UTSU)
   [LEFT STEP]

5. RIGHT WAR FIST STRIKE (MIGI KOBUSHI UTSU)
   [RIGHT STEP]

6. LEFT WAR FIST STRIKE (HADARI KOBUSHI UTSU)
   [LEFT STEP]

7. TURN CROSS BLOCK (MAWASU JIRERU KIRE)
   [STEP THROUGH AND DEEP WITH RIGHT LEG TO A STANCE]

8. LEFT BACK FIST STRIKE (HADARI URA KEN)
   [PERFORM A HEEL TOE PIVOT WITH STRIKE]

9. RIGHT WAR FIST STRIKE (MIGI KOBUSHI UTSU)
   [RIGHT STEP]

10. LEFT WAR FIST STRIKE (HADARI KOBUSHI UTSU)
    [LEFT STEP]

11. RIGHT WAR FIST STRIKE (MIGI KOBUSHI UTSU)
    [RIGHT STEP]

12. LEFT WAR FIST STRIKE (HADARI KOBUSHI UTSU)
    [LEFT STEP]

13. TURN (MAWASU)
    [USE A LEFT BACK HEEL SWEEP ON TURN]

14. LEFT REAR SWORD HAND STRIKE (HADARI URA SHUTO UTSU)

15. STAY SALUTE (YAMU KATA JIGI)

CATEGORY SEVENTEEN (YOSU JU-SHICHI): SHIROTO KATA

1. ENTRANCE FORM SALUTE (IRU KATA JIGI)

2. RIGHT BASIC STANCE (MIGI BUDO KAMAE)

3. RIGHT WAR FIST STRIKE (MIGI KOBUSHI UTSU)
   [RIGHT STEP]

4. LEFT WAR FIST STRIKE (HADARI KOBUSHI UTSU)
   [LEFT STEP]

5. RIGHT FRONT SNAP KICK (MIGI MAE ORU KERU)
   [SET DOWN IN A SADDLE STANCE WITH A DOUBLE FOREARM BLOCK. BE SURE AND HOLD FISTS PARALLEL TO EACH OTHER.]

6. RIGHT BACK FIST STRIKE (MIGI URA-KEN UTSU)
   [NO STEP]

7. RIGHT SIDE SNAP KICK (MIGI YOKO ORU KERU)
   [EXTEND THE RIGHT ARM OUT TO PROTECT THE KNEE. SET THE FOOT DOWN DEEPER FOR NEXT MOVE.]

8. LEFT BACK RIDGE HAND STRIKE (HADARI URA MINE-TE UTSU)
   [USE A RIGHT KNIFE HAND STRIKE TO LEAD INTO THE RIDGE STRIKE. HEEL-TOE PIVOT. NO STEP]

9. RIGHT WAR FIST STRIKE (MIGI KOBUSHI UTSU)
   [RIGHT STEP]

10. LEFT WAR FIST STRIKE TO GROIN (HADARI KOBUSHI UTSU NI MOMONE)
    [LEFT STEP. BLOCK LEFT ELBOW WITH RIGHT FIST.]

11. DOUBLE BACK FIST (NISOBAI URA-KEN)
    [AFTER DOUBLE STRIKE GRAPPLE THE TARGET. RIGHT STEP]

12. RIGHT FRONT LEG WHIP (MIGI MAE ASHI MUCHI KERU)
    [NO STEP. SPIN THROUGH WITH THE KICK AND SET FOOT DOWN IN BOW OUT POSITION]

14. STAY SALUTE (YAMU KATA JIGI)

CATEGORY EIGHTEEN (YOSU JU-HACHI): SPARRING TECHNIQUES (KUMITE JUTSU)

A. APEX

The point where the hands, legs, arms, and feet must pass through in order to strike their target. This area is located between the waist and collarbones, and the width of the body.

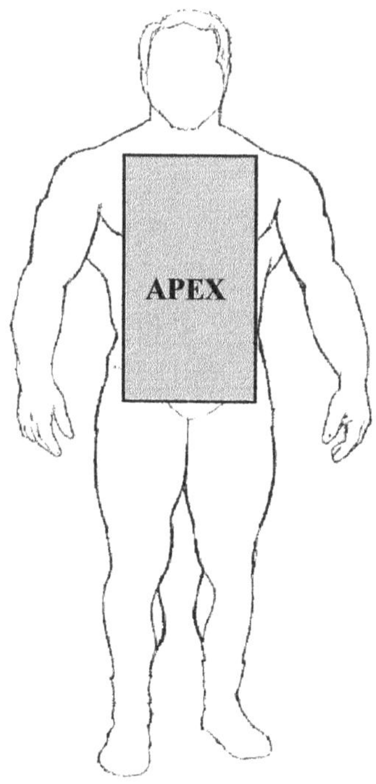

B. FOUR QUADRANTS

The four equal areas that the body divides into when an imaginary line is drawn through the waist and down the center of the body. In most cases, the quadrant you attack from your block will come from the quadrant diagonally across from your attacking quadrant.

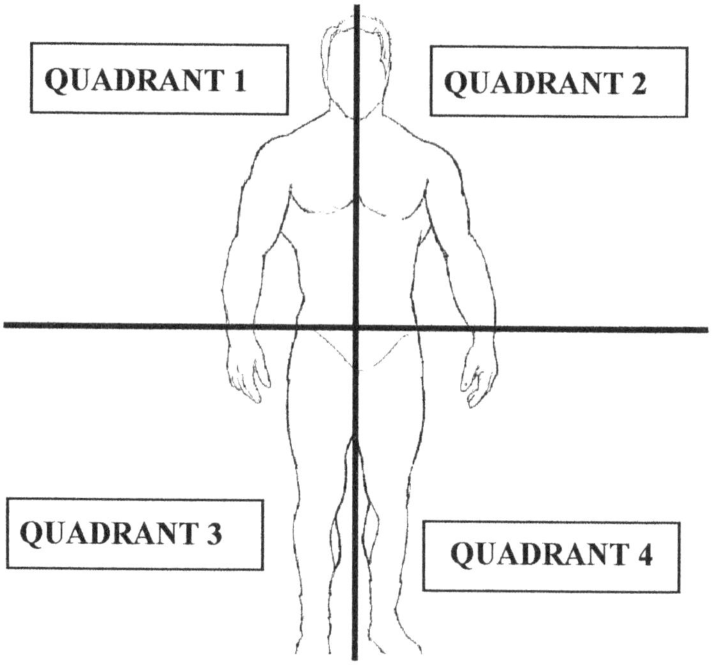

C. NINE FIGHTING ANGLES

The nine fighting angles are listed as follows and are in order from most wanted movements in a confrontation to least wanted movements

1 & 2- Right and left 45 degree angles forward.
3 & 4- Directly side to side.
5 & 6- Right and left 45 degree angles backward.
7- Directly forward.
8- Directly backward.
9- Ground zero.

RIGHT SIDE STANCE

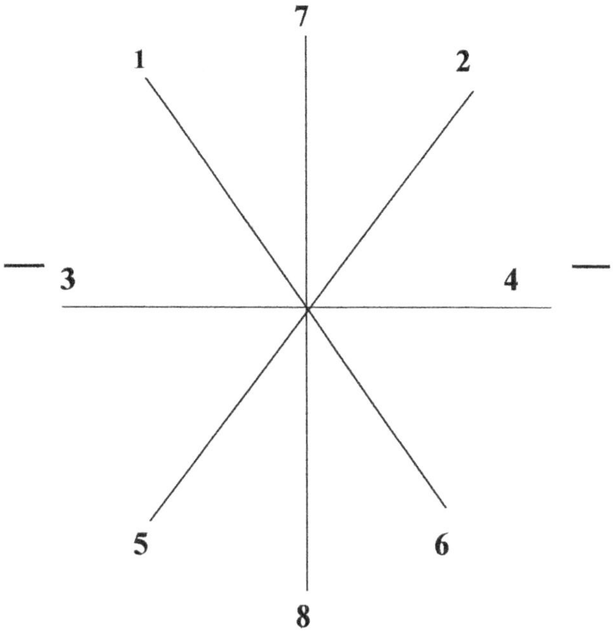

Center is Number 9

D. FIVE AURAS OF ATTACK AND DEFENSE

5th- Located fifteen feet away and used for communication.
4th- Located twelve feet away and uses rolls, cross steps, and shadow steps.
3rd- Located nine feet and uses rolls, stepping kicks, and glides.
2nd- Located six feet away and uses kicks, punches, and grapples.
1st- Located three feet away and uses knees, elbows, palm hands, and joint locks.
0** Body against body

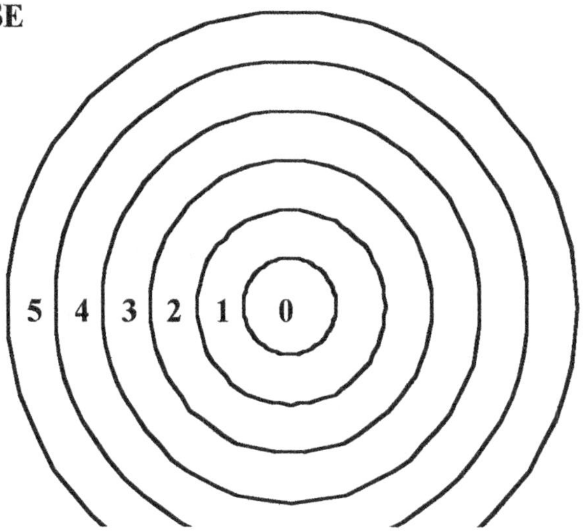

E. **SPARRING TIPS:**

1. Listen to all directions when learning moves.
2. Never lock your elbows or knees.
3. Do not redirect your attention and get distracted.
4. Never perform a technique that you are not sure about.
5. When on the ground, go for a joint lock on the hand, arm, or leg.
6. Never go for a pin.

NOTE: SPARRING WHAT IS NOT THERE

When sparring you should read or anticipate where your opponent will strike or move to next. You should never attack the existing position of your opponent. Most attackers attack and strike your existing position so your best defense is to relocate and attack the position that they will move to next; most often the one you just left. Although always beware of the 45 degree attacks.

CATEGORY NINETEEN (YOSU JU-KU): CONVERSATION (HANASHI):

1. YES SIR	(HIA SAN)
2. NO SIR	(IIA SAN)
3. STOP	(TOMERU)
4. BEGIN	(OSHIDO)
5. NOW	(IMA)
6. DISENGAGE	(AKU)
7. THANKS	(DOMO)
8. WELCOME	(YOI)
10. EXCUSE ME	(SUMIMASEN)
11. FORMATION	(GUROPU)
12. GATHER	(KAI)
13. FRATERNITY	(KYODAI)
14. HIGHER RANK BLACK SASH	(JOSHI)
15. LOWER RANK BLASK SASH	(BOKA)
16. BELT RANK	(KYU)
17. GENERAL STUDENTS	(MONTO)

CATEGORY TWENTY (YOSU NI-JU): BREAK FALLING (YABURERU)

DESHI

CATEGORY ONE (YOSU ICHI): STANCES (KAMAE)

** NOTE: The back foot in the stance can be on a 45-degree angle or perpendicular to the front foot. The foot positioning depends on whether you are progressively attacking or defending.

1. ADVANCE STANCE (AGERU KAMAE)

A. Stand with feet pointing forward at shoulder width.
B. For a right side stance the right foot will drop back and out. Make sure that the feet are a little more than shoulder width apart.
C. The front foot always stays pointed at the opponent.
D. The back foot is always perpendicular to the front foot.
E. Bend the knees and rise upon the balls of the feet. Make sure that the knees are over the ends of the toes. Do this while making sure that your feet are not in line with each other. If the feet are in line with each other, there will be no balance in the stance.
F. Shoulders should be at a 45-degree angle with the feet, and the head should always be pointed forward.
G. The front hand will be in a knife hand. The hand will extend out in front of the body at an angle greater than 90-degrees.
H. The back hand will be in a knife hand position. The hand will extent out in front of the body at an angle greater than 90-degrees.
I. The two shuto hands will divide the chest in one third and two thirds.

2. MASTER STANCE (SHUJIN KAMAE)

A. Stand with feet pointing forward at shoulder width.
B. For a right side stance the right foot will drop back and out. Make sure that the feet are a little more than shoulder width apart.
C. The front foot always stays pointed at the opponent.
D. The back foot is always perpendicular to the front foot.
E. Bend the knees and rise upon the balls of the feet. Make sure that the knees are over the ends of the toes. Do this while making sure that your feet are not in line with each other. If the feet are in line with each other there will be no balance in the stance.
F. Shoulders should be at a 45-degree angle with the feet, and the head should always be pointed forward.
G. The front hand will be in a shuto hand and will be positioned two inches above the knee with the fingers pointing down toward the ground along side the calf.
H. The back hand is in a shuto hand position and is placed between the eye brow and the ear. The hand is two inches from the side of the head, and arms are angled at a 45-degree angle with the elbow pointing toward the ground.

3. <u>SHADOW STANCE (KAGE KAMAE)</u>

A. Stand with feet pointing forward at shoulder width.
B. For a right side stance the right foot will drop back and out. Make sure that the feet are a little more than shoulder width apart.
C. The front foot always stays pointed at the opponent.
D. The back foot is always perpendicular to the front foot.
E. Bend the knees and rise upon the balls of the feet. Make sure that the knees are over the ends of the toes. Do this while making sure that your feet are not in line with each other. If the feet are in line with each other there will be no balance in the stance.
F. Shoulders should be at a 45-degree angle with the feet, and the head should always be pointed forward.
G. The front hand is in a kobushi position, and is place one to two inches above the knee. The hand points straight forward toward the ground in front of the knee.
H. The backhand is in a kobushi position, and is placed in the center of the chest. The hand is one to two inches away from the sternum. The thumb is in the upward position.

4. DRAW STANCE (KAKU KAMAE)

A. Stand with feet pointing forward at shoulder width.
B. For a right side stance the right foot will drop back and out. Make sure that the feet are a little more than shoulder width apart.
C. The front foot always stays pointed at the opponent.
D. The back foot is always perpendicular to the front foot.
E. Bend the knees and rise upon the balls of the feet. Make sure that the knees are over the ends of the toes. Do this while making sure that your feet are not in line with each other. If the feet are in line with each other there will be no balance in the stance.
F. Shoulders should be at a 45-degree angle with the feet, and the head should always be pointed forward.
G. The front hand is in kobushi position and is places across the from of the body, and the bottom of the arm points toward the ground. There should be an angle greater than 90-degrees between the arm block and the body. The wrist should be straightened so the fist will be level enough so that a glass of water will set on top of the fist and not spill.
H. The backhand is in a kobushi position, and is turned so that the top of the hand faces the ground. The hand is placed behind the arm block so that the middle finger knuckle will pass down, behind, or across the wrist joint of the arm block.

5. <u>SADDLE STANCE (KURA KAMAE)</u>

A. The legs are placed a little more than shoulders width apart.
B. The knee should be bent so that they extend over the toes.
C. Rise up on the balls of the feet.
D. Both arms will be in side block position.

CATEGORY TWO (YOSU NI): ADVANCE BLOCKS (AGERU KIRE)

1. DRAW STANCE
   (KAKU KAMAE)

2. LOWER CROSS BLOCK
   (SHITA NO JIRERU)

3. MIDDLE CROSS BLOCK
   (NAKABA JIRERU)

4. OVERHEAD BLOCK
   (NOKORU JIRERU)

5. LUNGE PUNCH
   (KOBUSHI UTSU)

CATEGORY THREE (YOSU SAN): SCISSORS (HASAMI)

1. <u>NECK (NODO)</u>

   A. Right side stance.
   B. Leap into the air with the legs spread apart.
   C. When opponent's neck is between the legs, slam the legs together.
   D. If you want to flip the opponent backward, strike the opponent in the lower back with the left leg, and strike him in the front of the neck with the right leg.
   E. If you want to flip the opponent forward, strike the opponent in the stomach with the right leg, and strike him in the back of the neck with the left

2. <u>WAIST (KOSHI)</u>

   A. Right side stance.
   B. Leap into the air with the legs spread apart.
   C. When opponent's waist is between the legs slam the legs together.
   D. If you want to flip the opponent backwards, strike him in the back of the knees with the left leg, and strike him in the waist with the right leg.
   E. If you want the opponent to flip forward, strike him in the kneecaps with the right leg, and strike him in the lower back with the left leg.

3. <u>LEG (ASHI)</u>

   A. Right side stance.
   B. Leap into he air with legs spread open.
   C. When the opponent's legs are between your legs, slam them together.
   D. If you want the opponent to fall backward, strike him in the back of the ankles with your left leg, and strike him in the kneecaps with your right leg
   E. If you want the opponent to fall forward, strike him in the ankles with the right leg, and strike him in the back of the knees with the left leg.

4. DIRECTIONAL SCISSORS (TORI-ATSUKAI HASAMI)

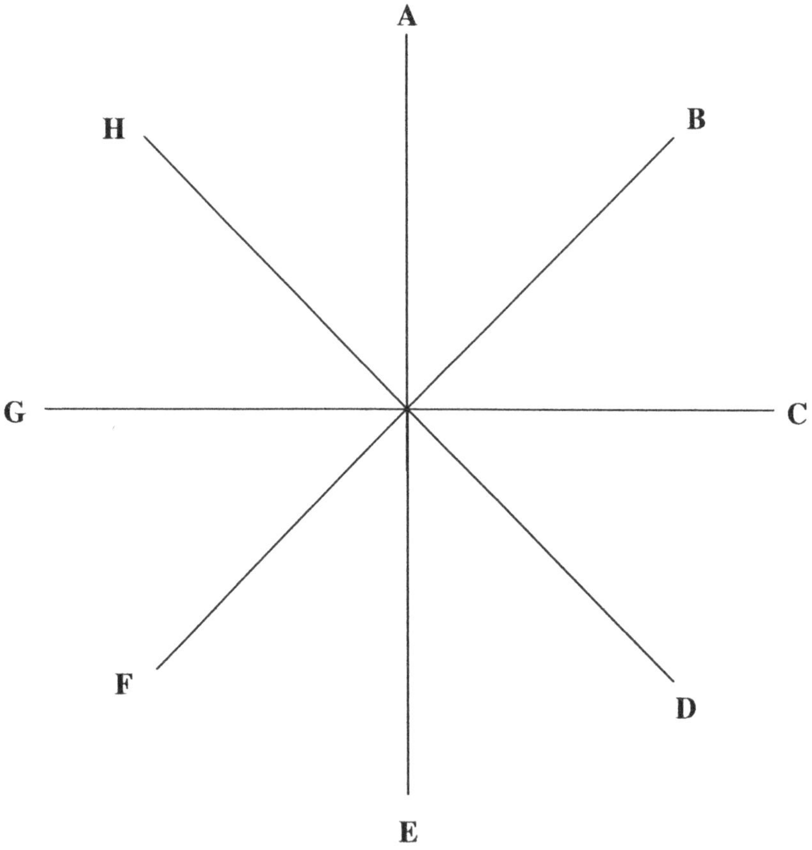

* NOTE: The sweeps can be done on either side. The following moves are illustrated from laying on the left side. The moves are designed to place the opponent on the letter. Your feet are located at the vortex point of the nine angles and your head is located at the letter (A) for this illustration.

A. Bottom, left heel pushes and top, right ankle joint pulls.

B. Bottom, left ankle joint pushes and top, right heel pulls and pushes.

C. Bottom, left ankle joint hooks and top, right heel pushes.

D. Bottom, left ankle joint pulls and top, right heel pushes.

E. Bottom, left ankle joint pulls and top, right heel pushes.

F. Bottom, left heel pulls and top, right ankle pushes.

G. Bottom, left heel pulls and top, right ankle joint pushes.

H. Bottom, left heel pushes and top, right ankle joint pulls.

CATEGORY FOUR (YOSU SHI): SWEEP KICKS (HAKU KERU)

1. <u>FRONT SWEEP USING TOP OF FOOT (ZETCHO HAKU)</u>

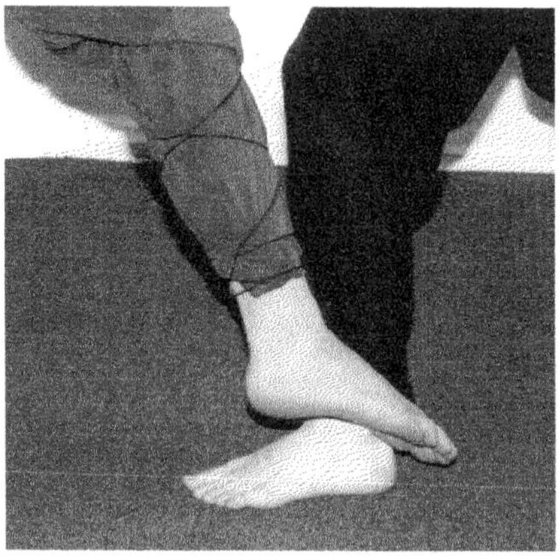

A. Right side stance.
B. Pick back leg up and point toes downward. (The foot placement is the same as the whip kick.)
C. The sweep will float about two inches off the ground, and will strike the ankle of the opponent.
D. Upon impact, jerk your foot straight up into the back of the opponent's knee. This will raise the opponent's leg off the ground and leave him off balance.
E. After the move is completed, you should be in a left side common stance

2. <u>FRONT SWEEP USING HEEL OF FOOT (KAGATO HAKU)</u>

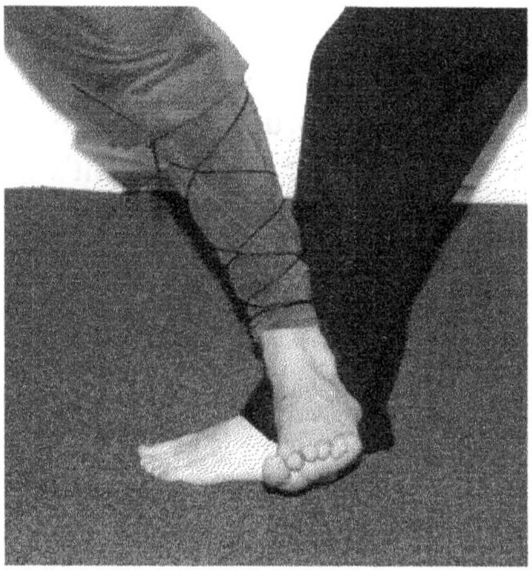

A. Right side stance.
B. Pick back leg up.
C. Bring the foot forward at an angle across the center of your stance
D. Once your foot reaches the inside of the opponent's front foot; slam the heel of your foot into the instep of the opponent's foot, and drive outwards.
E. This will throw the opponent's foot out and away from their center of gravity, leaving them off balance.
F. Once you have slammed the opponent's foot out, replace your feet into the common stance positions.

3. <u>BACK SWEEP USING HEEL OF FOOT (URA KAGATO HAKU)</u>

A. Right side stance.
B. Take a step forward with your right foot and plant it firmly in the ground.
C. Rise up on the ball of the foot and pivot, bringing your left leg spinning around.
D. Strike the ankle of the targeted leg with the heel of the pivoting leg.

4. <u>GRAPPLE SWEEP (HASUKAMI KAKU)</u>

A. Right side stance.
B. Pick up the back right leg and kick the back of the opponent's ankle joint.
C. This will drive the opponent's foot away and take him off balance.

5. HEEL AND TOE SWEEP (KAGATO NI ASHI NO YUBI HAKU)

A. Right side stance
B. Take a step forward with your right foot and plant it firmly in the ground.
C. Rise up on the ball of that foot and pivot, bringing your left leg spinning around.
D. Strike the backside of the front ankle of your opponent with the heel of your left foot, and drive outwards (drive outwards about one foot)
E. Plant that foot firmly in the ground and swing your right foot around so that the top of the foot connects with the backside of the opponent's back foot.
F. Drive through so that you pick the opponent off both of his feet, and end up in a right side stance.
G. This will leave you facing your opponent.

6. TOE AND HEEL SWEEP (ASHI NO YUBI NI KAGATO HAKU)

A. Right side stance.
B. Perform a toe sweep just as described above except do not pick your foot up. Simply drive through and position the now front foot, right foot, so you stand in a left sided common stance.
C. Once the right foot is placed, rise up on the ball of that foot, right foot, and pivot your body. The pivot will bring the heel of your left foot, back foot, spinning around so that your back will brush against the back of your opponent.
D. Strike the opponent's back ankle with the heel of your left foot. This will force his foot off the ground.
E. Follow on through with the left foot strike until you stand in a right side stance again. This will leave you facing the opponent.

NOTE: The double sweeps are also used when the first sweep does not strike the target, but the second sweep will usually strike the target.

CATEGORY FIVE (YOSU GO): KICK COMBINATIONS (KERU CHOGO)

1. FRONT SNAP/WHIP	(MAE ORU/MUCHI)
2. WHIP/BACK ROUND	(MUCHI/URA NARU)
3. FRONT SNAP/SIDE SNAP	(MAE ORU/YOKO ORU)
4. SIDE SNAP/BACK SNAP	(YOKO ORU/URA ORU)
5. BACK ROUND/WHIP	(URA NARU/MUCHI)
6. SIDE SNAP/BACK ROUND	(YOKO ORU/URA NARU)

*7. INNER ROUND/BACK SNAP (NAKA NARU/URA ORU)

8. FRONT SNAP/OUTER ROUND (MAE ORU/UWA NARU)

9. OUTER ROUND/BACK SNAP (UWA NARU/URA ORU)

*10. INNER ROUND/BACK ROUND (NAKA NARU/URA NARU)

11. SIDE SNAP/SIDE SNAP (YOKO ORU/YOKO ORU)

12. INNER ROUND/OUTER ROUND (NAKA NARU/UWA NARU)

*** THESE KICKS ARE PERFORMED WITH THE SAME LEG**

***** NOTE: EACH OF THE ABOVE COMBINATIONS ARE DESIGNED WITH A DIFFERENT LEG FOLLOWING UP THE FIRST LEG TO KICK.**

CATEGORY SIX (YOSU ROKU): ACROBATICS (KARUWAZA-SHI)

1. FULL SHOULDER ROLL WITH STRIKE
(AKU KA'TA KOROGARU UTSU)

2. HALF SHOULDER ROLL WITH STRIKE
(HAN KA'TA KOROGARU UTSU)

3. BACK SHOULDER ROLL WITH STRIKE
(URA KA'TA KOROGARU UTSU)

4. CARTWHEEL WITH STRIKE
(NI NIN NO NI GURUMA KURUMA UTSU)

*****ALL OVER THREE-FOOT OBJECT*****

CATEGORY SEVEN (YOSU SHICHI): GRAPPLING PRACTICE (TSUKAMU NERERU)

1. Practice all first moves to each of the counter moves until the teacher is satisfied that student can grapple.

CATEGORY EIGHT (YOSU HACHI): GRAPPLING TECHNIQUES (HASUKAAMU-JUTSU)

** Note: All techniques are illustrated from a right side stance.

1. ARM TO ARM (UDE NI UDE)

   A. Attacker throws punch.
   B. Block punch with left face block and grapple wrist.
   C. Twist the attacker's arm so that their elbow is locked by your elbow.
   D. Spin backwards down the side of their arm, and re-break their arm on your upper ribs.
   E. Continue spinning and elbow the attacker in between the shoulder blades.
   F. Back-fist the attacker in the base of the skull.

2. ARM TO OUTSIDE KNEE (UDE NI HOKA HIZA)

   A. Attacker throws right punch.
   B. Block punch with a left roll catch block, grapple it and carry it to the outside of the body.
   C. Twist the attacker's arm so that the elbow is pointing down.
   D. Bring the right knee up, knee opposite grapple, and break the elbow.
   E. With the same leg that broke the attacker's elbow, side snap the attacker's knee.

3. ARM TO INSIDE KNEE (UDE NI KANA HIZA)

   A. Attacker throws right punch.
   B. Block punch with a right roll catch block, grapple it and carry it across the body and to the outside.
   C. Twist the attacker's arm so that the elbow is pointing down.
   D. Bring the left knee up, knee opposite grapple, and break the elbow.
   E. With the same leg that broke the attacker's elbow, side snap the attacker's knee.

4. ARM BREAK WITH PALM HAND (UDE KOWASU TE NO URA)

   A. Attacker throws punch.
   B. Cross body roll catch block the punch and step at a 45 degree angle behind the punch
   C. Strike the elbow with a palm hand and roll the arm.

5. ARM BREAK WITH ELBOW (UDE KOWASU NO HIJI)

   A. Attacker throws punch.
   B. Cross body roll catch block the punch and step at a 45-degree angle behind the punch.
   C. Strike the elbow with an elbow and roll the arm.

6. <u>ARM BREAK COMBINATION (UDE KOWASU CHOGO)</u>

* NOTE: Lean with the strikes*

A. Attacker throws punch.
B. Cross body roll catch block simultaneously stepping at a forty-five degree angle behind the punch.
C. Strike the attacker's elbow with your elbow.
D. Back-fist the attacker's nose.
E. Elbow the attacker in the ribs.
F. Back-fist the attacker in the nose from underneath the attacker's grappled arm.
G. Cup hand strike the attacker's groin.
H. Ridge strike the attacker's jaw.
I. Rotate the grappled arm to palm up and the elbow down. As you tort the grappled arm down while pulling the attacker forward and down into your rising back leg knee to the attacker's face.
J. Step through with your back leg and sweep the opponent, simultaneous striking the attacker in the chest with the elbow that holds the grappled arm.

7. <u>BASIC UNIFORM GRAB (BUDO KI HITTAKURU)</u>

A. Attacker faces you and grabs you with both hands.
B. Break the grapple by striking the wrists with ridge hands. (Strike the wrists between the second and third lines on the wrist.)
C. Strike the attacker's collarbones with shuto hands.
D. Strike upward and gauge the eyes with the thumbs, and grab the head with the fingers.
E. Pull the attacker's head down while simultaneously bringing the knee up.
F. Slam the attacker's head into your knee.
G. Finish by front snapping the attacker in the groin.

8. <u>ADVANCED UNIFORM GRAB (AGERU KI HITTAKURU)</u>

A. Attacker faces you and grabs you with both hands.
B. Drive both elbows down and out between the arms.
C. Spear hand both the armpits of the attacker and grab.
D. Pull the attacker down simultaneously bringing your knee up.
E. Slam the attacker's diaphragm into your knee.
F. Front snap the attacker in the groin.

9. MASTER UNIFORM GRAB (SHUJIN KI HITTAKURU)

A. Attacker faces you and grabs you with both hands.
B. Cross-grab the wrists from the underneath. Be sure to strike upward hard enough to break the grapple.
C. Outside arm moves down and under the inside arm. This locks the attacker's arms at the elbows.
D. Push the inside arm down and away from you. This will twist the attacker so that his backside is turned toward you.
E. Knee the attacker in the back.
F. Stomp kick the backside of the attacker's knee. This will force the attacker to his knees.
G. Finish the counter by stomp kicking the attacker's Achilles tendons.

10. FOUR POINT DOUBLE HAND ON ELBOW (SHI MATO NISOBAI TE NI HIJI)

A. Attacker punches with right hand at face.
B. Upper cross-block. Left hand on inside of wrist and right hand on outside of elbow. This locks out the attacker's elbow.
C. Attacker punches with left hand at face.
D. Upper cross-block. Right hand on inside of wrist and left hand on outside of elbow. This will lock out the attacker's elbow.
E. Attacker punches with right hand at groin.
F. Downward cross-block. Left hand on inside of wrist and right hand on outside of elbow. This locks out the attacker's elbow.
G. Attacker punches with left hand at groin.
H. Downward cross-block. Right hand on inside of wrist and left hand on outside of elbow. This locks out the attacker's elbow.
I. Repeat steps a-d.
J. Repeat steps e-h but the hands in the cross-block are turned over to palm hands and the block is turned into a grapple.

11. INSIDE ARM WRAP (KANA UDE MAKU)

A. Attacker throws a right punch.
B. Block punch with a left roll catch block, and grapple.
C. Block punch with a shuto/ ridge combo.
D. Strike the jaw with a right shuto hand then strike the elbow joint of the attacker's grappled arm with a shuto hand and grapple. This causes the arm to fold.
E. Push down on the wrist and pull up on the elbow. This will spin the attacker around and expose his backside.
F. Knee the attacker in the back and stomp kick the knee.
*** There are two other endings to this counter and they begin at step E. **
I. Pull opponent down to the ground and put your right elbow into the opponent's throat.
II. Pull opponent down to the ground and put your left elbow into the opponent's jaw.

CATEGORY NINE (YOSU KU): HAND AND FOOT SPARRING (TAIJUTSU KUMITE)

1. The student must spar in hand and foot matches against another person until the sensei is satisfied with the student's ability.

CATEGORY TEN (YOSU JU): STAFF TECHNIQUE CONTEST OF SKILL (BOJUTSU SHIAI)

1. The student must spar in staff matches against another person until the sensei is satisfied with the student's ability.

CATEGORY ELEVEN (YOSU JU-ICHI): WAR FIST STRIKES (KOBUSHI UTSU)

1. 70 WARFIST STRIKES IN 1/3 MIN
   (SHICHI-JU KOBUSHI UTSU NI 1/3 FUN)

CATEGORY TWELVE (YOSU JU-NI): ADVANCE KICKS (AGERU KERU)

1. JUMPING SIDE SNAP	(TOBU YOKO ORU)
2. ROLL FRONT SNAP	(KOROGARU MAE ORU)
3. ROLL SIDE SNAP	(KOROGARU YOKO ORU)
4. ROLL WHIP	(KOROGARU MUCHI)
5. ROLL HOOK	(KOROGARU KAGI)
6. FRONT SNAP/INSIDE WHIP	(MAE ORU/NAKA MUCHI)
7. INSIDE WHIP	(NAKI MUCHI)
8. DOUBLE SIDE SNAP	(NISOBAI YOKO ORU)

CATEGORY THIRTEEN (YOSU JU-SAN): EXERCISE QUEST (UNDO)

1. 10 -10 COUNT PUSH UP	(JU O OSU KAMI JU KAZOERU)
2. 20-06 COUNT SIT UP	(NI-JU O SUWARU KAMI ROKU KAZOERU)
3. 20-10 COUNT JUMP HOP	(NI-JU O HANERU ODERU JU KAZOERU)

CATEGORY FOURTEEN (YOSU JU-SHI): KICK BLOCKS (KERU KIRE)

**Note: The inside and outside block are illustrated from a right side stance.

1. INSIDE BLOCK (NAKA KIRE)
   A. Opponent kicks with a right leg kick.
   B. Block the kick with a right downward roll block and carry the kick to the inside of body.

2. OUTSIDE BLOCK (UWA KIRE)
   A. Opponent kicks with a right leg kick.
   B. Block the kick with a left downward roll block and carry the kick to the outside of the body.

CATEGORY FIFTEEN (YOSU JU-GO): MONTO KATA

1. ENTRANCE FORM SALUTE (IRU KATA JIGI)

2. RIGHT COMMON MARTIAL ARTS STANCE (MIGI BUDO KAMAE)

3. RIGHT WAR FIST STRIKE (MIGI KOBUSHI UTSU)
   [RIGHT STEP]

4. RIGHT ROLLING BACKFIST STRIKE (MIGI KOROGARU URA-KEN)
   [NO STEP]

5. LEFT CLUTCH PALM (HADARI NIGIRU-TANAGOKORO)
   [LEFT STEP]

6. RIGHT FAKE JUMPING DOUBLE FRONT SNAP
   (MIGI MAGAI TOBU NISOBAI MAE ORU KERU)
   [LAND IN RIGHT STANCE]

7. LEFT BACK ROUND KICK (HADARI URA NARU KERU)
   [LOOK OVER LEFT SHOULDER BEFORE KICKING. LAND IN A RIGHT STANCE.]

8. RIGHT DOUBLE WHIP KICK (MIGI NISOBAI MUCHI KERU)
   [RIGHT LOWER WHIP HAND BLOCK AND RIGHT UPPER WHIP HAND BLOCK SIMULTANEOUS WITH THE KICKS. LAND IN A LEFT STANCE.]

9. RIGHT WHIP HAND (MIGI MUCHI TE)
   [FRONT HAND STRIKE. NO STEP]

10. LEFT WAR FIST STRIKE (HADARI KOBUSHI UTSU)
    [LEFT STEP]

11. LEFT ROLLING BACK FIST STRIKE (HADARI KOROGARU URA-KEN UTSU)
[NO STEP]

12. RIGHT CLUTCH PALM (MIGI NIGIRU TANAGOKARO)
[RIGHT STEP]

13. RIGHT SIDE CRADLE BLOCK (MIGI KOROGARU YOKO JIRERU KIRE)
REVERSE RIGHT LEG STEP TO RIGHT STANCE.]

14. ROLLING RIGHT GRAB WITH RIGHT ELBOW STRIKE
(MIGI KOROGARU HITTAKURU NO MIGI HIJI UTSU)
[RIGHT STEP INTO RIGHT STANCE FACING PERPENDICULAR TO LAST STANCE.]

15. UPPER RIGHT BACK FIST STRIKE (AGERU MIGI URA-KEN UTSU)
[STRIKE TO NOSE. NO STEP]

16. RIGHT DOWNWARD CUP HAND (MIGI SHIMO CHOKO TE)
[STRIKE TO GROIN. NO STEP]

17. RIGHT RIDGE HAND STRIKE (MIGI MINE TE UTSU)
[STRIKE TO JAW. NO STEP]

18. TURN (TO FACE FORWARD WITH HEEL TOE PIVOT), LEFT RIDGE HAND STRIKE
(MAWASU, HADARI MINE TE UTSU)
[LEAD INTO LEFT RIDGE STRIKE WITH A RIGHT KNIFE HAND STRIKE TO THE JAW. END IN RIGHT STANCE.]

19. RIGHT WAR-FIST STRIKE (MIGI KOBUSHI UTSU)
[WITH THE STRIKE PICK THE RIGHT LEG UP AND PLACE IN SADDLE STANCE. IT IS OPTIONAL WHETHER YOU PICK THE LEG UP IN A CHAMBERING MOTION OR BRUSH THE ARCH ACROSS YOUR LEFT LEG.]

20. STAY SALUTE (YAMU JIGI)

CATEGORY SIXTEEN (YOSU JU-ROKU): DESHI KATA

1. ENTRANCE FORM SALUTE (IRU KATA JIGI)

2. RIGHT DRAW STANCE (MIGI KAKU KAMAE)

3. RIGHT FRONT RIDGE HAND (MIGI MAE MINE TE)
   [RIGHT STEP]

4. LEFT FRONT RIDGE HAND (HADARI MAE MINE TE)
   [LEFT STEP]

5. RIGHT INNER ROUND HOUSE (MIGI NAKA NARU)
   [TRAVELING]

6. LEFT OUTER ROUND HOUSE (HADARI UWA NARU)
   [TRAVELING, BE SURE TO SET LEFT FOOT DEEP.]

7. LEFT CARTWHEEL ENDING WITH DOUBLE KNIFE HAND STRIKE
   (HADARI KURUMA NI NISOBAI SHUTO TE UTSU)
   [END IN RIGHT STANCE.]

8. RIGHT STANCE / MIDDLE CROSS BLOCK}
   (MIGI KAMAE / NAKABA JIRERU KIRE)
   [STEP WITH RIGHT LEG TO FACE REVERSE DIRECTION OF LAST STANCE.]

9. LEFT BACK FIST (HADARI URA-KEN)
   [STRIKE TO FRONT THEN RETURN TO CROSS BLOCK. NO STEP]

10. RIGHT GROIN STRIKE (MIGI NI MOMONE UTSU)
    [COVER RIGHT ELBOW WITH LEFT FOREARM BLOCK, AND USE A HEEL TOE PIVOT TO STRENGTHEN THE STRIKE. RETURN TO CROSS BLOCK, NO STEP]

11. LEFT BACK FIST (HADARI URA-KEN)
    [STRIKE TO FRONT. NO STEP AND HOLD HAND POSITION.]

12. RIGHT KNIFE HAND (MIGI SHUTO TE)
    [DROP BACK FIST TO A FOREARM BLOCK AND USE HEEL TOE PIVOT TO STRENGTHEN STRIKE. NO STEP AND HOLD HAND IN POSITION.]

13. LEFT UPPER SWEEPING KNIFE HAND
    (HADARI AGERU HAKU SHUTO TE)
    [STRIKE UPWARD FROM THE FOREARM BLOCK AND THE RIGHT HAND RETURNS TO READY POSITION AT HIP. NO STEP.]

14. RIGHT WAR FIST STRIKE (MIGI KOBUSHI UTSU)
[RIGHT STEP.]

15. FULL SHOULDER ROLL (AKU KA'TA KOROGARU)
[BEGIN ROLL IN LEFT STANCE.]

16. LEFT LUNGE PUNCH (HADARI KOBUSHI UTSU)
[COME OUT OF ROLL IN LEFT STANCE AND STEP WITH LEFT LEG WITH STRIKE. END IN RIGHT STANCE.]

17. LOOK BOTH WAYS (MIRU IDZURE-MO MICHI)
[LEFT THEN RIGHT]

18. RIGHT FAKE JUMPING DOUBLE FRONT SNAP
(MIGI MAGAI NISOBAI TORU MAE ORU KERU)
[THE LEFT LEG WILL KICK. LAND IN A RIGHT STANCE.]

19. LEFT HEEL SWEEP (HADARI KAGATO HAKU)
[USE A RIGHT KNIFE HAND STRIKE/ BLOCK WITH THE SWEEP. THE SWEEP SETS YOU UP FOR THE NEXT MOVE.]

20. THROAT PUNCH TAKE DOWN (NODO KOBUSHI SUWARU SHIMO)
[START THE MOVE OFF WITH A SHUTO BLOCK TO A GRAPPLE. ON THE TAKEDOWN SPIN - AROUND.]

21. STAND- UP {HANDS PARALLEL BLOCK}
(DAI KAMI {TE SOROTE ORU KIRE})
[REVERSE SPIN - AROUND ON STANDING MOTION. END WITH FEET IN BOW POSITION.]

22. STAY SALUTE (YAMU JIGI)

CATEGORY SEVENTEEN (YOSU JU-SHICHI): STAFFS (HAN-BO, BO, and KU-BO)

1. SALUTES (JIGI)

A. ENTRANCE SALUTE (IRU JIGI)

B. ADVANCED ENTRANCE SALUTE [HAND ROTATION] (AGARU KATA JIGI)

C. TURN-ABOUT/ EXIT SALUTE (MAWASU/ DE-GUCHI JIGI)

D. CROSSOVER/STAY SALUTE (WATARU/ YAMU JIGI)

2. STANCES (KAMAE)

A. BASIC STANCE (BUDO KAMAE)

B. ADVANCED STANCE (AGERU KAMAE)

C. SHADOW STANCE (KAGE KAMAE)

D. MASTER STANCE (SHUJIN KAMAE)

E. PRESENT STANCE (OKURU KAMAE)
[HANDS ARE FACE DOWN]

F. ON DUTY/ ON GUARD STANCE (TO-BAN KAMAE)
[STAFF IS AT 45 DEGREE ANGLE
IN FRONT OF BODY]

G. DRAW STANCE (KAKU KAMAE)

H. SADDLE STANCE (KURA KAMAE)

I. ATTENTION STANCE (JUSHA KAMAE)

Bo held at the side running the length of the arm and leg.

3. SPINS (TSUMUGU)

A. DOUBLE HAND SPIN (NISOBAI TE TSUMUGU)

B. TUCK UNDER SPIN (HASHORU SHITA TSUMUGU)

C. ROTATION SPIN (MAWARI TSUMUGU)

D. DOUBLE HAND SPIN OVERHEAD (NISOBAI TE TSUMUGU NOKORU)

E. MIDDLE SPIN (NAKABA TSUMUGU)

F. FAKE SPIN LOCK (MAGAI TSUMUGU TOJIRU)

G. REAR SPIN PENETRATION (URA TSUMUGU SATORI)

H. FINGER SPIN (YUBI TSUMUGU)

I. LONG END SPIN (NAGAI OWARI TSUMUGU)

J. OVERHEAD OPEN HAND SPIN (ICHI TE TSUMUGU NOKORU)

K. ROWING SPIN (KOGU TSUMUGU)

4. TUMBLES (OCHIRU)

A. FULL SHOULDER ROLL (AKU KA'TA KOROGARU)

B. HALF SHOULDER ROLL (HAN KA'TA KOROGARU)

C. CARTWHEEL (NI NIN NO NI-GURUMA KURUMA)

D. REVERSE ROLL (URA KOROGARU)

E. POLE VAULT (BO TOBU)

5. ACROBATICS (KARUWAZA-SIH): BLACK SASH ONLY

A. FRONT HANDSPRING (MAE TE HARU)

B. BACK HAND SPRING (URA TE HARU)

C. FRONT SOMERSAULT (MAE HIKKURI-KAYERU)

D. BACK SOMERSAULT (URA HIKKURI-KAYERU)

E. WALL RUN (KABE HASHIRU)

6. STRIKES (UTSU)

A. RIGHT AND LEFT PIVOT (MIGI TO HADARI MAWASU)

B. RIGHT AND LEFT REVERSE PIVOT (MIGI TO HADARI URA MAWASU)

C. RIGHT AND LEFT DOWN THRUST (MIGI TO HADARI SHIMO SASU)

D. RIGHT AND LEFT UPPER THRUST (MIGI TO HADARI AGERU SASU)

E. RIGHT AND LEFT DOWN SLASH (MIGI TO HADARI SHIMO KIRU)

F. RIGHT AND LEFT UPPER SLASH (MIGI TO HADARI AGERU KIRU)

G. PENETRATION (SATORI)

H. REVERSE PENETRATION (URA SATORI)

I. CENTER STRIKE (NAKABA USTU)

J. HIPNOTIZE (SAIMIN USTU)

K. TORNADO (TSUMUGUJI'KAZE UTSU)

7. ROTATIONS (MAWASU)

A. NECK ROLL (KUBI KOROGARU)

B. WAIST ROTATION [HORIZONTAL HAND ROLL WITH 4Ft. STAFF] (KOSHI MAWASU)

C. WAIST ROLL ROTATION [HAND PASS BEHIND THE BACK] (KOSHI KOROGARU MAWASU)

D. OVERHEAD OPEN HAND ROLL (SUGIRU KUBI TE KOROGARU)

E. FLOOR BOUNCE (YUKA HANARU)

F. SHOULDER ROTATION (KA'TA KOROGARU)

G. REVERSE OVERHEAD HAND ROTATION (URA NOKORU TE MAWASU)

H. OVERHEAD HAND ROTATION (NOKORU TE MAWASU)

I. LEG ROTATION [4Ft. STAFF] (ASHI MAWASU)

J. ARM ROTATION WITH PUNCH (UDE MAWASU NI KABUSHI UTSU)

K. REVERSE FRONT HAND ROTATION [STAFF ROTATION AROUND HAND LITTLE FINGER TO THUMB] (URA MAI TE MAWASU)

L. FRONT HAND ROTATION (MAI TE MAWASU)
[STAFF ROTATES AROUND HAND THUMB TO LITTLE FINGER]

8. STAFF COUNTER MOVES (BO SOMUKU HATARAKI)

A. UPPER HAND TAKE-AWAY (AGERU TE TORU RUSU)

B. DISTRACTION (NAGUSAMI)

C. SPIN UNDER (MAWASU SHITANO)

D. SPIN OVER (MAWASU SUGERU)

E. HAND STRIKE (TE UTSU)

9. BLOCKS (KIRE)

A. BEHIND HEAD BLOCK (URA NOKORU KIRE)

B. OVERHEAD BLOCK (NOKORU KIRE)

C. CENTER BLOCK (NAKABA KIRE)

D. LOWER BLOCK (SHITA NO KIRE)

E. SWEEP BLOCK (HAKU KIRE)

F. SIDE BLOCK [TOP THUMB UP] (YOKU KIRE)

G. REVERSE SIDE BLOCK [TOP THUMB DOWN] (URA YOKU KIRE)

H. SLASH BLOCK (KIRU KIRE)

I. PULL SLASH BLOCK (HIKI KIRU KIRE)

J. WALKING BLOCK (ARUKU KIRE)

K. REVERSE OPEN SIDE BLOCK [BOTTOM HAND OPEN] (URA HIRAITA YOKU KIRE)

L. OPEN SIDE BLOCK [TOP HAND OPEN] (HIRAITA YOKU KIRE)

10. PASSING (WATARU)

A. OVER SHOULDER (WATARU KA'TA)

B. AROUND WAIST (MAWARU KOSHI)

C. THROUGH LEGS (TORU ASHI)

D. OVER THE BACK (WATWRU SENAKA)

11. SWEEPS (HAKU):

A. LEG AND ANKLE PUSH (ASHI TO KURUBUSHI OSHIWAKE'RU)

B. LEG AND ANKLE PULL (ASHI TO KURUBUSHI NUKU)

12. STRIKE COMBO (USTU CHOGO):

A. BOX (TATAKU JUTSU)

B. REVERSE BOX (URA TATAKU JUTSU)

C. "X" (WATARU JUTSU)

D. REVERSE "X" (URA WATARU JUTSU)

CATEGORY EIGHTEEN (YOSU JU-HACHI): QUEST (NEGAU)

1. AT ONE'S REQUEST FROM THE TEACHER.
   (NEGAI NI YORI O KUDASAI SENSEI)

CATEGORY NINETEEN (YOSU JU-KU): CROSS GRAB TWO PEBBLES (JIRERU HITTAKURU NI KOISHI)

CATEGORY TWENTY (YOSU NI-JU): VERTICAL JUMP (TOBU)

1. UPWARD JUMP TO STERNUM. (KAMI TOBU NI MUNE)

MONJIN

YOSU ICHI: GRAPPLING COUNTER TECHNIQUES (KIHON HAPPO-JUTSU)

1. ELBOW TO CHEST (HIJI NI MUNE)

A. Right side stance.
B. Opponent punches with right arm.
C. Roll catch block the punch with the left arm.
D. Opponent punches with left arm.
E. Block the punch with a right ridge/ shuto combination.
F. Punch the chest with a right war fist.
G. Collapse the arm and right elbow the opponent's chest. Take a right step with this strike.
H. Roll back fist the nose with the right hand.
I. Elbow strike the chin with the right elbow.
J. Right back fist the side of the opponent's temple.
K. Right elbow strike the opposite side of the opponent's temple.
L. Right back fist strike the head.
M. Right clutch palm strike the groin.
N. Right forearm strike the under side of the opponent's right elbow as you push down on the opponent's right wrist.
O. Raise the opponent's right arm and slide your right hand under his shoulder and grab the opponent's back while putting your thumb into his armpit.
P. This will pin him face down to the ground.
Q. Once you have pinned him face down knee him in the chest with the left knee.
R. Kick him in the face with the left foot.
S. Heel kick him in the groin with the left heel.
T. Place a left jumping knee on the opponent's shoulder and drive them to the ground.

2. THROAT PUNCH TAKEDOWN (NODO UTSU OROSU)

A. Right side stance.
B. Opponent punches with right hand.
C. Roll catch block with left front hand.
D. If opponent punches with opposite hand, perform two hard blocks. (Ridge hand is followed by a knife hand with the same hand.)
E. Then with the right hand, strike the front of the neck with a clutch fist.
F. After you strike the neck with the clutch fist, open your hand and grab the sides of their neck with your right hand.
G. With the right leg, perform a heel sweep.
H. As the opponent falls, break their right arm over your left shin.
I. With your right arm, strike their collarbone with a knife hand.
J. Drop a right elbow into their groin.
K. Follow the groin strike with a right back fist strike to the xiphoid process.

L. Unfold your fist and strike the under side of the jaw with a spear hand.
M. Steps (H-M) are done immediately without any interruptions.

3. THROAT PUNCH PIN (NODO UTSU TOME-BARI DE TOMERU)

A. Right side stance.
B. Opponent punches with right hand.
C. Roll catch block with the left, front, hand.
D. If opponent punches with opposite hand, perform two hard blocks. (Ridge hand followed by a knife hand, with the same hand)
E. Then with the right hand, strike the front of the neck with a clutch fist.
F. Simultaneously with the clutch fist, take a step into your opponent with your right leg.
G. Once the clutch fist connects, immediately drop an elbow into the jaw, and drive through. Make sure that the elbow goes to the backside of the opponent's arm.
H. Lock the opponent's right wrist down with your left hand.
I. Slam your right elbow into the opponent's right elbow and drive down.
J. Right elbow strike the opponent in the back of the head.
K. Simultaneously with the elbow to the opponent's head, rotate your right hand down and grab their shoulder.
L. This will leave the opponent pinned face down.

4. THROAT PUNCH TURN-AROUND (NODO KOBUSHI UTSU MAWASU MAWARI

A. Right side stance.
B. Opponent punches with right hand.
C. Roll catch with left front hand.
D. If opponent punches with opposite hand, block with a ridge/ shuto combo.
E. Then with the right hand strike the front of the neck with a clutch fist.
F. Simultaneously with the clutch fist, take a step into your opponent with your right leg.
G. Once the clutch fist connects, immediately drop an elbow into the jaw, and drive through. Make sure that the elbow goes to the backside of the opponent's arm.
H. Next lock the wrist down with your left hand.
I. Slam your right elbow into the opponent's right elbow and drive down.
J. Simultaneously with the elbow break, raise the opponent's arm.
K. Then with the right elbow, elbow the opponent in the side of the head.
L. Once the elbow strikes the side of the head roll the arm around and place the opponent in an over the shoulder head lock.
M. While holding the neck and the opponent's arm, roll under so that the opponent's head is resting on your shoulder. This will allow you to put pressure on the opponent's neck or incapacitate him. Note that the arm you are holding will be locked out against you shoulder.
N. Step away from the opponent and throw him to the ground.

5. TWIST (YORU)

A. Right side stance.
B. Opponent punches with right arm.
C. Cross-body roll catch block the opponent's wrist.
D. Twist the opponent's arm so that his elbow points toward the ground and lift up. This locks out the opponent's arm.
E. Opponent punches with left arm.
F. Cross-body roll catch the opponent's wrist.
G. Step at a 45-degree angle down the side of the opponent and turn your body so that you are facing in the same direction as the opponent. As you come up behind him pull his lower arm into his under armpit and roll his upper arm so that it locks the lower arm out. Make sure your wrist, the wrist that is holding the opponent's arm that is locked in his armpit, is bent down and the palm is facing up.
H. Slam your lower forearm into the opponent's elbow and break it.
I. Knee the opponent in the backside and drive him away from you.

YOSU NI: WAR FIST STRIKES (KOBUSHI UTSU)

1. 90 WAR FIST STRIKES IN 1/3 MIN
(KU-JU KOBUSHI UTSU NI 1/3 FUN)

YOSU SAN: KICKING COUNTER TECHNIQUES (HAPPE KERU HEN KA-JUTSU)

1. SIDE SNAP CATCH (YOKO ORU TORU)

A. Right side stance.
B. Opponent throws a right side snap.
C. Strike block the ankle simultaneously with a left and right palm block, and grab the ankle.
D. Hold the opponent's ankle firm in your right hand while striking the opponent's knee joint with a right inner round kick.

2. SIDE SNAP KICK TO PUNCH (YOKO ORU KERU NI KOBUSHI)

A. Right side stance.
B. Opponent throws a right punch.
C. Cross-body roll catch block the punch with the right hand, and grapple the wrist.
D. Kick the opponent in the lower ribs or the shoulder joint with a side snap.

3. FRONT SNAP KICK TO PUNCH (MAE ORU KERU NI KOBUSHI)

A. Right side stance.
B. Opponent throws a right punch.
C. Cross-body roll catch block the punch with the right hand, and grapple the arm.
D. Kick the opponent in lower ribs or shoulder joint.

4. WHIP KICK TO PUNCH (MUCHI KERU NI KOBUSHI)

A. Right side stance.
B. Opponent throws a right punch.
C. Cross-body roll catch block the punch with the right hand, and grapple the arm.
D. Whip kick the opponent in the stomach.

5. DOUBLE ROUND TO PUNCH (NISOBAI NARU NI KOBUSHI)

A. Right side stance.
B. Opponent throws a right punch.
C. Right hand cross-body roll catch block the punch, and grapple the arm.
D. Strike the opponent in the jaw with a right inner round kick, and carry the leg over the arm. This will pull him forward and off balance.
E. Strike the opponent in the backside of the head with a left outer round kick and carry the leg over the opponent's arm.

6. PALM STRIKE TO FRONT SNAP CATCH (NIGIRU UTSU NI MAE ORU TORU)

A. Right side stance.
B. Opponent throws a right front snap kick.
C. Glide step to the inside of the kick at a 45-degree angle.
D. Simultaneously with the glide, perform a left downward roll catch to the opponent's kick and lift up.
E. Strike the opponent in the knee with a right palm hand strike.

7. KNIFE STRIKE TO HIP JOINT (SHUTO UTSU NI KOSHI FUSHI)

A. Right side stance.
B. Opponent throws a right front snap kick.
C. Glide step to the inside of the kick at a 45-degree angle.
D. Simultaneously with the glide, perform a left downward roll catch to the opponent's kick and lift up.
E. Strike the opponent in the hip joint with a right sliding knife hand strike.

YOSU SHI: KICKS (KERU)

1. DOUBLE ROUND KICK (NISOBAI NARU KERU)

   A. Right side stance.
   B. Perform a right inner round kick.
   C. Perform a left outer round kick.
   D. This kick can be used when crossing obstacles 2 to 4 feet in height.

2. SHADON SHADAN (SHADON SHADAN)

   A. Saddle stance.
   B. Right side snap.
   C. Cross step with the right leg behind the left leg.
   D. Perform a left side snap and set the foot down in a saddle stance.

3. SHIN SCRAPE (ASHI KOSURU)

   A. Right side stance.
   B. Chamber the right leg.
   C. Strike the opponent in the shin, just below the knee-cap, and push down with the blade of the foot.

4. HEEL TO BACK (KAGATO NI URA)

   A. Right side stance.
   B. Chamber the right leg.
   C. Hook kick the opponent in the lower back. Aim for the second and third vertebra

5. HOOK KICK WITH A WHIP (KAGI KERU NO MUCHI KERU NO MODORI) KICK ON THE RETURN

   A. Right side stance.
   B. Chamber the right leg
   C. Perform a hook kick and carry the kick just past the target.
   D. Once target is struck without setting the kicking leg down perform a whip kick to the opponent.
   E. Replace leg into a stance.

6. <u>WHIP KICK WITH A HOOK (MUCHI KERU NO KAGI KERU NO MODORI) KICK ON THE RETURN</u>

   A. Right side stance.
   B. Chamber the right leg.
   C. Perform a whip kick and carry the kick just past the target
   D. Once the target is struck, without setting the leg down, perform a hook kick to the opponent.
   E. Replace leg into a stance.

7. <u>STOMP KICK (TSU KU KERU)</u>

   A. Right side stance.
   B. Chamber the leg.
   C. Strike the opponent's ankle joint with stomp kick. The strike comes from the arch side of the foot.

8. <u>TIGER'S TAIL (TORA SHIPPO KERU)</u>

   A. Right side stance.
   B. Forward cross step with the right leg.
   C. Simultaneous with the cross step swing your head toward the ground.
   D. Simultaneous with the head movement kick with the left leg in a spinning heel kick position.
   E. The strike from this kick will come from the heel.
   F. The kick will spin you back around facing forward in a migi budo kamae.

9. <u>ROLLING AX KICK (KORAGARU ONO KERU)</u>

   A. Right side stance.
   B. Perform a full shoulder roll.
   C. On the forward roll motion, leave the left leg, straight. (Remember to keep the knee slightly bent)
   D. Strike the target with the heel of the left leg.

10. <u>INSIDE BLOCK (NAKA KIRE)</u>

   A. Right side stance.
   B. Opponent punches.
   C. Block punch to the inside with an outer round kick.

11. <u>OUTSIDE BLOCK (UWA KIRE)</u>

   A. Right side stance.
   B. Opponent punches.
   C. Block punch to the outside with an inside round kick.

YOSU GO: KNEE BREAKS (KOPPO-NINJUTSU NI HIZA)

1. FRONT SNAP KNEE BREAK (MAE ORU HIZA KOWASU)

   A. Right side stance.
   B. Chamber the right leg.
   C. Front snap the opponent at the base of the kneecap and drive backwards.

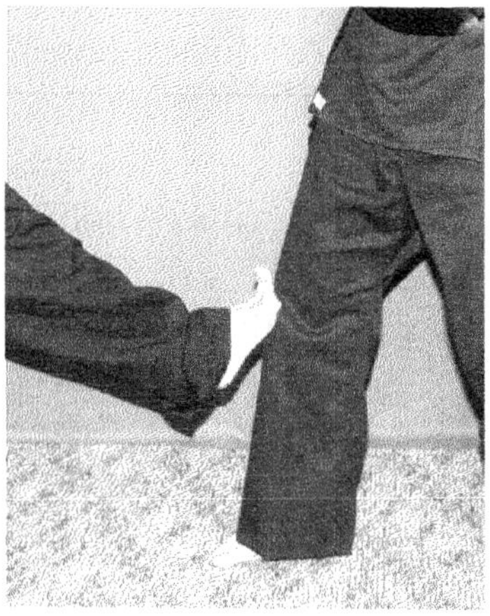

2. SIDE SNAP TO KNEE BREAK (YOKO ORU HIZA KOWASU)

   A. Right side stance.
   B. Chamber the right leg.
   C. Side snap the opponent at the top of the knee cap and drive backwards.

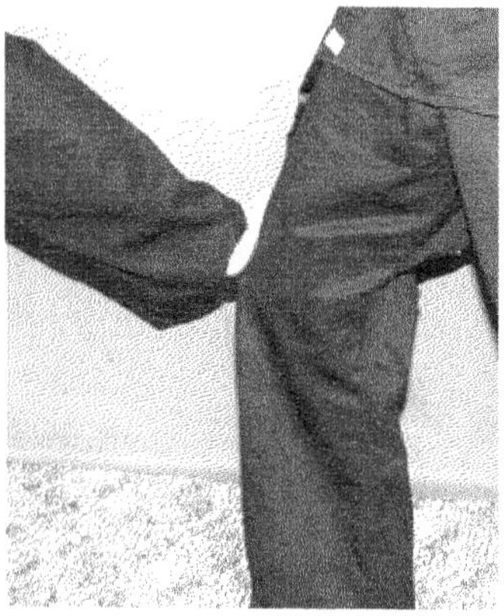

3. STOMP KICK KNEE BREAK (TSUKU KERU KOWASU)

   A. Right side stance.
   B. Chamber the right leg.
   C. Stomp kick the opponent above the kneecap and drive down.
      (Remember a stomp kick strikes with the arch side of the foot)

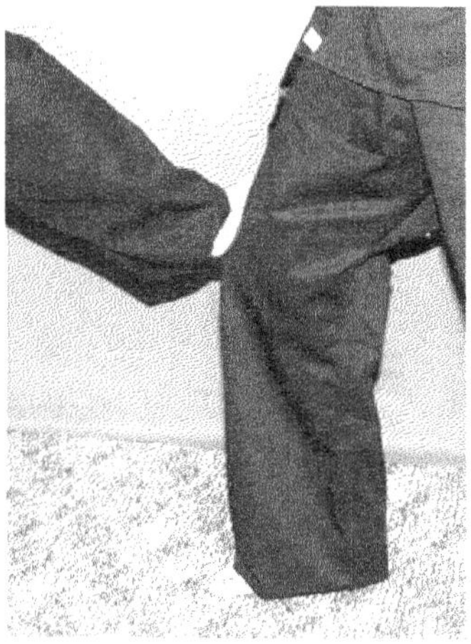

4. WHIP OR HOOK OUTER KNEE BREAK (MUCHI NO KAGI UWA HIZA KOWASU)

Note: The outer knee breaks pictures are the same as the inner knee break pictures seen below but on reverse side of the knee.

A. Right side stance.
B. Chamber the right leg.
C. Strike the outside of the knee directly in the center of the knee joint with either a hook or whip kick.

5. WHIP OR HOOK INNER KNEE BREAK (MUCHI NO KAGI NAKA HIZA KOWASU)

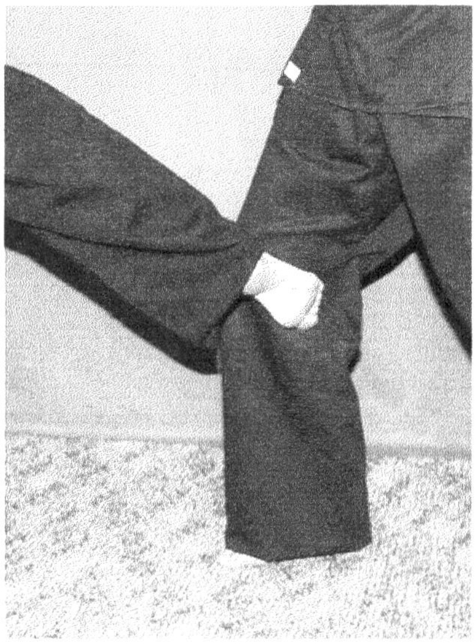

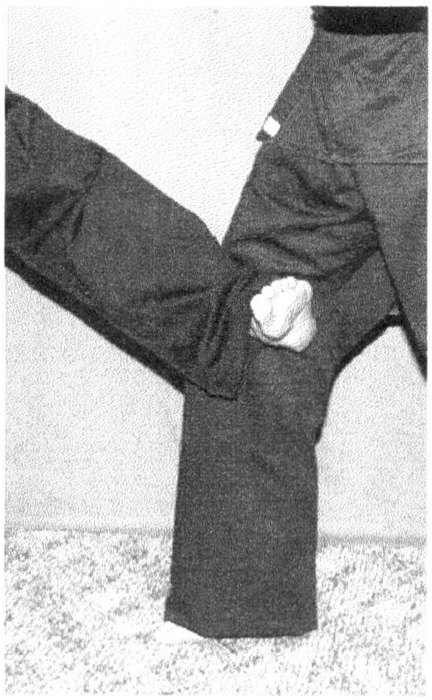

A. Right side stance.
B. Chamber the right leg.
C. Strike the inside of the knee directly in the center of the knee joint with either a hook or whip kick.

6. FRONT SNAP TO SIDE OF KNEE (MAE ORU NI YOKO HIZA KOWASU)

A. Right side stance.
B. Chamber the right leg.
C. Strike the center of the knee from the side with a front snap.

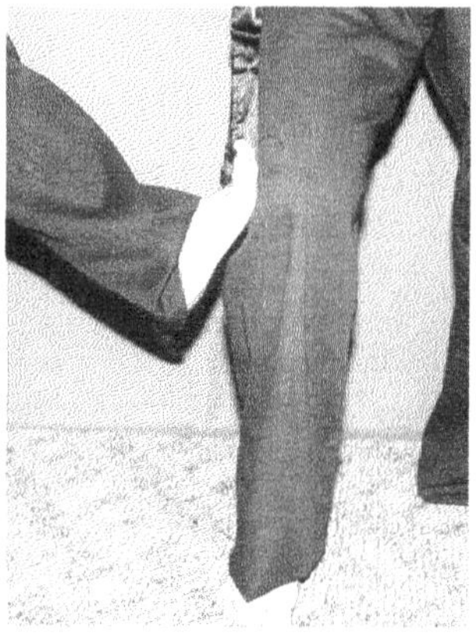

7. SIDE SNAP TO SIDE OF KNEE (YOKU ORU NI YOKO HIZA KOWASU)

A. Right side stance.
B. Chamber the right leg.
C. Strike the center of the knee from the side with a side snap.

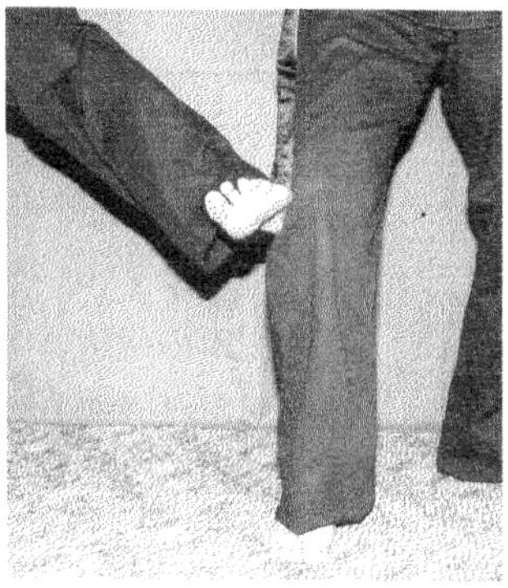

YOSU ROKU: BACK COUNTER TECHNIQUES (URA SOMUKU-JUTSU)

1. DOUBLE HAND UNDER COUNTER (NISOBAI TE SHITA SOMUKU)

A. Opponent grabs both shoulders from behind.
B. Twist left into the opponent and shuto strike him in the lower ribs.
C. Circle the left hand under the opponent's right arm and strike him in the back of the head with a palm hand.
D. Complete the circle motion and break the opponent's right elbow joint and torque your opponent to a face down position.
E. Right palm strike the side of the opponent's head.
F. Reach and grab the opponent's right wrist with your right hand and step to the side and throw the opponent away from you.

2. DOUBLE HAND OVER COUNTER (NISOBAI TE SUGIRU SOMUKU)

A. Opponent grabs both shoulders from behind.
B. Twist to the left while raising your left arm.
C. Strike the opponent in the side of the head with a shuto hand.
D. Carry the left arm on over and wrap it around the opponent's arms. This will break the opponent's right arm.
E. Strike the opponent's left elbow with a right palm strike. This will break his left elbow.

3. CROSS GRAB COUNTER (JIRERU HITTAKURU SOMUKU)

A. Opponent grabs left shoulder with right hand.
B. Grab opponent's right hand with your right hand.
C. Step back with left foot and twist toward opponent.
D. Slide your left forearm down the opponent's right arm.
E. Pull forward on the opponent's right arm while you slam your left elbow into their ribs.
F. Pull back on the opponent's wrist while you roll the opponent over using your forearm.
G. Step away from the opponent at a 45-degre angle and throw the opponent away from your position.

4. ONE HAND UNDER COUNTER (ICHI TE SHITA SOMUKU)

A. Opponent grabs right shoulder with right hand.
B. Twist left into the opponent while stepping through with the left foot.
C. Strike the opponent in the lower ribs with a left shuto hand.
D. Circle the left hand under the opponent's right arm and strike the opponent in the head with a palm hand.
E. Carry the hand on around and torque the opponent so that he is face down.

5. ONE HAND OVER COUNTER (ICHI TE SURIRU SOMUKU)

A. Opponent grabs right shoulder with right hand.
B. Grab the opponent's right hand with your left hand.
C. Step back with the right foot and turn to the right.
D. Move right arm in a circular motion and strike the opponent in the side of the head with a shuto hand.
E. Carry right arm on around and lock opponent's right arm in place.
F. Strike opponent's right elbow with a left palm hand.

YOSU SHICHI: GROUND COUNTER (MOTODZUKU SOMUKU)

Picture one is and example of being pinned on your back.

Picture two is an example of being pinned on your stomach.

1. BODY SPREAD (MI SHIKU)

   A. Opponent has you pinned on your back on the ground with your arms pinned above your head.
   B. Pull your hands from above your head down to your side of your body and roll your wrists. The hands will move in a circular motion down to your knees. The hand movement throws the opponent off balance.
   C. Simultaneously with the hand movement, thrust your pelvis into the air. This will send your opponent through the air and off of you.

2. EAR STRIKE (MIMI UTSU)

   A. Opponent has you pinned on your back on the ground and is choking you with both hands.
   B. Strike the opponent's elbows outward with two ridge hands.
   C. Strike both collarbones with shuto hands.
   D. Slam the ears.
   E. Gauge the eyes and grab the back of the head.
   F. Pull the opponent's head to one side of your head and raise the opposite leg. This will catapult the opponent into the ground head first.

3. STOMP ROLL (TSUKU MAWASU)

   A. You are lying on your back on the ground.
   B. Opponent throws a stomp kick at your head and chest area.
   C. Block kick with palm strikes and grab the foot.
   D. Twist the ankle. This will break the ankle.
   E. Feed the leg closest to the opponent between your body and the opponent's leg.
   F. Slam your leg toward the grouna. This will throw the opponent away from you.

4. STOMACH ROLL (I MAWASU)

   A. Opponent has you pinned on your stomach on the ground and is choking you with both hands.
   B. Put you right arm straight out and bring your left arm in by your side.
   C. Simultaneously with the moving of the arms, bring your left knee up to meet your left elbow.
   D. Push off with your left knee and left arm and roll to the right. This will roll the opponent off of you.
   E. Roll with the opponent and elbow him in the side with a left elbow.
   F. Roll on up and gauge your opponent's eyes.

5. STRIKE WITH ARM LOCK (USTU NI UDE TOJIRU)

   A. Opponent has you pinned on the ground on your back, and he is choking you with the left hand and punching you with the right.
   B. Block right punch with a right overhead block.
   C. Grapple the opponent's right arm, and slam the opponent's elbow with your left hand.
   D. Simultaneously with hand movements, slide the left foot up to your buttocks and press up. This will help with roll movement started by the hand movements.
   E. Follow through with the roll and come up on top of your opponent's right arm with the arm locked out.

6. SAND CRAB (SUNA KANI)

   A. Opponent has you pinned on the ground on your stomach, and is choking you with both hands.
   B. Raise up on both elbows and grab both of the opponent's wrists.
   C. Pull opponent's wrists to your pecks as you bring your knees up underneath you. This will slam your opponent on his face directly in front of you.

YOSU HACHI: ROPE OR BELT FIGHTING
(TORINAWAJUTSU <or> OBIJUTSU)

** Techniques are illustrated from a right side stance.

1. ARM WRAP (UDE TSUTSUMU)

   A. Attacker throws right punch.
   B. Wrap punch with belt. Make sure the belt is on the outside of the elbow and the inside of the wrist.
   C. Push the wrist up and pull the elbow down while stepping through with the right leg. This will spin the attacker around and expose the back.
   ** Alternate ending- Pull the wrist out and push the elbow in while stepping directly to the side. This will dislocate the shoulder.

2. ELBOW BREAK (HIJI KOWASU)

A. Attacker throws a right punch.
B. Wrap punch with belt. Make sure the belt is on the outside of the elbow and the inside of the wrist.
C. Glide step on a 45-degree angle with the arm wrapping. This will lock the attacker's arm out and break it. the arm lock can be done by pushing it out or up with the belt.

3. INSIDE DOUBLE HAND TIE (NAKA NISOBAI TE MUSUBU)

A. Attacker throws right punch.
B. Block the punch by sweeping the belt outward. When the belt makes contact with the punch bring the bottom (left) hand up in a circular motion.
C. Attacker throws left punch.
D. Wrap the punch by making a circle motion with the right hand.
E. This ties both hands together.
F. Glide step to the left on a 45-degree with the wrapping of the left arm.
G. Perform a right heel sweep and slam a left elbow into the opponent's right elbow.
H. Simultaneously with the slamming of the elbow, squat to one knee. This will throw our opponent to the ground.

4. BLOCK SWEEP (KIRE HAKU)

A. Attacker throws punch.
B. Hold belt loosely in the hands.
C. When punch draws near strike up, down, left, or right in a sweeping motion with the belt.
D. When the belt comes into contact with the arm pull the hands outward. This will pop the arm and send it out away from the body.

5. SIDE TO SIDE ROLL (YOKO NO YOKO KOROGARU)

** Note: If you roll to early then you will miss the grapple.

A. Attacker throws left punch.
B. Hold belt loosely between the hands in a bo draw stance.
C. When punch draws near, strike left in a sweeping motion with the belt.
D. When the belt comes into contact with the arm, pull the left hand up and the right down in a returning motion to the bo draw stance. This will grapple the arm.
E. Slam your right elbow into your opponent's left elbow.
F. Break the attacker's left elbow with a right knee strike and right stomp the attacker's closest knee.

** Alternate- If attacker throws right punch and you are in a right staff draw stance with the rope then you will strike left in a sweeping motion the same way as step C and grapple the punch. Drop your left elbow into the back of the opponent's right elbow. Right reverse heel sweep and throw your opponent away from you.

7. LEG WRAP (ASHI TSUTSUMU)

A. Attacker throws a right kick
B. Make a sweeping block (left hand on bottom of block) to the outside.
C. Once the belt makes contact with the leg bring the bottom hand up in a circular motion. This will wrap the leg.
D. Pick up on the leg as fast as you can. This will force the attacker back ward.

8. ARM TO KNEE WRAP (UDI NI HIZA TSUTSUMU)

A. Attacker throws a right punch.
B. Make a sweeping block (left hand on bottom of block) to the outside of the body
C. When the belt strikes the arm, make a circular motion with the bottom hand. This will wrap the arm.
D. Pull the belt down so that the attacker's arm twists and locks the elbow.
E. Strike the elbow with the outside knee.

9. ARM THROW (UDE NAGERU)

A. Attacker throws a right punch.
B. Perform a basic inside hand tie.
C. Step away from the attacker with the back leg while pulling the attacker off balance.
D. Jerk the attacker's arm toward the ground.
E. When the arm is 8 – 10 inches from the ground jerk it straight up. This will cause the attacker to flip.

10. DOUBLE ARM WRAP AND BREAK (NISOBAI UDE TSUTSUMU NI KOWASU)

A. Perform a double hand tie.
B. Once the hands are tied, pick them up over your shoulder while simultaneously twisting your back toward your attacker.
C. Pull the arms down onto your shoulders. This will break the elbows.

11. <u>OUTSIDE DOUBLE HAND TIE (URA NISOBAI TE MUSUBU)</u>

A. Attacker throws a right punch.
B. Block punch by sweeping the belt inward (right hand on top), across the body.
C. Wrap punch by bringing the top hand down.
D. The attacker throws a left punch.
E. Wrap the left punch by continuing the right hand on around.
F. This ties both hands together.
G. Glide step to the left on a 45-degree with the wrapping of the left arm.
H. Perform a right heel sweep and slam a left elbow into the opponent's right elbow.
I. Simultaneously with the slamming of the elbow, squat to one knee. This will throw opponent to the ground

YOSU KU: TONFA (A SHORT STAFF WITH A SIDE HANDLE)

A. SALUTE (JIGI)

1. ENTRANCE SALUTE (IRU JIGI)
2. ADVANCED ENTRANCE SALUTE (AGERU IRU JIGI)
3. CROSSOVER/ STAY SALUTE (WATARU/ YAMU JIGI)
4. TURN ABOUT/ EXIT SALUTE (MAWASU/ DE-GUCHI JIGI)

B. STANCES FOR TONFA, KAMA, AND HAN-BO (KAMAE)

1. TONFA STANCES (TONFA KAMAE)

A. DRAW STANCE (KAKU KAMAE)

B. MASTER STANCE (SHUJIN KAMAE)

C. SHADOW STANCE (KAGE KAMAE)

D. BASIC STANCE (BUDO KAMAE)

E. ADVANCE STANCE (AGERU KAMAE)

F. SADDLE STANCE (KURA KAMAE)

G. ATTENTION STANCE (JUSHA KAMAE)

H. PRESENT STANCE (OKURU KAMAE)

I. ON GUARD STANCE (TO-BAN KAMAE)

2. KAMA STANCES (KAMA KAMAE)

A. DRAW STANCE (KAKU KAMAE)

B. MASTER STANCE (SHUJIN KAMAE)

C. SHADOW STANCE (KAGE KAMAE)

D. BASIC STANCE (BUDO KAMAE)

E. ADVANCED STANCE (AGERU KAMAE)

F. SADDLE STANCE (KURA KAMAE)

G. ATTENTION STANCE (JUSHA KAMAE)

H. PRESENT STANCE (OKURU KAMAE)

I. ON GUARD STANCE (TO-BAN KAMAE)

5. HAN-BO STANCES (HAN-BO KAMAE)

A. DRAW STANCE (KAKU KAMAE)

B. MASTER STANCE (SHUJIN KAMAE)

C. SHADOW STANCE (KAGE KAMAE)

D. BASIC STANCE (BUDO KAMAE)

E. ADVANCED STANCE (AGERU KAMAE)

F. SADDLE STANCE (KURA KAMAE)

G. ATTENTION STANCE (JUSHA KAMAE)

H. PRESENT STANCE (OKURU KAMAE)

I. ON GUARD STANCE (TO –BAN KAMAE)

C. TONFA TOOLS

There are 9 tool of the tonfa and they consist of the six sides of the tonfa plus the handle and the two corners where the handle meets the short staff.

1. HANDLE (HANDORU)

2. BARREL (TARU)

3. BASE (MOTO)

4. JOINT (KANSETSU)

5. STUB (SUISASHI)

6. TAB [RIGHT AND LEFT] (HIMO)

7. TIP [TOP AND BOTTOM] (SAKI)

D. BLOCKS (KIRE)

1. SIDE BLOCK (YOKO KIRE)
2. OVERHEAD BLOCK (NOKORU KIRE)
3. NECK AND KIDNEY BLOCK (KUBI MURADO KIRE)
4. FACE BLOCK (TAN KAO KIRE)
5. UPPER CROSS BLOCK (AGERU JIRERU KIRE)
6. MIDDLE CROSS BLOCK (NAKABA JIRERU KIRE)
7. LOWER CROSS BLOCK (SHITA NO JIRERU KIRE)
8. CATCH BLOCK (TORU KIRE)
9. KIDNEY BLOCK (MURADO KIRE)
10. PARRALLEL BLOCK (SOROTE KIRE)
11. HORIZONTAL BLOCK (TAIRAKA NA KIRE)
12. JOINT ("Y") BLOCK (KANSETSU KIRE)
13. FORWARD BLOCK (MAE KIRE)

E. EXTENDED BLOCKS

1. KIDNEY BLOCK (MURADO KIRE)
2. SIDE BLOCK (YOKO KIRE)
3. UPPER CROSS BLOCK (AGERU JIRERU KIRE)
4. MIDDLE CROSS BLOCK (NAKABA JIRERU KIRE)
5. LOWER CROSS BLOCK (SHITA NO JIRERU KIRE)
6. PARRALLEL BLOCK (SOROTE KIRE)
7. HORIZONTAL BLOCK (TAIRAKA NA KIRE)
8. NECK AND KIDNEY BLOCK (KUBI MURADO KIRE)
9. FRONT PENETRATION (MAE SATORI)

F. STRIKES (UTSU)

1. INSIDE KNIFE STRIKE (NAKA SHUTO UTSU)
2. OVERHEAD BLOCK STRIKE (NOKORU KIRE UTSU)
3. DOUBLE OUTSIDE KNIFE STRIKE (NISOBAI UWA SHUTO UTSU)
4. OPEN HANDLE STRIKE (AITA YE UTSU)
5. REVERSE PENETRATION (FUSERU SATORI)
6. DOUBLE PENETRATION (NISOBAI SATORI)
   [STACK HANDS WITH STRIKE]
7. CLOSED HAND STRIKE WITH BACKFIST
   (SHIWAI TE UTSU NI URA-KEN)
8. BACK ARM STRIKE (URA UDE UTSU)
9. REVERSE BACK ARM STRIKE (FUSERU URA UDE UTSU)
10. DOWNWARD STRIKE (SHIMO UTSU)
11. DOUBLE OPEN HANDLE STRIKE (NISOBAI AITA YE UTSU)
12. INSIDE ROTATION STRIKE (ATAMA MAWASU UTSU)
13. OUTSIDE ROTATION STRIKE (UWA MAWASU UTSU)
14. BLOCKING STEP PENETRATION GROIN STRIKE
    (KIRE DAN SATORI MOMONE UTSU)
15. ROLL (TONFA) BACK ARM STRIKE WITH HANDLE
    (KOROGARU TONFA URA UDE UTSU NI YE)
16. FAN STRIKE (OGI UTSU)
17. HANDLE PULL BEHIND NECK (YE HIKU URA NI KUBI)
18. HANDLE PULL BEHIND KNEE (YE HIKU URA NI HIZA)
19. FAN HANDS (OGI TE)
20. BARREL STRIKE (TARU UTSU)

G. ROLLS WITH TONFA (KOROGARU NI TONFA)

1. REVERSE SHORT ROLL (TONFA)
   (FUSERU TAN KOROGARU TONFA)

2. DOUBLE SHORT ROLL (REQUIRES TWO TONFA)
   (NISOBAI TAN KOROGARU TONFA)

3. SHORT HANDLE SIDE ROLL
   [HOLD HANDLE AND ROLL DOWN BARREL]
   (TAN YE YOKO KOROGARU)

4. TWIST ROLL
   [HOLD HANDLE DOWN AND ROLL TONFA WHILE TURNING THE TONFA SO YOU FINISH HOLDING HANDLE]
   (YORU KOROGARU)

5. LONG ROLL (NAGAI KOROGARU)

6. REVERSE LONG ROLL (URA NAGAI KOROGARU)

7. TRIPPLE ROLL (SAN KOROGARU)
   [FRONT PENETRATION WITH OUTSIDE ROTATION STRIKE, SHORT HANDLE SIDE ROLL TO OPEN HANDLE STRIKE, TWIST ROLL TO BARREL STRIKE, THEN SHORT HANDLE SIDE ROLL TO OPEN HANDLE STRIKE TO KNEE AND PULL.]

8. WRIST ROLL (TE-KUBI KOROGARU)
   [TONFA ROLLS OVER OPPOSITE HAND]

9. 1 FINGER "Y" ROLL (ICHI YUBI KOROGARU)
   [HORIZONTAL ROLL]

10. OPEN HAND OVERHAND ROLL
    (AITA YE NOKORU KOROGARU)

11. 1 FINGER ROLL OVERHEAD (ICHI YUBI NOKORU KOROGARU)

12. 1 FINGER REVERSE ROLL (ICHI YUBI URA KOROGARU)
    [DIAGONAL ROLL]

13. OVERHAND BACKHAND ROLL (WATARU TE URA-KEN KOROGARU)

14. THROUGH FINGER ROLL (TORU YUBI KOROGARU)

15. AROUND BACK (MAWASU SENAKA)
    [PASS FROM ONE HAND TO THE NEXT]

YOSU JU: TONFA, HAN-BO, OR KAMA COUNTERS
(TONFA , HAN-BO OR KAMA SOMUKU)

** Note: Use the following diagram as an indicator in the proper direction that you should move when performing the techniques. All the techniques are illustrated by the tonfa and with the opponent attacking with a right punch.

RIGHT SIDE STANCE

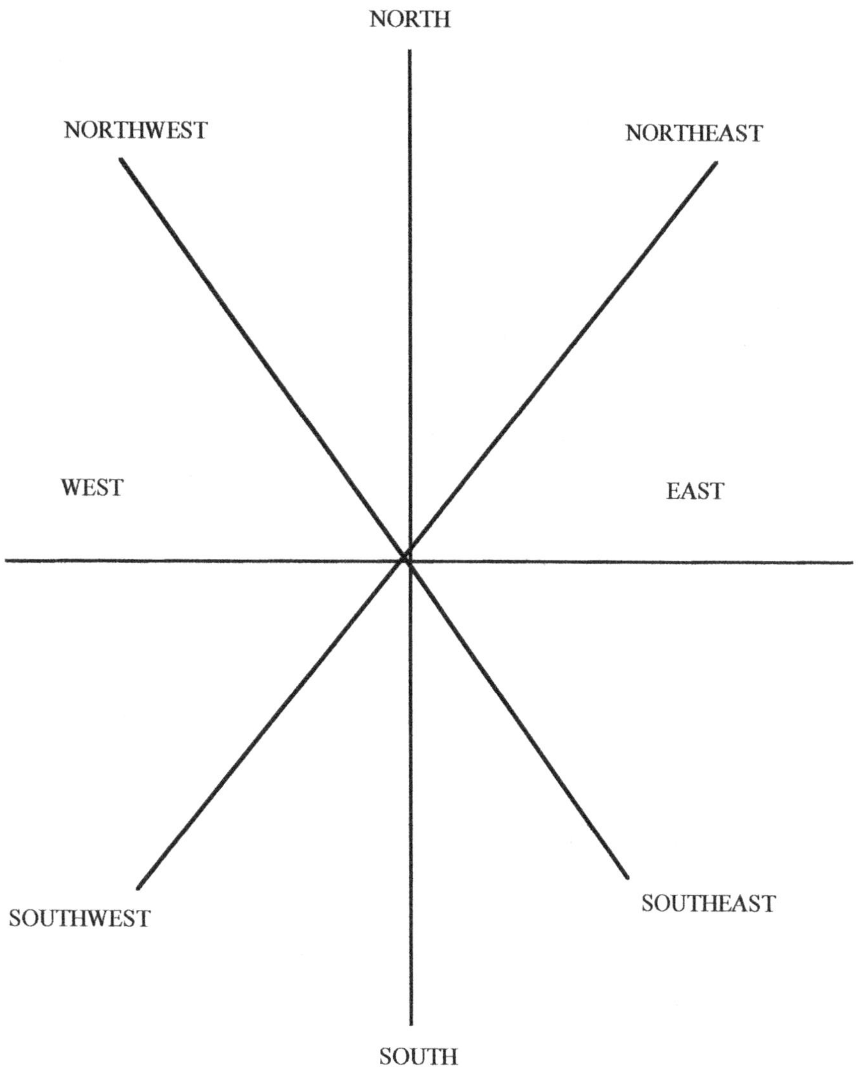

A. NORTH

1. BASIC STANCE (BUDO KAMAE)

A. THROAT PUNCH TAKEDOWN (NODO UTSU OROSU)

1. Make sure to hook the long end of the tonfa over the opponent's arm to help secure the grapple.

2. ADVANCED STANCE (AGERU KAMAE)

A. ARM WRAP (UDE TSUTSUMU)

1. Opponent throws a right punch.
2. Perform a left neck and head block and grapple the arm.
3. Punch the side of the throat with the short end of the tonfa.
4. Strike the face with the long end of the tonfa.
5. Strike the elbow with the long end of the tonfa and carry the strike through so that you can hook the elbow with the long end.
6. Wrap up the arm by twisting the opponent.

3. DRAW STANCE (KAKU KAMAE)

A. PASS UNDER (TSUKA SURU)

1. Opponent punches with a right punch.
2. Perform a left neck and head block and hook the wrist with the tonfa handle.
3. Punch the opponent's right floater ribs with the short end of the tonfa.
4. Step underneath the opponent's right arm and perform a left reverse penetration strike to the ribs.
5. Break the opponent's right elbow with a right downward tonfa strike.

4. SHADOW STANCE (KAGE KAMAE)

A. SCISSOR (HASAMI)

1. Opponent punches with a right punch.
2. Perform a left side block with the tonfa.
3. Simultaneously strike the back of the opponent's neck with the left tonfa handle as you strike the front of the opponent's neck with a right forearm strike.

5. MASTER STANCE (SHUJIN KAMAE)

A. ARM ROLL (UDE KOROGARU)

1. Opponent punches with a right punch.
2. Perform a left side block with the tonfa.
3. Lock out the opponent's elbow by wrapping the tonfa around the arm.
4. Strike the opponent in the throat with a right forearm.

B. <u>NORTHWEST</u>

1. BASIC STANCE (BUDO KAMAE)

A. SHOULDER LOCK (KA'TA TOJIRU)

1. Opponent punches with a right punch.
2. Perform a left side block with the tonfa.
3. Punch the opponent in the throat with a right short end strike.
4. Strike the opponent in the throat with a right forearm strike.
5. Right downward elbow to opponent's collarbone.
6. Feed the long end of the tonfa through the opponent's armpit and lock out the shoulder by pressing down.

2. ADVANCED STANCE (AGERU KAMAE)

A. DOUBLE HAND ON ELBOW (NISOBAI TE NI HIJI)

3. DRAW STANCE (KAKU KAMAE)

A. ARM TO ARM (UDE NI UDE)

1. Opponent punches with a right punch.
2. Block inward with a left face block and capture the opponent's wrist with the tonfa handle.
3. Perform the standard arm to arm counter from this point on.

4. SHADOW STANCE (KAGE KAMAE)

A. DOUBLE FAN (NISOBAI OGI)

1. Opponent punches with a right punch.
2. Perform a double fan block to the right.
3. Strike the face with a left short end punch.

5. MASTER STANCE (SHUJIN KAMAE)

A. SHOULDER BACK LOCK (KA'TA SENAKE JO)

1. Start the technique out by blocking the opponent's right punch with a left neck and head block.
2. Break attacker's arm with a right side block that fans under the grappled arm and strike outward against the elbow.
3. Grab wrist with right hand.
4. Pull down on the attacker's right wrist with your right hand while pushing up with your right elbow.

C. <u>NORTHEAST</u>

1. BASIC STANCE (BUDO KAMAE)

A. SHOULDER STRIKE (KA'TA UTSU)

1. Opponent punches with a right punch.
2. Block punch with a left side block.
3. Strike the opponent's right shoulder with a right short end punch.

2. ADVANCED STANCE (AGERU KAMAE)

A. SINGLE FAN (ICHI OGI)

1. Opponent punches with a right punch.
2. Block the punch outward with a left outside fan.
3. Strike the underside of the opponent's chin with a right short end punch.

3. DRAW STANCE (KAKU KAMAE)

A. SIDE BLOCK (YOKO KIRE)

1. Opponent punches with a right punch.
2. Block opponent's strike with a left side block and grapple.
3. Strike the opponent's right ribs with a right short end punch.
4. Strike the opponent's right elbow with a right forearm strike or handle strike and carry over.
5. Slam short end of weapon into the back of the opponent's shoulder and lock out face down.

4. SHADOW STANCE (KAGE KAMAE)

A. THROAT PUNCH PIN
(NODO USTU TOME-BARI DE ROMERU)

5. MASTER STANCE (SHUJIN KAMAE)

A. ELBOW TO CHEST (HIJI NI MUNE)

D. <u>WEST</u> (Opponent will step with punch.)

1. BASIC STANCE (BUDO KAMAE)

A. RIB STRIKE (ROKKOTSU UTSU)
1. Opponent punches with a right punch.
2. Block punch with a left side block.
3. Strike the opponent's left ribs with a right short end punch.

2. ADVANCED STANCE (AGERU KAMAE)
[When the following move is performed with the tonfa hold the tonfa by the barrel and not the handles.]

A. HANDLE LOCK (HANDORU TOJIRU)
1. Opponent punches with a right uppercut.
2. Use the left handle to hook the opponent's right wrist.
3. Simultaneous with the hooking of the wrist use the right handle to hook the opponent's right elbow.

3. DRAW STANCE (KAKU KAMAE)

A. THROAT PIN (NODO PIN DE TOMERU)
1. Opponent punches with a right punch.
2. Block the punch with a left outward fan block.
3. Strike the opponent's elbow with a right strike.
4. Spin tonfa out and use long end to pin throat.

4. SHADOW STANCE (KAGE KAMAE)

A. THROAT STRIKE (NODO UTSU)
1. Opponent punches with a right punch.
2. Block the punch with a left side block.
3. Punch the opponent in the throat with the short end of the tonfa.

5. MASTER STANCE (SHUJIN KAMAE)

A. KNEE STRIKE (HIZA USTU)
1. Opponent punches with a right punch.
2. Block the opponent's punch with a right side block.
3. Strike the back of the opponent's right knee with a short end punch as you go to a left knee.
4. Left forearm strike the opponent in the back of the neck or head.

E. <u>EAST</u> (Opponent will step with punch.)

1. BASIC STANCE (BUDO KAMAE)

A. DOUBLE FAN BLOCK (NISOBAI OGI KIRE)
(Left fan strikes the opponent's wrist while the second fan strikes the opponent's jaw.)

2. ADVANCED STANCE (AGERU KAMAE)

A. HOOK (TOMERU)
1. Opponent punches with a right punch.
2. Block strike with a left side block.
3. Strike the underside of the opponent's right elbow with the right tonfa and feed under so that you hook the neck with the tonfa handle.

3. DRAW STANCE (KAKU KAMAE)

A. DOUBLE LUNGE PUNCH (NISOBAI KOBUSHI UTSU)
(Throat and sternum)

4. SHADOW STANCE (KAGE KAMAE)

A. HEAD STRIKE (ATAMA UTSU)
1. Opponent punches with a right punch.
2. Block punch with a left side block.
3. Strike the opponent in the throat with a right short end punch and drive through so that the entire tonfa is past the head.
4. Hook the head between the tonfa handle and the arm.
5. Pull down and right knee strike the opponent in the face.

5. MASTER STANCE (SHUJIN KAMAE)

A. HIP STRIKE (KOSHI FUSHI UTSU)
1. Opponent punches with a right punch.
2. Block the punch with a left outside fan block.
3. Strike the opponent's right hip joint with a right short end punch.

F. VOID

1. SADDLE STANCE (KURA KAMAE)

   A. BASIC GI GRAB (BUDO KI HITTAKURU)

2. ADVANCED STANCE (AGARU KAMAE)

   A. SNAKE ARM (HEBI UDE)

3. DRAW STANCE (KAKU KAMAE)

   A. ADVANCED BLOCK (AGERU KIRE)

YOSU JU-SAN: MONJIN KATA

** NOTE: The raising of the foot in unison with the strikes can be in a chambering motion, or the foot can brush the leg and make noise. Moves number 2, 3, and 4, are done fast; and when moving from move 1 to move 2, carry the hands all the way above the head.

1. ENTRANCE FORM SALUTE (IRU KATA JIGI)

2. DOUBLE KIDNEY BLOCK / SADDLE STANCE [NO STEP]
   (NISOBAI MURADO KIRE / KURA KAMAE)

3. LOWER CROSS BLOCK / SADDLE STANCE [NO STEP]
   (SHITA NO JIRERU / KURA KAMAE)

4. MIDDLE CROSS BLOCK / SADDLE STANCE [NO STEP]
   (NAKABA JIRERU / KURA KAMAE)
   [RIGHT HAND IS ON THE INSIDE]

5. RIGHT BACK FIST (MIGI URA-KEN)
   [MAKE A FULL CIRCLE AROUND THE LEFT FIST. RAISE THE RIGHT FOOT UP TO KNEE HEIGHT IN UNISON WITH THE STRIKE AND REPLACE IT IN THE SADDLE STANCE]

6. LEFT BACK FIST (HADARI URA-KEN)
   [MAKE A HALF CIRCLE AROUND THE RIGHT FIST. RAISE THE LEFT FOOT UP TO KNEE HEIGHT IN UNISON WITH THE STRIKE AND REPLACE IT IN THE SADDLE STANCE.]

7. RIGHT DOWNWARD BACK FIST (MIGI SHIMO URA-KEN)
   [STEP BACK INTO A SADDLE STANCE WITH THE RIGHT LEG IN UNISON WITH THE STRIKE.]

8. LEFT ELBOW STRIKE (HADARI HIJI UTSU)
[RAISE LEFT LEG AND REPLACE IN STANCE.]

9. DOUBLE LUNGE PUNCH (NISOBAI KOBUSHI UTSU)
[RAISE RIGHT LEG AND REPLACE IN STANCE.]

10. RIGHT RIDGE HAND (MIGI MINE-TE)
[RIGHT REVERSE HEEL SWEEP TO A LEFT STANCE.]

11. RIGHT KNIFE HAND (MIGI SHUTO TE)
[RIGHT STEP TO A LEFT STANCE.]

12. LEFT RIDGE HAND (HADARI MINE-TE)
[TURN UPPER BODY TO A RIGHT STANCE WITH A LEFT HEEL SWEEP. USE A RIGHT KNIFE STRIKE TO LEAD INTO THE RIDGE]

13. FOUR WAY KICK (SHI-DO KERU)
[KICK WITH RIGHT LEG AND SET DOWN IN A LEFT STANCE.]

14. RIGHT OVERHEAD BLOCK (MIGI NOKORU KIRE)
[THE BLOCK IS DONE IN UNISON WITH THE PLACEMENT OF THE LEFT LEG]

15. REVERSE ROLL (FUSERU KOROGARU)
[ROLL ON A 45-DEGREE ANGLE TO A RIGHT DRAW STANCE.]

16. LEFT TIGER'S EYE (HADARI TORA-ME)
[USE A RIGHT FOREARM BLOCK. PICK UP THE RIGHT LEG AND SET IT INTO A SADDLE STANCE.]

17. RIGHT HEART GRAB (HADARI SHINZO HITTAKURU)
[USE A LEFT FOREARM BLOCK. PICK UP THE LEFT LEG AND REPLACE IT INTO A SADDLE STANCE.]

18. FORWARD RIGHT PALM STRIKE (MAE MIGI NIGIRU UTSU)
[PICK UP THE RIGHT LEG AND REPLACE IT INTO A SADDLE STANCE.]

19. LEFT REVERSE SWEEP (HADARI URA HAKU)
[USE A LEFT KNIFE HAND STRIKE/ BLOCK WITH THE SWEEP.]

20. THROAT PUNCH TAKE DOWN WITH GROUND TECHNIQUE
(NODO KOBUSHI UKERU SHIMO NO MOTOD'ZUKU-JUTSU)
[SPIN AROUND ON THE TAKEDOWN TECHNIQUE. THE GROUND COUNTER INCLUDES A RIGHT SHUTO TO THE LEFT COLLARBONE, A RIGHT ELBOW TO THE GROINS, A RIGHT BACK-FIST TO THE STERNUM, AND A RIGHT SPEAR-HAND TO THE THROAT.]

21. STAY SALUTE (YAMU JIGI)
[REVERSE SPIN AROUND ON THE STAND UP MOTION, AND PLACE FEET IN BOW OUT POSITION.

YOSU JU-SHI: SHOSEI KATA

** NOTE: The raising of the foot in unison with the strikes can be in a chambering motion or the foot can brush the leg and make noise. When moving from move 1 to move 2 carry the hands all the way above the head.

1. ENTRANCE FORM SALUTE
(IRU KATA JIGI)

2. OPEN DOUBLE FAN BLOCK (BUILDING CHI)/ SADDLE STANCE
(AITA NISOBAI KIRE/ KURA KAMAE)

3. DOWNWARD DOUBLE PALM STRIKE
(SHIMO NISOBAI TANAGOKORO UTSU)
[STAY IN SADDLE STANCE.]

4. RETRACT AND CONCENTRATE (BUILDING CHI)
(HIKKOMERU NO YOSE-ATSUMERU)
[STAY IN SADDLE STANCE.]

5. DOUBLE PALM STRIKES TO THE FRONT
(NISOBAI TANAGOKORO UTSU NI MAE)
[STAY IN SADDLE STANCE.]

6. RETRACT AND CONCENTRATE (BUILDING CHI)
(HIKKOMERU NO YOSE-ATSUMERU)
[STAY IN SADDLE STANCE.]

7. DOUBLE SIDE PALM STRIKES
(NISOBAI YOKO TANAGOKORO UTSU)
[STAY IN SADDLE STANCE.]

8. RIGHT FAN BLOCK TO THE LEFT
(MIGI OGI KIRE NI HADARI)
[STAY IN SADDLE STANCE.]

9. LEFT SPEAR HAND TO THE SOLAR PLEXUS
(HADARI YARI-TE UTSU NI MUNE)
[STAY IN SADDLE STANCE.]

10. ROLL BACK TO RIGHT SPEAR HAND TO THE THROAT
(KONOGARU URA NI MIGI YARI-TE NI NODO)
[STAY IN SADDLE STANCE.]

11. ROLL HANDS BACK TO OPEN FAN BLOCK
(KONOGARU TE URA NI AITA OGI KIRE)
[STAY IN SADDLE STANCE.]

12. DOUBLE KNIFE HANDS TO THE GROIN
(NISOBAI SHUTO UTSU NI MOMONE)
[STAY IN SADDLE STANCE.]

13. BRING HANDS UP TO A MIDDLE CROSS BLOCK.
(MOTTE-KURU TE KAMI NI NAKABA JIRERU KIRE)
[SAY IN SADDLE STANCE. RIGHT HAND IS ON THE INSIDE OF THE BLOCK.]

14. RIGHT BACK FIST
(MIGI URA-KEN)
[MAKE A FULL CIRCLE AROUND THE LEFT FIST. RAISE THE RIGHT FOOT UP TO KNEE HEIGHT IN UNISON WITH THE STRIKE AND REPLACE IT IN THE SADDLE STANCE.]

15. LEFT BACK FIST
(HADARI URA-KEN)
[MAKE A HALF CIRCLE AROUND THE RIGHT FIST. RAISE THE LEFT FOOT UP TO KNEE HEIGHT IN UNISON WITH THE STRIKE AND REPLACE IT IN THE SADDLE STANCE.]

16. RIGHT OVERHEAD BACK FIST
(MIGI SUGIRU ATAMA URA-KEN)
[STEP BACK INTO A SADDLE STANCE WITH THE RIGHT LEG IN UNISON WITH THE STRIKE.]

17. LEFT ELBOW STRIKE
(HADARI HIJI UTSU)
[RAISE LEFT LEG AND REPLACE IN STANCE.]

18. DOUBLE LUNGE PUNCH
(NISOBAI KOBUSHI UTSU)
[RAISE RIGHT LEG AND REPLACE IN STANCE.]

19. REVERSE SWEEP (RIGHT) WITH A RIGHT RIDGE HAND
(FUSERU HAKU (MIGI) NI MIGI MINE-TE)
[END IN A LEFT STANCE.]

20. RIGHT KNIFE HAND STRIKE TO THE COLLAR BONE
(MIGI SHUTO UTSU IN SAKOTSU HONE)
[RIGHT STEP TO A LEFT STANCE.]

21. REVERSE HEEL SWEEP (LEFT) WITH A LEFT RIDGE HAND STRIKE
(FUSERU KAGATO HAKU (HADARI) NI HADARI MINE-TE)
[USE A RIGHT KNIFE HAND STRIKE TO LEAD INTO THE RIDGE. END IN A RIGHT STANCE.]

22. HEEL TOE PIVOT TO RIGHT WITH A RIGHT RIDGE HAND
(KAGATO ZETCHO MAWASU NI MIGI NI MIGI MINE-TE)
[END IN A LEFT STANCE.]

23. LEFT STEP WITH A LEFT RIDGE HAND
(HADARI DAN NO HADARI MINE-TE)
[END IN RIGHT STANCE.]

24. RIGHT INNER ROUND KICK
(MIGI NAKA NARU KERU)
[TRAVELING]

25. LEFT OUTER ROUND KICK
(HADARI UWA NARU KERU)
[LAND DEEP FOR CARTWHEEL.]

26. CART WHEEL
(KURUMA)
[END IN RIGHT STANCE.]

27. DOUBLE KNIFE HAND STRIKE
(NISOBAI SHUTO UTSU)
[NO STEP.]

28. RIGHT STEP TURN WITH A MIDDLE CROSS BLOCK
(MGI DAN MAWASU NO NAKABA JIRERU KIRE)
[END IN A RIGHT STANCE TO FACE REVERSE DIRECTION OF LAST STANCE.]

29. BACKFIST (LEFT)
(URA-KEN (HADARI))
[STRIKE TO FRONT THEN RETURN TO CROSS BLOCK. NO STEP.]

30. GROIN STRIKE (RIGHT)
(MOMONE UTSU (MIGI))
[COVER RIGHT ELBOW WITH LEFT FOREARM BLOCK, AND USE A HEEL TOE PIVOT TO STRENGTHEN THE STRIKE. RETURN TO CROSS BLOCK, NO STEP.]

31. BACKFIST (LEFT)
(URA-KEN (HADARI))
[STRIKE TO FRONT. NO STEP, HOLD POSITION.]

32. KNIFE HAND STRIKE (RIGHT)
(SHUTO UTSU (MIGI))
[DROP THE LEFT BACKFIST INTO A FOREARM BLOCK AND USE A HEEL TOE PIVOT TO STRENGTHEN THE STRIKE. NO STEP, HOLD POSITION.]

33. KNIFE HAND STRIKE TO THE THROAT (LEFT)
(SHUTO UTSU NI NODO (HADARI))
[STRIKE UPWARD FROM THE FOREARM BLOCK. THE RIGHT HAND RETURNS TO READY POSITION AT THE HIP. NO STEP.]

34. RIGHT WAR FIST STRIKE
(MIGI KOBUSHI UTSU)
[RIGHT STEP.]

35. FULL SHOULDER ROLL
(AKU KA'TA KONOGARU)
[BEGIN ROLL IN LEFT STANCE.]

36. LEFT LUNGE PUNCH
(HADARI KOBUSHI UTSU)
[COME OUT OF ROLL IN LEFT STANCE AND STEP WITH THE LEFT LEG WITH THE STRIKE. END IN RIGHT STANCE.]

37. LOOK BOTH WAYS
(MIRU RIYO-HO DO)
[LEFT THEN RIGHT.]

38. RIGHT FAKE JUMPING DOUBLE FRONT SNAP WITH A ROLL PARALLEL BLOCK
(TOBU NISOBAI MAE ORU KERU NI MAWASU SOROTE ORU KIRE)
[THE LEFT LEG WILL KICK. LAND IN A RIGHT STANCE.]

39. LEFT ROLLING TIGER'S EYE
(HADARI MAWASU TORE-ME)
[REVERSE STEP WITH THE RIGHT LEG TO A SADDLE STANCE . USE A RIGHT FOREARM BLOCK WITH THE STRIKE.]

40. RIGHT ROLLING HEART GRAB
(MIGI MAWASU SHINZO HITTAKURU)
[RAISE LEFT LEG IN UNISON WITH THE STRIKE. USE A RIGHT FOREARM BLOCK WITH THE STRIKE.]

41. RIGHT CLUTCH PALM TO THE FRONT
(MIGI NIGIRU NI MAE)
[RAISE RIGHT LEG IN UNISON WITH THE STRIKE.]

42. STAY SALUTE (YAMU JIGI)

YOSU JU-ROKU: QUEST (NEGAU)

1. AT REQUEST FROM THE TEACHER
(NEGAI NI YORI O KUDASAI SENSEI)

YOSU JU-SHICHI: NATURE SKILLS (SHO TEGIWA)

1. 4 NATURE SKILLS (SHI SHO TEGIWA)

YOSU JU-HACHI: HARD BLOCKS (KATAI KIRE)

1. RIDGE HAND (MINE-TE)

2. SWORD HAND (SHUTO-TE)

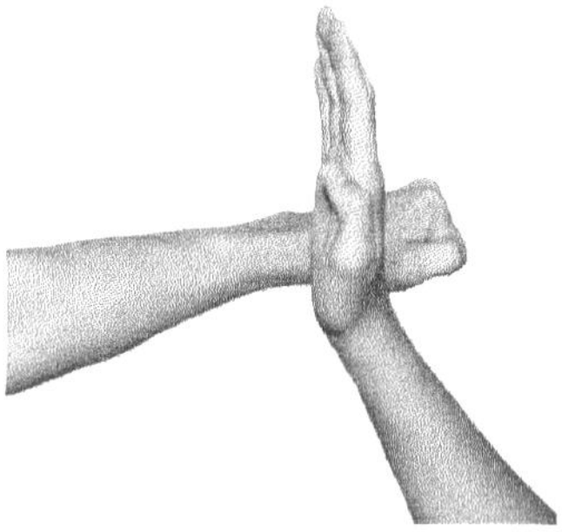

3. SWORD TO RIDGE HAND (SHUTO NI MINE-TE)

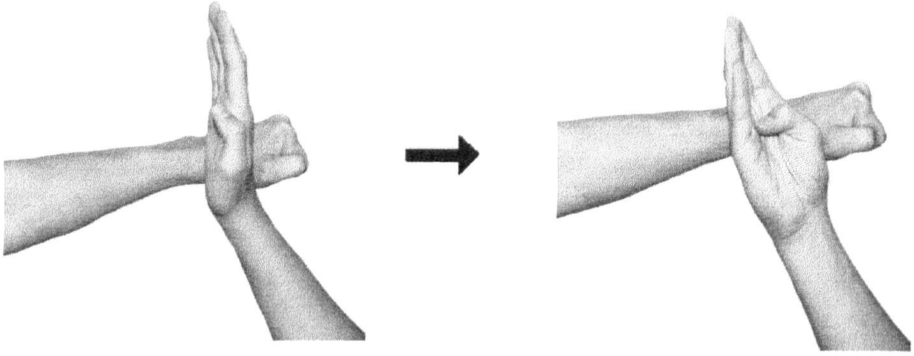

4. RIDGE TO SWORD HAND (MINE NI SHUTO-TE)

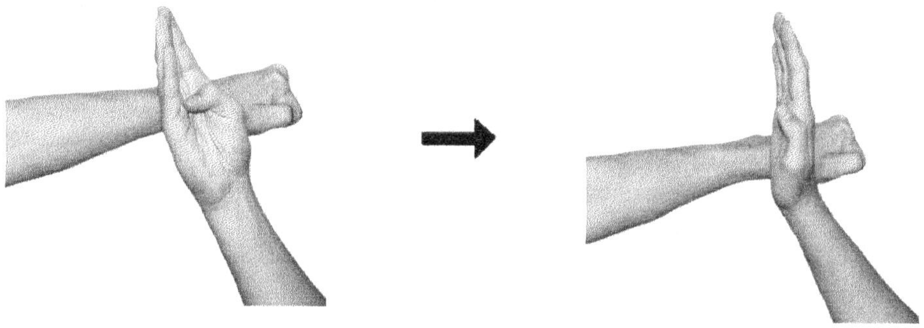

5. SWORD TO RIDGE HAND (SHUTO NI MINE-TE)
(WALK THE ARM)

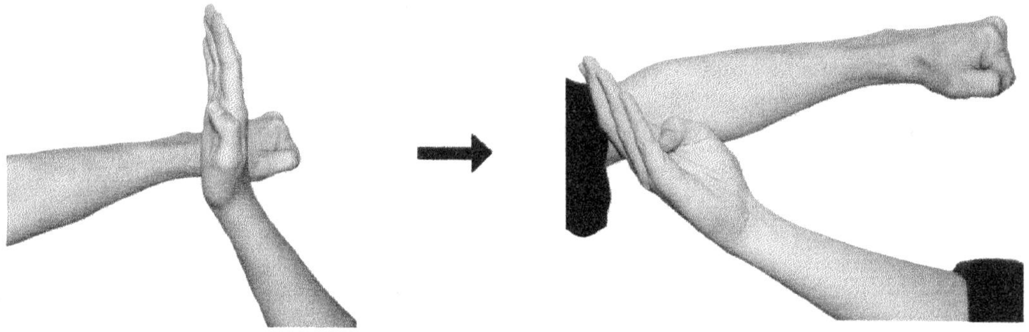

6. RIDGE TO SWORD HAND (MINE NI SHUTO-TE)
(WALK THE ARM)

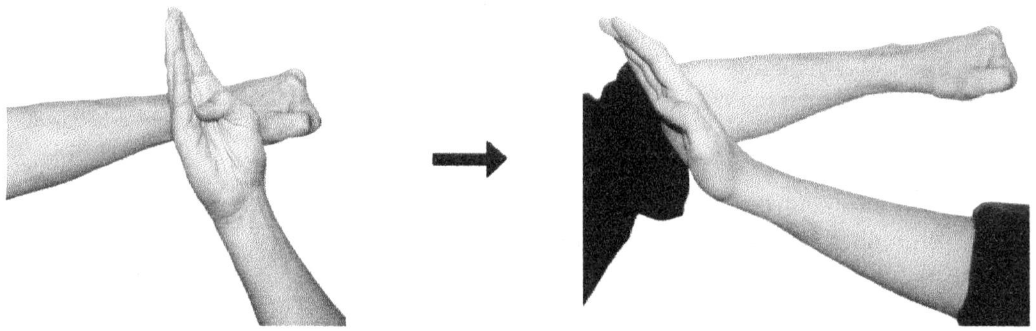

YOSU JU-KU: FAN HANDS (OGI TE)

A. THREE HAND STRIKE TECHNIQUE (SAN-UTSU-JUTSU)

1. Left forearm horizontal strike block.

2. Right palm strike over top of forearm block.

3. Right palm hand drops over front of forearm block and rotates back inside as you do a rolling back fist to face

4. Clockwise fan hands. (The right shuto hand strikes the jaw as the left shuto hand strikes the inside of the hip. Then continue the fan by rotating the hands on around. Then a left shuto strikes the jaw as a right ridge strikes the lower two ribs.

5. As the left hand pulls jaw out of socket as it will travel down to a left forearm block. Then the right hand comes underneath the forearm block and strikes the chin with a ridge hand.

6. Right ridge continues over the left forearm block. The left forearm strikes out at the already broken ribs with a back fist. Then the right fist strikes the pelvis bone as the left arm returns to a forearm block.

7. Right hand comes up outside of the left forearm block and strikes the chin with an ox hand.

8. Right ox hand continues over left forearm block to the left armpit. Then the left back fist strikes the jaw followed by a right catch palm strike to the throat as the left back fist returns to a ready war fist at the defender's side.

B. OUTSIDE FAN HANDS (HOKA OGI TE)

1. Fan hands will rotate in a clockwise and counter clockwise motion toward the center of your chest. This set of fan hands is done in a vertical motion.

2. The fan or circular motion should come from the elbow and not the shoulder.

3. As your hands pass down the center of your chest, along your sternum, they should be set up for hard blocks and grapples.

C. HORIZONTAL CIRCLES (TAIRAKA NA MARU WA)

THERE ARE TWO TYPES OF HORIZONTAL FAN HANDS:

A. FORWARD HORIZONTAL FANS:

1. When moving toward your opponent, the hand pattern is a short, tight, horizontal circular motion using shuto hands.

2. The pattern will move from your shoulder in a downward diagonal motion across your chest toward your opponent's body.

B. REVERSE HORIZONTAL FANS:

1. When moving away from your opponent, the hand pattern is a short, tight, horizontal circular motion using ridge hands.

2. The pattern will move from your opponent's waist and travel backward diagonally across your chest heading toward your shoulder.

D. HAND ROLLS (TE MAWASU)

1. The shuto and ridge hands move in a circular motion directly in front of your body.

2. The hand motion starts at the defender and rolls like a combine toward the attacker, or the hand motion begins at the attacker and rolls toward the defender.

E. WRIST TURNS (TE-KUBI MAWASU)

1. Hands will move in a vertical circular motion.

2. When striking upward, an ox hand strike will be used.

3. When striking downward, a tiger's paw strike will be used.

4. When one hand is striking upward, the other hand will be striking downward.

YOSU NI-JU: CROSS GRAB (JIRERU HITTAKURU SHI KOISHI)

1. CROSS GRAB FOUR PEBBLES (JIRERU HITTAKURU SHI KOISHI)

YOSU NI-JU-ICHI: TWO DIRECTIONAL KICKS (NI-DO SHOCHI KERU)

1. ICHI KERU CHOGO
   (WHIP WITH DROP RETURN HOOK)

2. NI KERU CHOGO
   (HIGH WHIP TO LOW WHIP)

3. SAN KERU CHOGO
   (FRONT SNAP TO SIDE SNAP WITH SAME LEG)

4. SHI KERU CHOGO
   (FRONT SNAP TO WHIP)

5. GO KERU CHOGO
   (DOUBLE WHIP TO DROP HOOK)

YOSU NI-JU-NI: FOUR WAY SPARRING (SHI-DO KUMITE)

SENPAI

YOSU ICHI: OVER ARM PIN COUNTER
(SOMUKU O TOMERU UDE NI TOME-BARI)

Note: For all the counters in category Ichi, use this picture as an example of how to grab.

1. THUMB PULL (OYAYUBI HIKU)

   A. Opponent grabs you over the top of your arms, and pins them down the side of your body.
   B. Reach with the left hand and grab their left thumb
   C. Pull down and out on the opponent's thumb. This will give you an escape hole.
   D. Spin under the opponent's left grappled arm.
   E. Slam the opponent's elbow with a palm or elbow strike.

2. DROP STRIKE (YAMU UTSU)

   A. Opponent grabs you over the top of your arms, and pins them down the side of your body
   B. Grab the opponent's right wrist with your right hand.
   C. Simultaneously with the grab, squat down and thrust your elbows up and out.
   D. Left elbow strike to opponent's left ribs.
   E. Slip under the opponent's right arm and lock out the opponent's right elbow with your left palm.

3. <u>ANKLE GRAB (KURUBUSHI HITTAKURU)</u>

A. Opponent grabs you over the top of your arms, and pins them down the side of your body.
B. Opponent picks you off the ground.
C. Curl your feet up to your chest. This will add extra weight and force the opponent to put you down.
D. When the opponent sets you down land with your feet wide and bend your knees. This will pull the opponent over.
E. Reach through your legs and grab the opponent's ankles. As you bend over straighten your leg, and lift the opponent off his feet.
F. Stand straight up and pull the opponent's legs through your legs. This will slam the opponent on the ground

4. <u>ARM PRESS (UDE GUNJU)</u>

A. Opponent grabs you over the top of your arms, and pins them down the side of your body
B. Grab opponent's left thumb with your left hand.
C. Grab opponent's left wrist with your right hand.
D. Carry opponent's left arm over your head and break opponent's arm over your right shoulder. Simultaneous with the arm break step with right leg and go to your knee. This will catapult your opponent onto his face

5. <u>HIP STRIKE (KOSHI UTSU)</u>

A. Opponent grabs you over the top of your arms, and pins them down the side of your body
B. Strike the right knee with a right shuto hand
C. Using the right knee strike as a distraction pivot the hips to the right and strike the opponent's left hip joint with a left elbow followed by a left shuto strike to the opponent's left knee.
D. Grapple the opponent's left leg and pull the opponent around so that he is directly in front of you.
E. Strike the opponent's groin with a knee.

YOSU NI: UNDER ARM COUNTER TECHNIQUES (SOMUKU NI SHITA-NO UDE)

PRESSURE POINT NOTE: If you cannot pull the thumb out to break the grip make a shuto hand and bend your middle finger at the middle knuckle joint. Place your finger on the opponent's hand just behind their index and middle finger. Slap the top of you hand and drive your finger into their hand. This will cause the thumb to involuntarily pop up.

Note: For all the counters in category Ni, use this picture as an example of how to grab.

1. <u>ARM LOCK (UDE YEYA)</u>

   A. Opponent grabs you under you arms.
   B. Grab opponent's left thumb with your left hand.
   C. Roll the thumb down and spin out around and behind the arm.
   D. Strike the elbow with a palm hand. This will lock out the opponent's arm.

2. <u>ARCH STOMP (ASHI-NO-KO TSUKU)</u>

   A. Opponent grabs you under your arms.
   B. Stomp the arch of the opponent's foot with your foot. This will crush the opponent's arch and let you free.

3. <u>ONE FINGER PRESS (ICHI YUBI GUNJU)</u>

   A. Opponent grabs you under your arms.
   B. Grab opponent's left index finger with your right hand.
   C. Leave your left arm hanging down over opponent's left arm.
   D. Roll index finger down and spin out. The spinout automatically torts the opponent face first toward the ground, and pins him.

4. SIDE STEP TWIST (YOKO DAN YORU)

   A. Opponent grabs you under your arms.
   B. Grab opponent's left thumb with left hand and roll down.
   C. Grab opponent's right wrist with your right hand.
   D. Step back with the right foot and slip underneath the opponent's left arm. This will leave you with the opponent's left hand pulled across his chest and pinned between his right arm and his right side, in a twist position.
   E. Simultaneously with the sliding underneath your opponent's arm, buckle the opponent's right arm and heel sweep the front side of the opponent's ankle joint. This will drive the opponent's face into the ground.

YOSU SAN: HEAD HOLD COUNTER (ATAMA TEGAKARE SOMUKU)

1. HEAD LOCK (ATAMA TOJIRU)

   A. Opponent puts you in a right side headlock.
   B. Turn your face toward the side of the body while punching the opponent's right knee with a right war-fist.
   C. Simultaneously with the striking of the opponent's knee, strike the opponent's groin with a left ridge hand.
   D. Right spear hand to the opponent's lower ribs. This will make the opponent let go with his left arm.
   E. Grapple opponent's right wrist with the left hand and pull your head back.
   F. Step back with the right leg and break the opponent's right elbow with a right palm strike. This will force the opponent down.
   G. Cross stomp kick the opponent's right knee with a right stomp kick.

2. HEAD LOCK WITH PUNCH (ATAMA TOJIRU NI UTSU)

   A. Opponent puts you in a right side headlock.
   B. Turn your face into the opponent's side while blocking the opponent's punch with the left hand.
   C. Grapple the opponent's left hand with your left hand, and grapple the opponent's right hand with your right hand.
   D. Step back with the left leg while drawing the left arm with you and locking the left wrist in the opponent's right armpit.
   E. Force the attacker forward to the ground by pulling back on the opponent's right arm and pushing forward on the opponent's left arm.
   F. Cross stomp kick the opponent's outside knee with a right stomp kick.

YOSU SHI: NATURE SKILLS (SHO TEGIWA)

1. 4 NATURE SKILLS (SHI SHO TEGIWA)

YOSU GO: WARFIST STRIKES (KOBUSHI UTSU)

1. 110 WARFIST STRIKES IN 1/3 MINUTE
   (HYAKU-JU KOBUSHI UTSU NI 1/3 FUN)

YOSU ROKU: EYE PLACEMENT (ME-TíSUKE)

1. <u>THE UNDERSTANDING</u>

   A. Eye placement is a key to fighting. The defender should look at his opponent through his peripheral vision. Direct sight is conscious thought and peripheral vision is subconscious thought. Subconscious reactions are faster than conscious reactions because subconscious reactions are more like instincts.
   B. When placing your eyes, you need to focus just past your opponent. Never focus on your opponent or another object behind your opponent because this will distract your eyes and allow sneaky punches.
   C. When looking at your opponent, make sure that you range of eyesight is from their ankles to just over their head.
   D. Do not move your eyes, just keep looking through your peripheral vision because your eyes will immediately pick up and track all of your opponent's strikes.

YOSU SHICHI: SPEAR (YARI)

1. SPEAR FORM (YARI KATA)

2. THROWING OF THE YARI FROM 30 FEET THROUGH A 6 INCH TARGET EIGHT OUT OF TEN TIMES.

   A. Stand in a right stance. The front foot and knee should point at the target. The front hand will point at the target.
   B. Throw with the backhand. The spear is one of the few times that a reverse throw is used.
   C. Hold the spear in one-third two-thirds with the hand gripping on the back third. Do not hold the spear in a full grip. Hold it with the three grapple fingers.
   D. Throw with elbow action not shoulder action.
   E. Do not look down the spear when throwing let the eyes line the spear up with the target.

   The ninja would throw the spear with a straight throw and not a lob throw. The spear hand many uses ranging from knocking men off horses, stopping horses, disabling sentries, and delivering oil or snake filled pottery through windows.

3. SPEAR STANCES (YARI KAMAE)

YOSU HACHI: KNIFE (MAMBA)

1. THROWING (NAGE-KOMU)

   A. Glide release: the knife is released from the palm of the hand.

   B. Tip release: the knife is released from the tip of the thumb and the side of the index finger.

2. STANCES (KAMAES)

   Note: Stances are illustrated from a left stance

A. BASIC STANCE (BUDO KAMAE)

1. The feet are in the same position as a normal right side stance.
2. The left, front, hand is in a horizontal forearm block.
3. The right, back, hand is about 6 inches behind the forearm block.
4. The right hand will hold the knife in a reverse grip.

B. ADVANCED STANCE
(AGERU KAMAE)

1. The feet are in the same position as a normal right side stance.
2. The hands are held the same way as the advanced stance.
3. The knife will be held in the right hand in a reverse grip. The blade of the knife will face outward toward your opponent.

C. DRAW STANCE (KAKU KAMAE)

1. The feet are in the same position as a normal right side stance.
2. The hands are held the same way as the draw stance.
3. The knife will be held in the right hand in a reverse grip. The blade of the knife will face out away from the body.

D. SHADOW STANCE (KAGE KAMAE)

1. The feet are in the same position as a normal right side stance.
2. The hands are held the same way as the shadow stance.
3. The knife will be held in the right hand in a reverse grip. The blade of the knife will face toward the ground.

E. MASTER STANCE
(SHUJIN KAMAE)

1. The feet are in the same position as a normal right side stance.
2. The hands are the same way as the master stance.
3. The knife will be held in the right hand in a reverse grip. The blade will face forward.

F. SADDLE STANCE (KURA KAMAE)

1. The feet are in the same position as a normal right side stance.
2. The hands are held the same as the saddle stance.
3. The knife will be held in one hand in a reverse grip. The blade will face forward.

3. STANCE USE (KAMAE TSUKAU)

A. BASIC STANCE (BUDO KAMAE)
   1. This is and aggressive or traveling stance.
   2. The stance is also used for close quarters combat.

B. ADVANCED STANCE (AGERU KAMAE)
   1. This is a defensive stance used against a stronger or more superior opponent.

C. MASTER STANCE (SHUJIN KAMAE)
   1. This stance is used when treading water.
   2. The hand is down in the water feeling around for the opponent, while the hand holding the knife is used to block attacks from above.

D. DRAW STANCE (KAKU KAMAE)
   1. This stance is used when going through doors or over thresholds.

E. SHADOW STANCE (KAGE KAMAE)
   1. This stance is used when traveling down walls.
   2. The stance is mostly used outside.

F. SADDLE STANCE (KURA KAMAE)
   1. This stance is used against multiple attackers or when your back is against the wall.

4. KNIFE STRIKES (MAMBA UTSU)

[The strikes listed below can also be referred to as forward and reverse strikes. If a person performs a right pivot or right forward pivot, then the knife is held in the right hand and the strike is coming from the right and traveling to the left. If the knife is held in the right hand and the strike comes from the left to the right then it is call a reverse strike.]

A. RIGHT & LEFT DOWN THRUST
   1. MOTION IS ON A 90-DEGREE DOWNWARD ANGLE

B. RIGHT & LEFT UPPER THRUST
   1. MOTION IN ON A 90-DEGREE UPWARD ANGLE

C. RIGHT & LEFT DOWN SLASH
   1. MOTIONIS ON A 45-DEGREE DOWNWARD ANGLE

D. RIGHT & LEFT UPPER SLASH
   1. MOTION IS ON A 45-DEGREE UPWARD ANGLE

E. RIGHT & LEFT PIVOT

1. HORIZONTAL CUT TO THE INSIDE OF THE BODY

F. RIGHT & LEFT REVERSE PIVOT

1. HORIZONTAL CUT TO THE OUTSIDE OF THE BODY

G. RIGHT & LEFT DRAG PIVOT

1. HOLD THE KNIFE REVERSE AND DRAG THE KNIFE TO CUT.

H. RIGHT & LEFT PENETRATION

1. PUSH KNIFE STRAIGHT INTO TARGET.

I. RIGHT & LEFT REVERSE PENETRATION

1. HOLD THE KNIFE REVERSE AND PUSH SRAIGHT BACK INTO THE TARGET.

J. THE RIP

1. USE BACK OF POINT OR BLADE TO CUT.

5. <u>COUNTER MOVES [FRONT ATTACK] (SOMUKU)</u>

A. DOWN THRUST (SHIMO SASU)

1. ELBOW LOCK (HIJI YEYA)
   A. Opponent strikes downward with right thrust.
   B. Upper cross block the strike at the elbow. Make sure that the right hand is the outside hand on the block.
   C. Slide your right hand down and grapple the wrist.
   D. Lock the opponent's elbow out with your left hand.

2. SHOULDER BREAK (KA'TA YABURERU)
   A. Opponent strikes downward with a right thrust.
   B. Left overhead block the strike at the elbow.
   C. Fold the opponent's elbow by striking it with a right side block.
   D. Reach up with the right hand and grapple the opponent's right arm.
   E. Step directly to the side and pull down on the opponent's right arm with your right arm.

3. GLIDE (NAGARERU)
   A. Opponent strikes downward with a right thrust.
   B. Right overhead block the strike and grapple the opponent's arm.
   C. Simultaneously with the block glide, step on a 45-degree angle and slam the opponent's knife into his right leg.

4. FAN BLOCK (OGI KIRE)
   - A. Opponent strikes downward with a right thrust.
   - B. Right fan block the strike as you glide step by on a 45-degree angle.
   - C. Grapple the wrist and carry it on by your opponent.
   - D. Raise the grappled arm higher the opponent's shoulder.
   - E. Reverse step with the left leg under the opponent's arm.
   - F. Simultaneously with the spin, left elbow strike the opponent's floater ribs.
   - G. Left shuto strike the opponent's floater ribs.
   - H. Break opponent's right elbow with a left palm strike.

B. UPPER THRUST (AGERU SASU)

1. CROSS BLOCK (JIRERU KIRE)
   - A. Opponent strikes with right upper thrust.
   - B. Block strike with a lower cross block.
   - C. Glide step with the lower cross block.
   - D. Trap opponent's arm between your body and your left elbow.
   - E. Spin to the right and lock out opponent's arm on the ground.

2. DOUBLE HAND ON ELBOW (NISOBAI TE NI HIJI)
   - A. Opponent strikes with a right upper thrust toward stomach/groin area.
   - B. Block down and out with the left hand in a circular motion and grapple the wrist as you step slightly in with the front left foot.
   - C. Reach with the right hand and grab the opponent's right elbow.
   - D. Glide step to the right of your opponent and pin his arm behind his back with his face toward the ground.

C. DOWN SLASH (SHIMO KIRU)

1. THROAT PUNCH TAKEDOWN (NODO UTSU OROSU)
   - A. Opponent strikes with a right downward slash.
   - B. Block the strike with a left overhead block.
   - C. Grapple the punch.
   - D. Perform throat punch takedown.

2. ARM TO KNEE (UDE NI HIZA)
   - A. Opponent strikes with a downward slash.
   - B. Block the strike with a left overhead block.
   - C. Grapple the punch.
   - D. Perform arm to outside knee.

D. UPPER SLASH (AGERU KIRU)

1. OUTER ROUND KICK (UWA NARU KERU)

   A. Opponent strikes with a right upper slash.
   B. Kick the opponent in the wrist or forearm area with a right outer round kick.

2. FAN BLOCK (OGI KIRE)

   A. Opponent strikes with a right upper slash.
   B. Block the opponent's strike with a left downward fan.
   C. Carry the fan on around and grapple the wrist.
   D. Reach with the right hand and re-grapple the opponent's hand.
   E. Lock out opponent's arm.

3. DOUBLE HAND ON ELBOW (NISOBAI TE NI HIJI)

   A. Opponent strikes with a right upper slash.
   B. Block down and out with the left hand in a circular motion and grapple the wrist as you step slightly in with the front left foot.
   C. Reach with the right hand and grab the opponent's right elbow.
   D. Glide step to the right of your opponent and pin his arm behind his back with his face toward the ground.

E. PENETRATION (SATORI)

1. DOUBLE HAND ON ELBOW (NISOBAI TE NI HIJI)

   ** Note: This technique is used on an outward slashing motion to an inward penetration strike.

   A. Opponent strikes with a right forward penetration toward stomach/ groin area.
   B. Block down and out with the left hand in a circular motion and grapple the wrist as you step slightly in with the front left foot.
   C. Reach with the right hand and grab the opponent's right elbow.
   D. Glide step to the right of your opponent and pin his arm behind his back with his face toward the ground.

2. ARM TO ARM (UDE NI UDE)

   ** Note: This technique is used on a straight in penetration strike.

   A. Opponent strikes with a forward penetration.
   B. Block punch with left face block and grapple wrist.
   C. Twist the opponent's arm so that your elbow locks their elbow.
   D. Spin backwards, down the side of their arm, and re-break their arm on your upper ribs.
   E. Continue spinning and elbow the opponent in between the shoulder blades.
   F. Back-fist the attacker in the base of the skull

3. SPIN UNDER (TSUMUGU SHITA)
   A. Opponent Strike with a right forward penetration.
   B. Block the strike with a left overhead block and grapple the arm.
   C. Punch the opponent in the floater ribs with a right punch. Take a step with the right foot on this technique.
   D. Collapse the right punch into a right elbow strike to the floater ribs.
   F. Spin under the opponent's grappled arm and lock out his elbow with your right hand.

F. BACK PENETRATION (URA SATORI)

[When pivoting away from an oncoming knife attack from behind pivot on the front foot, which will carry you away from the knife and pull you off the blade. If you pivot on the back foot then you could burry the blade deeper in the body.]

1. HIGH (TAKERU)
   A. Opponent strikes at the head area with a right back penetration strike.
   B. Block the strike with a left outside fan block and grapple the arm.
   C. Drop to a right knee as you carry the block over your head.
   D. Stand straight up and dive your right elbow into the opponent's right shoulder joint.

2. LOW (SHIMO)
   A. Opponent strikes toward the waist with a right back penetration strike.
   B. Block the strike with a right palm hand strike to the elbow and stop the knife's momentum.
   C. Stomp kick the opponent's right knee.

G. REVERSE GRIP PENETRATION (URA TSUKAMI SATORI)

1. FRONT PENETRATION (MAE SATORI)
   A. Opponent holds knife in the right hand in a reverse grip in the center of his chest.
   B. Opponent strikes forward by flicking the knife out in a stabbing motion.
   C. Glide step to the right as you block the strike with a right knife hand strike to the wrist. Turn the body as you block the knife in order to pull the center-line of the knife attack from chest to shoulder.
   D. Grapple the opponent's right wrist with your right hand.
   E. Pull the opponent off balance and break his elbow with your elbow.

   [Do not grab with the same side hand, opponent right strike you left block, because the opponent can perform the gate and still cut you.]

6. COUNTER MOVES (REAR ATTACK)

** Note: To help defend against back knife attacks, step to the right because most people fight with their knife in their right hand. If you step to the right on a forward 45-degree angle from your starting position, it will help in slowing down your opponent because he must change his angle of attack.

A. DOWN THRUST (SHIMO SASU)

1. RIGHT OVERHEAD (MIGI NOKORU)
   A. Opponent strikes with a right downward thrust.
   B. Look over your right shoulder.
   C. Spin out to the right as you block the strike with a right overhead block.
   D. Grapple the opponent's right wrist.
   E. Spin your left leg on around to the right and break the opponent's right elbow with a left palm strike.

2. LEFT OVERHEAD (HADARI NOKORU)
   A. Opponent strikes with a right downward thrust.
   B. Look over your left shoulder.
   C. Spin inward to the left as you block the strike with a left overhead block.
   D. Grapple the opponent's right wrist.
   E. Spin the right leg on around to the left and break the opponent's right elbow with a right upward palm strike.

B. PENETRATION (SATORI)

1. CRADLE BLOCK (TSUGURO KIRE)
   A. Opponent strikes with a right forward penetration strike.
   B. Look over your right shoulder.
   C. Spin to the outside or right while stepping on the forward 45-degree angle and performing a right downward fan block.
   D. Spin the left leg around to the right and carry the fan block around to a cradle catch.
   E. Break the opponent's right elbow with a left palm hand.
   F. Stomp kick the opponent's knees.

C. UPPER THRUST (AGERU SASU)

1. CRADLE BLOCK (TSUGURO KIRE)
   - A. Opponent strikes with a right upper thrust.
   - B. Look over your right shoulder.
   - C. Spin to the outside or right while stepping on the forward 45-degree angle and performing a right downward fan block.
   - D. Spin the left leg around to the right and carry the fan block around to a cradle catch.
   - E. Break the opponent's right elbow with a left palm hand.
   - F. Stomp kick the opponent's knees.

D. UPPER SLASH (AGERU KIRU)

1. CRADLE BLOCK (TSUGURO KIRE)
   - A. Opponent strikes with a right upper slash.
   - B. Look over your right shoulder.
   - C. Spin to the outside or right while stepping on the forward 45-degree angle and performing a right downward fan block.
   - D. Spin the left leg around to the right and carry the fan block around to a cradle catch.
   - E. Break the opponent's right elbow with a left palm hand.
   - F. Stomp kick the opponent's knees.

E. DOWN SLASH (SHIMO KIRU)

1. CATCH BLOCK (TORU KIRE)
   - A. Opponent strikes with a right down slash.
   - B. Look over your right shoulder.
   - C. Spin to the outside or right while stepping on the forward 45-degree angle and performing a right downward fan block.
   - D. Spin the left leg around to the right and carry the fan block around to a catch.
   - E. Break the opponent's right elbow with a left palm hand.
   - F. Stomp kick the opponent's knees.

F. HORIZONTAL SLASH (TAIRAKANA KIRU)

1. CRADLE BLOCK (TSUGURO KIRE)
   - A. Opponent strikes with a right horizontal slash or pivot.
   - B. Look over your right shoulder.
   - C. Spin to the outside or right while stepping on the forward 45-degree angle and performing a right downward fan block.
   - D. Spin the left leg around to the right and carry the fan block around to a cradle catch.
   - E. Break the opponent's right elbow with a left palm hand.
   - F. Stomp kick the opponent's knees.

7. <u>RAKE AWAY (KAKU RUSU)</u>

A. FORWARD PENETRATION (MAE SATORI)
1. Opponent thrust at you with a forward left penetration strike.
2. Right roll block and clasp the hand.
3. Press the opponent's thumb down with your palm.
4. Hook your thumb behind the knife hilt and pull down. This will strip the knife from their hand.

B. CROSS FORWARD PENETRATION (JIRERU MAE SATORI)
1. Opponent thrust at you with a forward right penetration strike.
2. Right roll block and clasp the hand.
3. Grip the thumb with your little and ring fingers.
4. Break the wrist with your thumb.
5. Grip the knife hilt with your index and middle fingers and pull down. This will strip the knife from their hand.

8. <u>KNIFE DEFLECTION (MAMBA SORERU)</u>

A. KNIFE HANDS (SHUTO TE)
1. Opponent hold knife with point pointed toward you.
2. Strike the wrist on both sides with double knife hands.

B. PALM HANDS (TANAGOKORO TE)
1. Opponent holds knife with point pointed toward you.
2. Strike the wrist on a 45-degree angle to the top and bottom with double palm hands.

YOSU KU: GENERAL KNOWLEDGE OF TRAINING GROUND CONSTRUCTION

A. BALANCE BEAM

B. HIGH JUMP BAR

C. CLIMB ROPE

D. TIGHT ROPE

E. KICK STUMP

F. HANG BAG

G. HANG BAR

H. MAKIWARI

YOSU JU: SENPAI KATA

1. ENTRANCE FORM SALUTE (IRU KATA JIGI)

2. SADDLE STANCE (KURA KAMAE)

3. BASCI KI GRAB (BUDO GI HITTAKURU)
   [KICK OFF WITH THE RIGHT LEG TO A LEFT STANCE.]

4. RIGHT SIDE BLOCK (MIGI YOKO KIRE)
   [LAND IN THIS POSITION FROM PREVIOUS KICK.]

5. LEFT SIDE BLOCK (HADARI YOKO KIRE)
   [STEP WITH LEFT LEG TO TIGER WALK.]

6. [R] NECK AND [L] KIDNEY BLOCK
   (MIGI KUBI KIRE TO HADARI MURADO KIRE)
   [RIGHT STEP TO TIGER WALK.]

7. [L] NECK AND [R] KIDNEY BLOCK
   (HADARI KUBI KIRE TO MIGI MURADO KIRE)
   [LEFT STEP TO TIGER WALK.]

8. ARM BREAK COMBINATION (UDE KOWASU CHOGO)
   [PIVOT UPPER TORSO WITH CATCHING OF HAND. SLAM THE OPPONENT INTO YOUR RIGHT KNEE AND SET DOWN INTO THE NEXT MOVE.]

9. RIGHT ADVANCED STANCE (MIGI AGERU KAMAE)
   [NO STEP]

10. ADVANCED BLOCK TECHNIQUE (AGERU KIRE JUTSU)
    [NO STEP]

11. RIGHT VORTEX BLOCK WITH LEFT PALM STRIKE
    (MIGI UDZU KIRE DE HADARI NIGIRU-TE UTSU)
    [STEP WITH RIGHT LEG TO TIGER WALK.]

12. LEFT VORTEX BLOCK WITH RIGHT PALM STRIKE
    (HADARI UDZU KIRE DE MIGI NIGIRU-TE UTSU)
    [STEP WITH LEFT LEG TO TIGER WALK.]

13. RIGHT DOWN FOREARM BLOCK WITH LEFT PALM STRIKE
    (MIGI SHIMO KO-UDE KIRE NO HADARI NIGIRU-TE UTSU)
    [RIGHT STEP TO TIGER WALK.]

14. LEFT DOWN FOREARM BLOCK WITH RIGHT PALM STRIKE
(HADARI SHIMO KO-UDE KIRE NO MIGI NIGIRU-TE UTSU)
[LEFT STEP TO TIGER WALK.]

15. RIGHT FRONT SNAP WITH RIGHT INSIDE WHIP
(MIGI MAE ORU NO MIGI NAKA MUCHI)
[SET FOOT DOWN IN A LEFT STANCE. PERFORM HORIZONTAL CIRCLES TO NEXT MOVE.]

16. RIGHT SHADOW STANCE (MIGI KAGE KAMAE)
[NO STEP]

17. LEFT TIGER PAW BLOCK (HADARI TORA ASHI KIRE)
[RIGHT FORWARD STEP.]

18. RIGHT TIGER PAW BLOCK (MIGI TORA ASHI KIRE)
[LEFT FORWARD STEP.]

19. LEFT TIGER PAW BLOCK (HADARI TORA ASHI KIRE)
[LEFT REVERSE STEP.]

20. RIGHT UPPER DOUBLE HAND ON ELBOW
(MIGI KAMI NISOBAI TE NI HIJI)
[LEFT STEP TO TIGER WALK.]

21. LEFT LOWER DOUBLE HAND ON ELBOW
(HADARI SHIMO NISOBAI TE NI HIJI)
[RIGHT STEP TO TIGER WALK.]

22. THROAT PUNCH TAKEDOWN (NODO UTSU UKERU)
[1/4 SPIN, TECHNIQUE ENDS AT KNIFE HAND TO COLLARBONE.]

23. RIGHT MASTER STANCE (MIGI SHUJIN KAMAE)
[NO STEP]

24. DOUBLE PALM BLOCK (NISOBAI NIGIRU KIRE)
[SIMULATES A CATCH BLOCK FOR A MIDDLE STRIKE FROM A STAFF. RIGHT STEP]

25. TURN STAFF TO 90- DEGREE AND BREAK WITH A RIGHT 90-DEGREE KNIFE HAND STRIKE.
(MAWASU BO KU-NI DO DE YABURERU NO MIGI KU-NI DO SHUTO UTSU)
[NO STEP]

26. GRAB WRIST AND PULL DOWN TO WAIST LEVEL.
(HITAKURU TE-KUBI NI HIKI SHIMO NI KOSHI MIDZUMORI)
[LEFT STEP]

27. RIGHT WOOD HAND STRIKE WRIST.
(MIGI KI-TE USTU TE-KUBI)
[NO STEP]

28. RIGHT SPEAR HAND STRIKE (MIGI YARI-TE UTSU)
[TO THROAT, RIGHT STEP]

29. LEFT ROLL BLOCK WITH GRAPPLE
(HADARI MAWASU KIRE DE HASUKAAMU)
[LEFT STEP]

30. ELBOW TO CHEST COUNTER TECHNIQUE
(HIJI NI MUNE SOMUKU-JUTSU)
[1/4 SPIN. ONCE AT KNEE ON GROUND FINISH TECHNIQUE WITH KNIFE HAND TO RIGHT COLLARBONE, RIGHT ELBOW STRIKE TO GROIN, RIGHT BACK FIST TO STERNUM, AND RIGHT SPEAR TO THROAT.]

31. STAY SALUTE (YAMU JIGI)
[STAND STRAIGHT UP. YOU SHOULD END EXACTLY WHERE YOU BEGAN.]

YOSU JU-ICHI: QUEST (NEGAU)

1. AT ONE'S REQUEST FROM THE TEACHER
(NEGAI NI YORI O KUDASAI SENSEI)

YOSU JU-NI: BREAKING TECHNIQUES (YABURERU-JUTSU)

1. ONE MID-AIR (ICHI NAKABA SARSAU)
2. THREE HORIZONTAL (SAN TAIRAKA NA)
3. ONE WHIP HAND (ICHI MUCHI TE)
4. BO STAFF OVER STOMACH (BO SUGIRU ONAKA)

YOSU JU-SAN: STRIKING TARGETS (UTSU NI MATO)

1. EAR (MIMI)
2. EYE (ME)
3. NOSE (HANA)
4. BASE OF SKULL (ATAMA)
5. TEMPLE (TERA)
6. SIDE OF THROAT (YOKO NODO)
7. FRONT OF THROAT (MAE NODO)
8. COLLARBONE (SAKOTSU)
9. ARMPIT (WAKI NO SHITA)
10. STERNUM (MUNE NO HONE)
11. TWO LOWER RIBS (NI ABARA HONE)
12. SPINE (SEBO-HONE)
13. SHOULDER JOINT (KA'TA FUSHI)
14. ELBOW (HIJI)
15. WRIST (TE-KUBI)
16. HIP JOINT (KOSHI FUSHI)
17. GROIN (MOMONE)
18. LEG (ASHI)
19. KNEE (HIZA)
20. SHIN (MAE ASHI)
21. ANKLE (KURUBUSHI)
22. TOP OF FOOT (ZETCHO)

YOSU JU-SHI: COUNTER TECHNIQUES (SOMUKU KAPPO JUTSU)

** Note: All techniques are illustrated from a right side stance.

1. WRIST RELEASE ["**Gate**"] (TE-KUBI HANASU)

A. Attacker grabs wrist.
B. Defender twists his wrist toward the attackers thumb and pulls away.

Or

If gate technique can not be applies.

A. Turn/kick the fingers horizontally toward your body thus pivoting the wrist.
B. With the free hand drive your thumb between the opponent's middle and ring fingers simultaneous with grabbing the opponent's thumb with the little and ring fingers.
C. Roll the opponent's hand toward his thumb and peel his hand off your wrist.

2. SHOULDER BACK LOCK (KA'TA SENAKE JO)

A. Attacker throws right punch.
B. Block punch with left face block and grapple wrist.
C. Break attacker's arm with a right side block that fans under the grappled arm and strike outward against the elbow.
D. Grab wrist with right hand.
E. Pull down on the attacker's right wrist with your right hand while pushing up with your right elbow.

3. DOUBLE HAND ON ELBOW (NISOBAI TE NI HIJI)

A. Attacker throws right punch toward groin area.
B. Strike the right wrist of the attacker with a left palm hand and strike the right elbow with a left palm hand. This breaks the elbow.
C. Twist arm up with the hand on the elbow while moving the hand on the wrist to the shoulder blade.
D. This locks the attacker out.

4. INSIDE ELBOW (NAKA HIJI)

A. Attacker throws punch.
B. Block with left ridge hand.
C. Roll left hand over attacker's arm and lock the wrist under your left armpit.

5. <u>ELBOW STRIKE (HIJI UTSU)</u>

A. Attacker throws punch.
B. Block with left face block and grapple.
C. Break arm with right side block.
D. Defender grabs attacker's throat with right hand and throws to ground.

6. <u>WRIST SPIN (TE-KUBI MAWASU)</u>

A. Attacker throws punch.
B. Block punch with right roll catch block.
C. Twist attacker's arm so that attacker turns face down.
D. Pull attacker's arm toward ground.
E. When attacker's hand is 8 to 10 inches from ground jerk straight up.
F. This flips attacker's over.

7. <u>HORIZONTAL BLOCK (TAIRAKA NA KIRE)</u>

A. Attacker charges.
B. Get into a good stance with a right horizontal block on top and a left horizontal block on bottom.
C. Attacker rams defender.
D. Defender absorbs attacker's kinetic energy with horizontal block.
E. Grab shirt with top hand and grab pants with left hand.
F. Defender pushes with right hand and pulls with left hand while striking the opponent in the back of his left leg with his right knee.
G. This allows the defender to cut the attacker for a flip.

8. <u>THROAT STRIKE (NODO UTSU)</u>

A. Attacker throws punch.
B. Block with a ridge/ shuto combo strike to the wrist.
C. The block is followed by a wood hand strike to the side of the neck. Both strikes are made with the same hand.

9. <u>DOUBLE HAND ON ELBOW COUNTER (NISOBAI TE NI HIJI SOMUKU)</u>

A. Opponent grabs the defender's right arm using double hand on elbow technique with the right hand on the defender's wrist and his left hand on the defender's elbow.
B. Twist the right wrist out of the block using the gate/wrist release technique, and grab the opponent's left elbow.
C. Pin the opponent's left wrist against your chest as you roll the opponent's left arm over to a locked position.
D. Knee the opponent in the face with a left knee as you push his face toward the ground.

YOSU JU-GO: A TEST OF HUMILITY AND HONOR

YOSU JU-ROKU: BALANCE ROPE (TSURIAI O TORU NO OBI)

YOSU JU-SHICHI: HYPNOTIZING DISTRACTION (SAIMIN NAGUSAMI)

1. OPEN HAND (HIRATE)

    A. Hold palm hand in front of face.
    B. Roll fingers into a fist as you strike the face with a fist.

2. MASTER HAND (SHUJIN TE)

    A. Hold master hand in front of face.
    B. Waive the hand in front of opponents face until the opponent is concentrating on hand.
    C. Pull fingertips back while you strike with a palm hand to the face.

3. WEAPONS HYPNOTIZING (DOGU SAIMIN)

    A. Both hands are held at shoulder height.
    B. Perform an open hand hypnotizing distraction with the hand diagonally across from the weapon.
    C. Slap the hand holding the weapon with the hand directly across from the weapon and grapple it.
    D. Strike the elbow joint of the grappled arm with a wood hand.
    E. With the same hand ox strike the chin.
    F. With the same hand reach around and grab the back of the neck.
    G. Punch the face/ throat area with the hand holding the opponent's grappled arm.
    H. Drag the weapon across the opponent's neck area for a finishing move.

YOSU JU-HACHI: TWO PERSON HOLD COUNTERS (NI HITO TEGAKARE SOMUKU)

** Note: The counters are done with the opponent on the right side hold the defender's wrist with his right hand and the elbow with his left hand. The opponent on the left side is holding the defender's wrist with his left hand and the elbow with his right hand.

1. <u>WRIST THROW (TE-KUBI NAGERU)</u>

   A. Two opponents hold both arms to either side.
   B. Break the hold on the right wrist by using the gate technique.
   C. Reach and grab the left opponent's left wrist.
   D. Simultaneously with the reach, break the left opponent's hold on your left wrist and grapple their left wrist.
   E. Right back sweep and throw the left opponent into the right opponent.

2. <u>ELBOW THROW (HIJI NAGERU)</u>

   A. Two opponents hold both arms to either side.
   B. Break both holds by performing the gate technique.
   C. Reach with your right hand and grapple the left opponent's right wrist.
   D. Place your left elbow over the left opponent's right elbow.
   E. Right back heel sweep and throw the left opponent into the right opponent.

3. <u>SHADON SHADAN (SHADON SHADAN)</u>

   A. Two opponents hold both arms to either side.
   B. Perform technique as described in Monjin Rank.

4. <u>WRIST GRAPPLE (TE-KUBI TSUKAMU)</u>

   A. Two opponents hold both arms to either side.
   B. Break both holds by performing the gate technique.
   C. Grapple the opponents' front wrists and roll the wrists to the back.
   ** Note: If opponent grapples your wrists with their back hand then roll your hand to the front after you grapple their wrists.

YOSU JU-KU: CROSS GRAB (JIRERU HITTAKURU ROKU HOISHI)

1. CROSS GRAB SIX PEBBLES (JIRERU HITTAKURU ROKU KOISHI)

YOSU JU-JU: BALANCE BEAM SPARRING (TSURIAI O TORU NO HARI NI KUMITE)

YOSU NI-JU-ICHI: SIX ON ONE SPARRING WITH HAND AND WEAPONS (ROKU NI ICHI KUMITE NO TE TO DOGU)

BUSHI

YOSU ICHI: NATURE SKILLS (SHO TEGIWA)

1. FOUR NATURE SKILLS (SHI SHO TEGIWA)

YOSU NI: QUEST (NEGAU)

1. AT ONE'S REQUEST FROM THE TEACHER
   (NEGAI NI YORI O KUDASAI SENSEI)

YOSU SAN: WARFIST STRIKES (KOBUSHI UTSU)

1. 130 WARFIST STRIKES IN 1/3 MINUTES (130 KOBUSHI NI 1/3 FUN)

YOSU SHI: ACROBATICS (KARUWAZA-SHU)

1. FRONT HANDSPRING (MAE TE HARU)
2. BACK HANDSPRING (URA TE HARU)
3. FRONT SOMERSAULT (MAE HIKKURI-KAYERU)
4. BACK SOMERSAULT (URA HIKKURI-KAYERU)
5. WALL RUN SOMERSAULT (KABE HASHIRU HIKKURI-KAYERU)

YOSU GO: BLIND SPARRING (MOMOKU NO KUMITE)

1. THE STUDENT WILL PERFORM THIS TASK UNTIL THE TEACHER IS SATISFIED WITH THE STUDENTS SKILL.

YOSU ROKU: HAND AND WEAPON SPARRING SKILL (KUMITE NO JUTSU TO TE NI ASHI)

1. A TEST OF SKILL SATISFACTORY TO THE TEACHER

YOSU SHICHI: LANGUAGE (KOTOBA)

NOTE: THIS CATEGORY IS CONCERNED ONLY WITH THE LANGUAGE.

SWORD TYPES

1. WOOD (BOKEN)
2. WOODEN SAMURAI SWORD (BOKUDO)
3. BAMBOO (SHINAI)
4. NINJA (NINJA-TO
5. SHORT NINJA (TANTO)
6. SHORT SAMURAI (WAKAZASHI)
7. MIDDLE SAMURAI (SHOTO)
8. LONG SAMURAI (DAITO)

UNDERSTANDING

1. BODY MANAGEMENT (TAISABARI)
2. PERSISTANCE (MA-AI)

SWORD ACTION

1. PIVOT OR HORIZONTAL CUT (KIRU)
2. STAB OR PENETRATION (T'SUKU)
3. THRUST OR THROW (NAGURU)
4. SLASH (UTSU)
5. DRAWING (KIRISUKI)
6. UPWARD SLASH (GYAKU KESA GIRI)
7. STANCE (KAMAE)
8. LOCKED TOGETHER BLADES (BAZERIAI)
9. SWORD WIND (TAICHI-KAZI)
10. FAST DRAW (IAIDO)
11. SWORD MOUNTING ON PERSON (HANDACHI-DO-KOSHIRAE)

SWORD PARTS

1. HANDEL (T'SUKA)
2. BRAID (ITO)
3. SCABBERD (SAYA)
4. METAL SLEEVE ON SWORD (FUCHI)
5. CORD (HIMO)
6. CORD KNOB (KURIKATA)
7. HANDLE BUTT (T'SUKAGASHIRIA)
8. HANDLE BUTT CAP (KASHIRA)
9. BELT (OBI)
10. ROUND HAND GUARD (T'SUBA)
11. SQUARE HAND GUARD (SHIBEN)
12. BLADE (KEN)
13. BACK OF BLADE (MINE)
14. WRAP (SA-ME)
15. HANDLE ORNAMENT (MENUKI)
16. ETCHED CUTTING BLADE (HAMON)
17. SWORD POINT (DAI KISSAKI)

YOSU HACHI: SWORD STANCES (DIATO KAMAE)

1. <u>JODAN NO KAMAE (UPPER LEVEL POSTURE)</u>

Holding the sword overhead at a 45 angle.

2. <u>SAIGAN NO KAMAE (TRUE EYES POSTURE)</u>

The sword handle is at hip level with the tip aiming at your adversary's eyes

3. HASSO NO KAMAE

Holding the sword at your side in a manner similar to a baseball bat.

4. GEDAN NO KAMAE

Holding the sword handle at hip height so tip aims towards the opponent's feet.

YOSU KU: SWORD GRIP (TO NIGIRU)

1. HANDLE GRIP (T'SUKA NIGIRU)
   Hold the sword in the top left hand and let the thumb rest on top of the index finger, in the same manner as a war fist. The bottom hand or right hand can be held in two different manners. It can be held in the same manner as the top left hand or it can be held with the middle finger, index finger, and thumb on the very end of the handle.

YOSU JU: ELEMENT HANDS (GO-GIYO TE)

1. EARTH (JIMEN)
2. WIND (FU)
3. FIRE (KA)
4. WATER (SUI)
5. MIND (SHIN)
6. BODY (TAI)
7. SOUL (KI)
8. ENERGY (CHI)
9. VOID (KU)

YOSU JU-ICHI: ELEMENT SALUTE (GO-GIYO JIGI)

1. FULL CEREMONY

   A. <u>NINJA SEAT</u>

   B. <u>EARTH HAND</u>.

      1. Starts in the center of the chest.
      2. Moves to the left shoulder.
      3. Moves diagonally to the center of the chest.
      4. Moves to the right shoulder.
      5. Twists so that the bottom of the weave moves horizontally to the left shoulder.
      6. Push the hand weaves out away from the body simultaneously twisting the hands back to their proper position.

C. WIND HAND.

1. Begins where earth stopped.
2. Moves directly up the center of the body toward the mouth. Simultaneous with the hand movement take a deep breath.
3. Moves back down the center of the body to its beginning position. Simultaneous with the hand movement exhale the deep breath.
4. Perform a counter clockwise circle with the hand weave in front of your chest. Circle begins and ends at waist level.
5. Re-perform steps 1 & 2 and stop.

D. FIRE HAND.

1. Begins where wind stopped.
2. Moves from the center of the body to the left shoulder.
3. Moves diagonally to the right knee.
4. Moves back to its beginning position and stops.
5. Fire then dips down into the water.
6. The hand weave comes back to the center of the chest as water.

E. WATER HAND.

1. Water hand opens in the center of the chest.
2. Move the hand weave up toward the sky bringing it directly in front of the body.
3. When the hands reach just above your head they will separate and fall down the sides of your body.
4. The hands will meet back in the center of the chest as mind.

F. MIND HAND

1. Mind hand starts in the center of the chest. The hand weave will make a small jarring motion forward and change into body.

G. BODY HAND.

1. Body hand starts in the center of the chest. The hand weave will make a small jarring motion forward and change into soul.

H. SOUL HAND

1. Soul hand starts in the center of the chest. The hand weave will make a small jarring motion forward and change into power.

I. <u>POWER HAND</u>.

1. Power hand starts in the center of the chest. The hand weave will move straight to the ground into void position.

J. <u>SALUTE</u>.

1. Place both hands simultaneously on the ground with palms down in the triangle formation.
2. Bow so that your forehead touches the hand pattern on the ground.
3. Raise your body/ head back up.
4. Then place your hands back on your knees. Right hand first then left hand.

YOSU JU-NI: ADVANCED BLOCK ELEMENT COUNTERS (AGERU KIRE GO-GIYO SOMUKU)

RIGHT SIDE STANCE

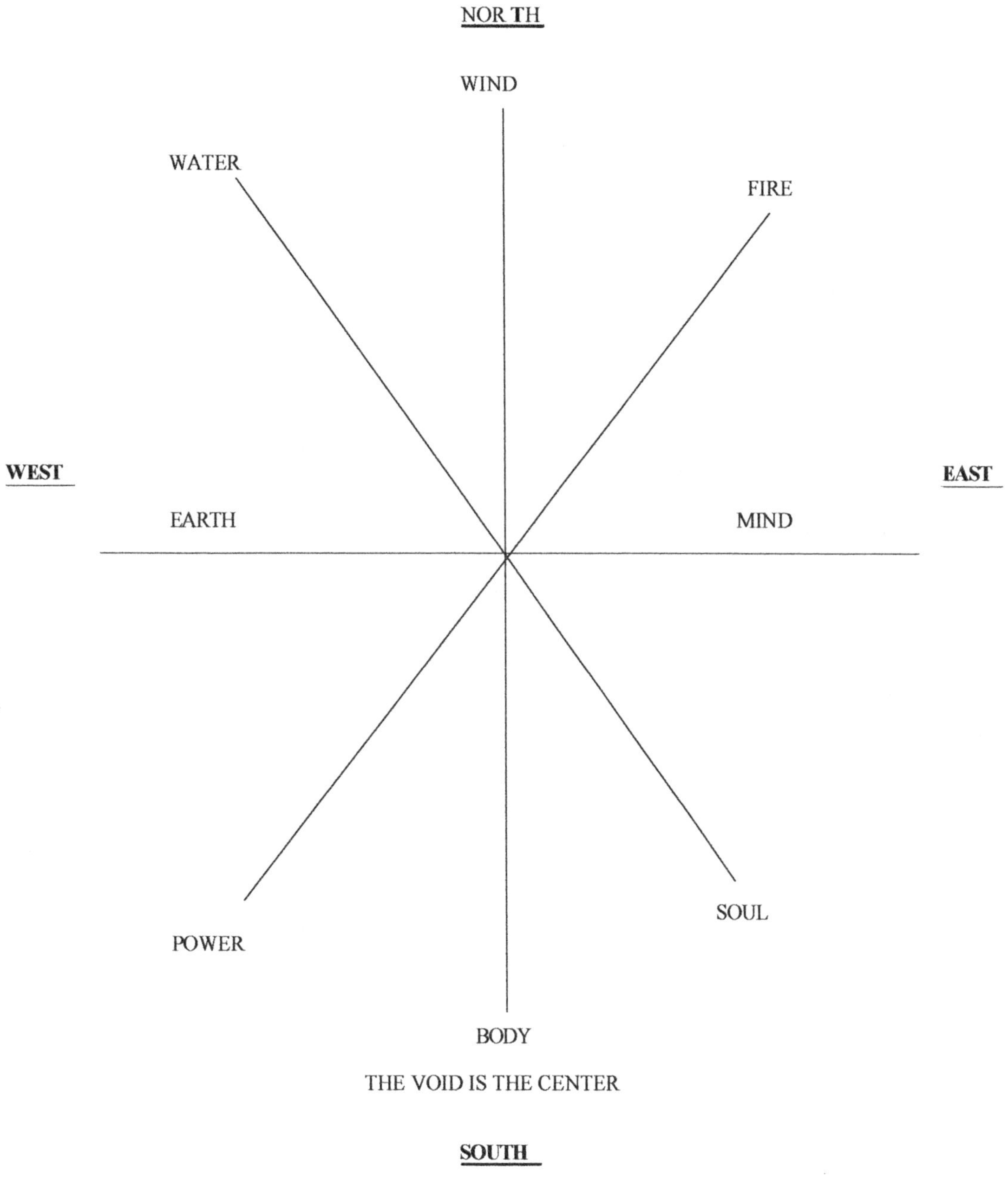

NOTE: The counter moves are illustrated from a right side draw stance. If the opponent kicks with his left leg use a left draw stance. The counters are illustrated with the starting position being the vortex of the nine angles.

1. EARTH COUNTER
    A. Start in a right draw stance.
    B. Opponent throws a right kick.
    C. Block kick with a lower cross block and grapple.
    D. Step with back leg in the direction of EARTH.
    E. While holding onto the grappled kick perform a full shoulder roll toward MIND.

2. WATER COUNTER
    A. Start in a right draw stance.
    B. Opponent throws a right kick.
    C. Block kick with a lower cross block and grapple.
    D. Glide step with your front left leg in the direction of WATER. This will flip your opponent face first toward the ground.
    E. Simultaneous with the glide step sweep the opponent's standing leg with your right foot.

3. WIND COUNTER
    A. Start in a right draw stance.
    B. Opponent throws a right kick.
    C. Block kick with a lower cross block and grapple.
    D. Step directly into your opponent in the direction of WIND.
    E. While stepping inward push back and pick up on your opponent's leg. This will throw your opponent backwards in a flipping motion.

4. FIRE COUNTER
    A. Start in a right draw stance.
    B. Opponent throws a right kick.
    C. Block kick with a lower cross block and grapple.
    D. Glide step into a left stance in the direction of FIRE. This will spin your opponent away from you.
    E. Simultaneous with the glide stomp your opponent's standing leg with a left stomp kick to the knee.

5. MIND COUNTER
    A. Start in a right draw stance.
    B. Opponent throws a right kick.
    C. Block kick with a lower cross block and grapple.
    D. Pivot on your back (right) foot and bring your front (left) foot out in the direction of MIND.
    E. Simultaneous with the foot movement hammer-fist the side of the opponent's knee. This will fold the leg.
    F. Push your opponent backwards to the ground and figure four lock his leg with your body.

6. SOUL COUNTER
    A. Start in a right draw stance.
    B. Opponent throws a right kick.
    C. Block kick with a lower cross block and grapple.
    D. Stance hop backwards in the direction of SOUL. This will pull your opponent off balance.
    E. While opponent is in mid air double knife hand strike him in the throat and lower ribs. This will flip him.

7. BODY COUNTER
    A. Start in a right draw stance.
    B. Opponent throws a right kick.
    C. Block kick with a lower cross block and grapple.
    D. Stance hop backwards in the direction of BODY. This will pull the opponent into the splits or off balance for an easier strike.

8. POWER COUNTER
    A. Start in a right draw stance.
    B. Opponent throws a right kick.
    C. Block kick with a lower cross block and grapple.
    D. Stance hop backwards in the direction of POWER. This will pull your opponent off balance.
    E. Twist your upper body so that the opponent's knee is over your front knee.
    F. Press down and break the opponent's knee over your knee.

9. VOID COUNTER
    A. Start in a right draw stance.
    B. Opponent throws a right kick.
    C. Block kick with lower cross block and grapple with left hand.
    D. Pull your opponent past you while striking his right hip joint with a right palm hand.

YOSU JU-SAN: ELEMENT STANCES (GO-GIYO KAMAE)

EARTH

In a right earth stance both arms should be extended over a 90-degree angle in advanced type stance using earth hands (master hands). Left leg should be facing opponent while right leg is in 45-degree angle.

WIND

In a right wind stance position the upper body is like a master stance except the stance is made using wind hands. Front leg (left) facing opponent. The right leg is in a 45-degree angle from the front leg.

FIRE

In a right fire stance a mid chest block should be used as the upper body of the fire stance. Front leg (left) is facing the opponent. Right leg is in a 45-degree angle from the left.

WATER

In a right water stance left arm will be extended upward toward center of the chest, palm up. Right arm will be extended downward toward center of abdomen, palm down. Right and left legs will be in saddle stance

YOSU JU-SHI: BUSHI KATA

1. ELEMENT SALUTE (GO-GIYO JIGI)

2. LEAP TO FEET (TOBU NI ASHI)

3. DOUBLE MASTER HAND [TO ESOPHAGUS AND SOLAR PLEXUS]
(NISOBAI SHUJIN TE)
[NO STEP]

4. RIGHT REAR OX/ PALM STRIKE
(MIGI O'SHIRI KOTOI TANAGOKORO UTSU)
[RIGHT REVERSE STEP. STRIKE TO REAR.]

5. TURN LEFT FRONT ROLL BLOCK
(MAWASU HADARI MAE KONOGARU KIRE)
[NO STEP]

6. RIGHT FORWARD PUNCH AND ELBOW STRIKE [TO STERNUM]
(MIGI MAE KOBUSHI NI HIJI UTSU)
[RIGHT STEP]

7. RIGHT BACK ELBOW STRIKE [TO RIBS] (MIGI URA HIJI UTSU)
[NO STEP]

8. ELBOW BREAK WITH RIGHT RIDGE
(HIJI YABURERU NI MIGI MINE-TE)
[NO STEP]

9. SIDE SNAP [TO RIBS] (YOKO ORU KERU)
[HOLD LEG IN AIR]

10. LOOK LEFT (MIRU HADARI)

11. WRIST SPIN TECHNIQUE (TE-KUBI MAWASU JUTSU)
[HOLD LEG IN AIR]

12. RIGHT STOMP KICK [TO FACE] (MIGI TSU KU KERU)

13. DIVE ROLL (HAN KA'TA KONOGARU)

14. RIGHT EARTH STANCE (MIGI CHI KAMAE)
[COME UP FACING THE REVERSE DIRECTION]

15. LEFT CROSS GRAB BLOCK (HADARI JIRERU TORU KIRE)
[45-DEGREE LEFT GLIDE]

16. RIGHT RAIN DROP HAND [TO ESOPHAGUS]
(MIGI SOUI TAICAZI TE)
[NO STEP]

17. RIGHT UPWARD ELBOW [TO CHIN] (MIGI KAMI HIJI)
[NO STEP]

18. RIGHT DOWNWARD BACK FIST [TO NOSE]
(MIGI SHIMO URA-KEN)
[NO STEP]

19. DOUBLE PALM STRIKE [TO CHEST]
(NISOBAI KONOGARU UTSU)
[RIGHT STEP TO SADDLE STANCE]

20. LEFT BACK ROUND KICK (HADARI URA NARU KERU)

21. LEFT DRAGON'S TAIL SWEEP (TATSU SHIPPO HAKU)

22. RIGHT WIND STANCE (FU KAMAE)

23. RIGHT PALM TO KNEE/ UPWARD LEFT EAGLE'S CLAW TO THROAT
(MIGI TANAGOKORO NI HIZA/ KAMI HADARI WASHI T'SUME NI NODO)
[RIGHT STEP]

24. RIGHT KNIFE HAND [TO GROIN] (MIGI FUME SHUTO TE)
[RIGHT REVERSE STEP TO RIGHT STANCE.]

25. RIGHT UPWARD MASTER HAND [TO ESOPHAGUS] & LEFT DOWNWARD MASTER HAND [TO BASE OF SKULL]
(MIGI KAMI SHUJIN TE NO HADARI SHIMO SHUJIN TE)
[NO STEP]

26. RIGHT MASTER SPEAR HAND [TO EYE SOCKET]
(MIGI SHUJIN TE)
[NO STEP. STRIKE TO RIGHT SIDE.]

27. LEFT OX HAND [TO CHIN] & RIGHT UPWARD RIDGE [TO GROIN]
(HADARI KOTOI TE NO MIGI KAMI MINE)
[NO STEP. STRIKE TO FRONT.]

28. DOUBLE DEM MAC [TO CHEST] (NISOBAI ANA UTSU)
[RIGHT STEP TO SADDLE STANCE]

29. THUMB PULL TECHNIQUE (OYAYUBI HIKU JUTSU)

30. LEFT KNEE TO ARM PIT, DRIVE TO THE GROUND
(HADARI HIZA NI WAKI NO SHITA, MORO DZUKUNI)

31. ELBOW BREAK (HIJI YABURERU)
[LEFT HAND PUSHES THE WRIST AND THE RIGHT HAND PULLS THE ELBOW.]

32. HALF SHOULDER ROLL (HAN KA'TA KONOGARU)

33. RIGHT FIRE STANCE (MIGI KA KAMAE)

34. LEFT KNIFE BLOCK (HADARI SHUTO KIRE)

35. LEFT KNIFE HAND [TO NECK], RIGHT TIGER'S PAW [TO THROAT]
(HADARI SHUTO TE, MIGI TORU TE)

36. LEFT REAR SWEEP WITH A LEFT BACK ELBOW BLOCK
(HADARI URA HAKU NI HADARI URA HIJI KIRE)
[TO A RIGHT STANCE]

37. RIGHT HEART GRAB [THROUGH ARM PIT]
(MIGI SHINZO HITA KURU)
[NO STEP]

38. DOUBLE DEM MAC PUSH OFF
(NISOBAI ANA UTSU OSU DEHODAS)
[NO STEP]

39. FAN BLOCK (OGI KIRE)
[RIGHT STEP. OUTSIDE FANS.]

40. LEFT EARTH STANCE (HADARI CHI KAMAE)

41. LEFT OUTER ROUND KICK (HADARI UWA NARU KERU)
[TRAVELING]

42. WATER STANCE (SOUI KAMAE)
[RIGHT HAND ON TOP]

43. RIGHT CROSS GRAB BLOCK [TO OPPONENT'S RIGHT PUNCH]
(MIGI HITAKURU TORU KIRE)
[NO STEP]

44. LEFT SIDE BLOCK ELBOW BREAK
(HADARI YOKO KIRE HIJI YABURERU)
[NO STEP]

45. RIGHT FORWARD ELBOW [TO JAW] (MIGI MAE HIJI)
[NO STEP]

46. RIGHT BACK ELBOW [TO NOSE] (MIGI URA HIJI)
[NO STEP]

47. FAN DOWN [INTO NEXT MOVE]
(OGI SHIMO)
[RIGHT STEP]

48. LEFT FOREARM BLOCK WITH RIGHT BACK-FIST STRIKE.
(HADARI KO-UDE KIRE NI MIGI URA-KEN UTSU)
[RIGHT STEP.]

49. OUTSIDE FANS (HOKA OGI TE)
[TO LEFT FOREARM BLOCK AND RIGHT RIDGE STRIKE TO JAW.
LEFT STEP TO SADDLE STANCE.]

50. DOUBLE OX STRIKES (NISOBAI KOTOI TE USTU)
[TO BOTH SIDES. NO STEP]

51. DOUBLE PALM STRIKES (NISOBAI TANAGOKORO)
[TO BOTH SIDES. NO STEP]

52. BODY STANCE (TAI KAMAE)

53. RIGHT DOWN PALM BLOCK (MIGI SHIMO TANAGOKORO KIRE)
[RIGHT STEP]

54. RIGHT OX STRIKE WITH DOWNWARD PALM STRIKE
(MIGI KOTOI TE UTSU NO MIGI SHIMO TANAGOKORO UTSU)
[GLIDE STEP STRAIGHT IN]

55. HORIZONTAL BLOCKS (TAIRAKA NA KIRE)
[GRAPPLE, LEFT STEP TO SADDLE STANCE]

56. BACK BREAK (SENAKA YABURERU)
[RIGHT SPIN TO LEFT KNEE]

57. STAY KATA SALUTE (YAMU KATA SALUTE)

YOSU JU-GO: THREE SECTIONAL STAFF (SAN-SETSU-KAN)

1. SALUTES (JIGI):

A. BASIC ENTRANCE SALUTE (IRU JIGI)

B. ADVANCED ENTRANCE SALUTE (AGERU IRU JIGI)
[HAND ROTATION]

C. TURN-ABOUT/ EXIT SALUTE (MAWASU/ DE-GUCHI JIGI)

D. CROSSOVER/ STAY SALUTE (WATARU/ YAMU JIGI)

2. STANCES (KAMAE):

On the basic stances the middle bar is down and on element stances the middle bar is up.

A. BASIC STANCE (BUDO KAMAE)
[The staff is held with hands in basic stance position.]

B. ADVANCED STANCE (AGARU KAMAE)
[The staff is held with hands in advance stance position.]

C. SHADOW STANCE (KAGE KAMAE)
[The staff is in a "Z" formation in front of the body.]

D. MASTER'S STANCE (SHUJIN KAMAE)
[The hands are held in master stance position.]

E. PRESENT STANCE (OKURU KAMAE)
[The staff is folded up and held in both hands palm down.]

F. ON DUTY/ ON GUARD STANCE (TO-BAN KAMAE)
[The staff is held with the middle bar down and the two ends making an "X" in front of the body.]

G. DRAW STANCE (KAKU KAMAE)
[The staff is held the same as the bo draw stance.]

H. SADDLE STANCE (KURA KAMAE)
[The staff is held in front of the body with the middle bar down and the ends of the staff pointing straight up.]

I. ATTENTION STANCE (JUSHA KAMAE)
[The staff is folded up and held in the right hand at the individual's side.]

3. SPINS (TSUMUGU):

A. DOUBLE HAND SPIN (NISOBAI TE TSUMUGU)

B. ROTATION SPIN (MAWARI TSUMUGU)

C. DOUBLE HAND SPIN OVERHEAD (NISOBAI TE TSUMUGU NOKORU)

D. MIDDLE SPIN (NAKABA TSUMUGU)

E. END SPIN (NAGI OWARI TSUMUGU)

4. TUMBLES (OCHIRU):

A. FULL SHOULDER ROLL (AKU KA'TA KOROGARU)

B. HALF SHOULDER ROLL (HAN KA'TA KOROGARU)

C. CARTWHEEL (NI NIN NO NI-GURUMA KURUMA)

D. REVERSE ROLL (URA KOROGARU)

5. ACROBATICS (KARUWAZA-SIH): BLACK SASH ONLY

A. FRONT HANDSPRING (MAE TE HARU)

B. BACK HAND SPRING (URA TE HARU)

C. FRONT SOMERSAULT (MAE HIKKURI-KAYERU)

D. BACK SOMERSAULT (URA HIKKURI-KAYERU)

E. WALL RUN (KABE HASHIRU)

6. STRIKES (UTSU):

A. RIGHT AND LEFT PIVOT (MIGI TO HADARI MAWASU)

B. RIGHT AND LEFT REVERSE PIVOT (MIGI TO HADARI URA MAWASU)

C. RIGHT AND LEFT DOWN THRUST (MIGI TO HADARI SHIMO SASU)

D. RIGHT AND LEFT UPPER THRUST (MIGI TO HADARI AGERU SASU)

E. RIGHT AND LEFT DOWN SLASH
(MIGI TO HADARI SHIMO KIRU)

F. RIGHT AND LEFT UPPER SLASH
(MIGI TO HADARI AGERU KIRU)

G. PENETRATION (SATORI)

H. REVERSE PENETRATION (URA SATORI)

I. MIDDLE SECTION STRIKE (NAKABA SHO UTSU)

J. DISTRACTION (NAGUSAMI)

K. JOINT VERTICAL STRIKE (FUSHI MASSU-GU-NI TATSU UTSU)

L. JOINT HORIZONTAL STRIKE (FUSHI TAIRAKA NA UTSU)

7. COUNTER MOVES (SOMUKU HATARAKI)

A. UPPER HAND TAKE-AWAY (AGERU TE TORU RUSU)

B. DISTRACTION (NAGUSAMI)

C. SPIN UNDER (MAWASU SHITANO)

D. SPIN OVER (MAWASU SUGERU)

E. HAND STRIKE (TE UTSU)

F. STAFF SWEEPS (BO HAKU)

8. BLOCKS (KIRE):

A. HIGH BLOCK (TAKAI KIRE)

B. LOW BLOCK (SHITA KIRE)

C. BEHIND HEAD BLOCK (URA KUBI KIRE)

D. SIDE BLOCK (YOKO KIRE)

E. REVERSE SIDE BLOCK (TURNING) (URA YOKO KIRE {MAWASU})

F. TRAVELING BLOCK (ARUKU KIRE)

G. UPPER SLASH BLOCK (AGERU KIRU KIRE)

H. DOWN SLASH BLOCK (SHIMO KIRU KIRE)

I. MID-SECTION BLOCK (NAKABU SHO KIRE)

J. SWEEP BLOCK (HAKU KIRE)

9. STRIKE COMBO (USTU CHOGO):

A. "X" (WATARU JUTSU)

B. REVERSE "X" (URA WATARU JUTSU)

10. ROLLS (KOROBU):

A. HAND ROLL (TE KOROBU)

B. REVERSE HAND ROLL (URE TE KOROBU)

C. PUNCH ROLL (KOBUSHI KOROBU)

D. LEG ROLL (ASHI KOROBU)

E. NECK ROLL (KUBI KOROBU)

F. WAIST ROTATION (KOSHI MAWASU)

G. WAIST ROLL ROTATION (KOSHI KOROBU MAWASU)

H. OVERHEAD OPEN HAND ROLL (SUGIRU KUBI TE KOBORU)

I. FLOOR BOUNCE (YUKA HANARU)

J. FLOOR ROLL (YUKA KOROBU)

YOSU ROKU: NUN-CHAKU
(TWO 12 TO 14 INCH STAFFS CONNECTED BY CHAIN OR ROPE)

1. Be able to perform eighty individual moves not counting left and right side moves. Each grapple technique is counted as one move.

A. ROLLS (KONOGARU)

1. HORIZONTAL ROLL OVER BACK OF HAND
   (TAIRAKA KONOGARU AGERU SENAKE TE)

2. VERTICAL ROLL OVER BACK OF HAND
   (KONOGARU AGERU SENAKE TE)

3. DOUBLE ROLL OVER BACK OF HAND
   (NISOBAI NO SENAKE URA-TE KONOGARU)

4. UPWARD CROSS CHEST BACKHAND ROLL
   (KAMI JIRERU TO MUNE NO URA-TE KONOGARU)

5. NECK ROLL [BOTH WAYS] (KUBI KONOGARU)

6. UPSIDEDOWN NECK ROLL (ACROSS FINGERTIPS)
   (KAMI-YOKO-SHIMO KUBI KONOGARU)

7. DOWNWARD CROSS CHEST BACKHAND ROLL
   (SHIMO JITERU MINE NO URA-TE KONOGARU)

8. FOOT ROLL (ASHI KONOGARU)

9. WRIST ROLL (TE KUBI KONOGARU)

10. ARM ROLL (UDE KONOGARU)

11. FRONTAL HAND ROLL (MAE TE KONOGARU)

12. OUTSIDE LEG ROLL (SOTO ASHI KONOGARU)

13. REPEATING ROLL OVER ARM (KONOGARU AGERU UDE)

B. PASSES (WATARU)

1. PASS AROUND WAIST(WATARU AGERU HASHI)

2. PASS THROUGH LEGS [BOTH WAYS]
   (WATARU SHITA NO ASHI)

3. PASS THROUGH LEGS WITH HAND ROLL [BOTH WAYS]
   (WATARU SHITA NO ASHI NI TE KONOGARU)

4. PASS CROSS BACK (WATARU JIRERU SENAKE)

5. PASS OVER SHOULDER (WATARU AGERU KA'TA)

6. SHOULDER TO SHOULDER TWIST (KA'TA NI KA'TA MAWASU)

7. SIDE TO SIDE PASS (YOKO MI YOKO WATARU)

8. SIDE TO SIDE TOSS PASS (YOKO NI YOKO NAGERU WATARU)

9. REVERSE CROSS BACK PASS
   (URA JIRERU NO URA WATARU)

C. STRIKES (UTSU)

1. SNAKE SNAP (HEBI ORU)

2. BUTTERFLY STRIKE (CHO UTSU)

3. REVERSE BUTTERFLY STRIKE (URA CHO UTSU)

4. BUTTERFLY STRIKE WITH HAND ROLL
   (CHO UTSU NI TE MAWASU)

5. REVERSE BUTTERFLY STRIKE WITH HAND ROLLS
   (URA CHO UTSU NI TE MAWASU)

6. STRIKES (SWING IN A DOWNWARD DIAGONAL MOTION)
   (UTSU)

7. REVERSE GRAB STRIKES (URA TSUKAMU UTSU)
   [SWING IN AN UPWARD DIAGONAL MOTION]

8. THRUSTS (SASU)
   [SWING IN A DOWNWARD VERTICAL MOTION]

9. REVERSE GRAB THRUSTS (URA TSUKAMU SASU)
(SWING IN AN UPWARD VERTICAL MOTION)

10. HORTZONTAL STRIKES (TAIRAKA NA UTSU)

11. REVERSE GRAB HORIZONTAL STRIKES
(URA TSUKAMU TAIRAKA NA USTU)

12. PENETRATION (SATROI)

13. REVERSE PENETRATION (URA SATORI)

D. SPINS & ROTATIONS (TSUMUGU NI MAWASU)

1. SIDE SPIN (YOKO TSUMUGU)

2. SIDE ROTATION [USES HAND] (YOKO MAWASU)

3. 1 FINGER SPIN (ICHI YUBI TSUMUGU)

4. LONG END SPIN (NAGAI OWARI TSUMUGU)

E. BLOCKS (KIRES)

1. UPPER CROSS BLOCK (AGERU JIRERU)

2. LOWER CROSS BLOCK (SHITA NO JIRERU)

3. BEHIND HEAD BLOCK (URA NOKORU KIRE)

4. OVER HEAD BLOCK (NOKORU KIRE)

5. SIDE BLOCK (YOKO KIRE)

6. REVERSE SIDE BLOCK [ELBOW EXPOSED] (URA YOKO KIRE)

7. LOWER BLOCK (SHITA NO KIRE)

8. CENTER STRIKE BLOCK (NAKABA UTSU KIRE)

9. SWEEP BLOCK (HAKU KIRE)

10. STRIKE BLOCK (UTSU KIRE)

11. STRIKE COUNTER BLOCK (UTSU SOMUKU KIRE)

12. JOINT STRIKE BLOCK (FUSHI UTSU KIRE)

F. STANCES (KAMAES): Basic stance is single chuck and double chuck is element stances.

1. BASIC STANCE (BUDO KAMAE)
[The hands are in the basic stance posture and the chucks are held in the backhand.]

2. ADVANCED STANCE (AGARU KAMAE)
[The chuck is held with one end in each hand. The hands are in the middle of the chuck and the chain is on the topside.]

3. MASTER STANCE (SHUJIN KAMAE)
[The hands are in the master stance posture and the chuck is held in the backhand.]

4. DRAW STANCE (KAKU KAMAE)
[The hands are held in the draw stance position and the chucks are held with one handle in each hand.]

5. ON GUARD STANCE (TO-BAN KAMAE)
[The hands are in front of the body at waist level and the chuck is held in one hand with the palms down.]

6. PRESENT STANCE (OKURU KAMAE)
[The chuck is folded up and held in both hands at waist level with palms down.]

7. SHADOW STANCE (KAGE KAMAE)
[The hands are in shadow stance position with the chuck in the top hand.]

8. SADDLE STANCE (KURA KAMAE)
[The hands are in saddle stance position with the chuck held in one hand at shoulder height.]

9. ATTENTION STANCE (JUSHA KAMAE)
[The hands are held in jusha kamae position with the chuck at the right side.]

G. SALUTES (JIGIS)

1. ENTRANCE SALUTE (IRU JIGI)
2. ADVANCED ENTRANCE SALUTE (AGERU IRU JIGI)
3. TURN ABOUT/ EXIT SALUTE (MAWASU/ DE-GUCHI JIGI)
4. CROSSOVER/ STAY SALUTE (WATARU/ YAMU JIGI)

H. HANDLING

1. IN THE STANDARD WAY WITH NUN-CHAKU THE HANDLES ARE TOGETHER.

I. THROWING (NAGERU)

1. TARGETING (MATO)

J. ACROBATICS (KARUWAZA-SHI)

1. FULL SHOULDER ROLL (AKU KA'TA KONOGARU)
2. HALF SHOULDER ROLL (HAN KA'TA KONOGARU)
3. REVERSE SHOULDER ROLL (URA KONOGARU)
4. SIDE ROLL (YOKO KONOGARU)
5. CARTWHEEL (NI NIN NO NI-GURUMA KURUMA)

K. GRAPPLES (HASUKAAMU)

1. CHUCK WRAP (NUN-CHAKU MAKU)
2. ELBOW LOCK (HIJI YEYA)
3. NECK WRAP (NODO MAKU)
4. THROAT PUNCH PIN (NODO UTSU TOME-BARI DE TOMERU)
5. THROAT PUNCH TAKEDOWN (NODO UTSU UKERU)
6. BODY STRIKES (FREESTYLE)(MI JO)

SAMURAI

YOSU ICHI: COUNTER (SOMUKU)

** Note: When performing the ox walks; block, strike then glide strike.

1. HAND WALK WITH PALM (ARUKE-SUGIRU NO TANAGOKORO)

    A. Opponent punches.
    B. Right palm strike block the opponent's punch down.
    C. Right ox strike the opponent's chin.
    D. Right palm strike the opponent's chest.
    E. Right ox strike the opponent's chin.
    F. Right palm strike the opponent's left collarbone.

2. HAND WALK WITH OX (TE ARUKE-SUGIRU NO KOTOI-TE)

    A. Opponent punches.
    B. Right ox strike block the opponent's punch upward.
    C. Right palm strike the opponent's chest.
    D. Right ox strike the opponent's chin.
    E. Right palm strike the opponent's right collarbone.
    F. Right ox strike the opponent's left collarbone.

3. UNDER ARM WITH ONE ARM (SHIMO UDE NO ICHI UDE)

    A. Opponent punches.
    B. Right ox strike block opponent's punch upward.
    C. Strike the opponent's exposed two lower ribs with a right palm strike.
    D. Right ox strike opponent's chin.
    E. Flick the wrist up and around. This brings the ox hand into a shuto hand, and pushes the opponent's head back.
    F. Right shuto strike the opponent's left collarbone.

4. HORIZONTAL OX WALK (TAIRAKA NA KOTOI-TE ARUKE-SUGIRU)

    A. Opponent holds hands like a boxer.
    B. Right ox strike the opponent's front hand outward.
    C. Right palm strike the opponent's second hand outward.
    D. Right shuto strike the left side of the opponent's neck.

5. HORIZONTAL PALM WALK
(TAIRAKA NA TANAGOKORO ARUKE-SUGIRU)

A. Opponent holds hands like a boxer.
B. Right palm strike opponent's front hand outward.
C. Right ox strike the opponent's second hand outward.
D. Right palm strike the opponent's cheek.

6. FAN WALK (OGI ARUKI-SUGIRU)

1. PALM HANDS OR SHUTO HANDS.

A. RIGHT HAND FIRST.
1. Opponent punches
2. Right palm strike block the opponent's punch down.
3. Left palm strike the opponent's elbow.
4. Right palm strike the opponent's collarbone.
5. Left palm strike to opponent's jaw.

B. LEFT HAND FIRST.
1. Opponent punches.
2. Left palm strike block the opponent's punch down.
3. Right palm strike the opponent's elbow.
4. Left palm strike the opponent's shoulder.
5. Right sliding knife strike to opponent's throat.

NOTE: Step 5 on both sets A & B remains the same if palm hands or shuto hands are used.

YOSU NI: MASTER BLOCKS (SHUJIN KIRE)

1. SPEAR HAND TO SHOULDER (YARI-TE NI KA'TA)

A. Opponent punches.
B. Block punch with a left roll catch block.
C. Grapple the blocked arm.
D. Strike the opponent's shoulder joint with a right spear hand.

2. PALM HAND TO KNEE CAP (NIGIRU-NI HIZA)

A. Opponent kicks.
B. Defender side steps and blocks kick with a palm hand strike to the kneecap.

3. <u>SHIN BLOCK (MAE-ASHI KIRE)</u>

   A. Opponent kicks.
   B. Defender side steps and blocks opponent's kick by punching the shin of the opponent's kicking leg.

4. <u>ELBOW BLOCK (HIJI KIRE)</u>

   A. Opponent punches.
   B. Block with a right face block.
   C. Opponent punches with opposite hand.
   D. Block second punch by raising his right elbow up and to the right.

5. <u>INNER ROUND KICK BLOCK (NAKA NARU KERU NO KIRE)</u>

   A. Opponent punches.
   B. Block punch by kicking the wrist, elbow, or forearm area with an inner round kick.

6. <u>OUTER ROUND KICK BLOCK (UWA NARU KERU NO KIRE)</u>

   A. Opponent punches.
   B. Block punch by kicking the wrist, elbow, or forearm area with an outer round kick.

YOSU SAN: MASTER KICKS (SHUJIN KERU)

1. <u>THIGH KICK (SHUJIN ASHI KERU)</u>

   A. Opponent confronts defender.
   B. Defender strikes opponent's thigh with a side snap kick thrown at a 45-degree angle.

2. <u>STERNUM KICK (SHUJIN MUNE KERU)</u>

   A. Opponent confronts defender.
   B. Defender strikes opponent's sternum with a front snap kick.
   C. The defender can also strike the opponent's sternum with an outer round kick, but making sure that the strike is made with the ball of the foot and not the instep.

YOSU SHI: BAMBOO SWORD SPARRING (SHINAI KUMITE)

1. TEACHER WILL APPROVE (SENSEI O YOSHI TO SURU)

YOSU GO: QUEST (NEGAU)

1. AT ONE'S REQUEST FROM THE TEACHER.
   (NEGAI NI YORI O KUDASAI SENSEI)

YOSU ROKU: SWORD MAINTENANCE (KEN O YASHINAU)

1. HOW TO WRAP SWORD HANDLE (KEN-T'SUKA O TSUTSUMU)
2. HOW TO SHARPEN BLADE (NAIFU O TOGU)
3. HOW TO WRAP A SWORD IN A SOCK TYPE COVER
   (KEN O KORI-KA-TAMARU)

YOSU SHICHI: THE WAY OF THE BLADE (KENDO)

A. DRAW AND RE-PLACEMENT OF SWORD IN SHEATH
(DAN-JIKI KAKU NI SAYA)

B. HANDLING ONE TO ANOTHER THE SWORD (TSUTAYERU-KEN)

When handing the sword to one another the handle of the sword is always to the right side of the giver's body. Hold the sword in both hands with the hands placed in one-third and two-thirds position on the scabbard. The feet will be in bow-in-position. The giver of the sword will have his palms faced up. The receiver of the sword will receive the sword palms up by placing his hands between the giver's hands. Never grab the hilt to accept a sword and only a sword master can receive a sword palms down. When a sword is passed the receiver will say " Domo" to signify that he has control of the blade and the giver will say " Yoi" to inform the receiver that he is letting go.

When handing the sword to another Konigun Brother the handle of the sword is always to the left side of the body. Hold the sword in both hands with the hands placed in one-third and two-thirds position on the scabbard. The giver of the sword will have his palms faced down. The receiver of the sword will receive the sword palms up. This is to show trust in the brotherhood.

If the receiver of the sword reaches to the center then he will receive it with one hand and this gesture signifies the receiver's intentions of drawing the blade. This is for students and teachers in class.

An instructor is permitted to accept a sword one handed but the palm is still face up. If the receiver of the sword reaches to the center then he will receive it with one hand and this gesture signifies the receiver's intentions of drawing the blade.

If the sword is unsheathed then the sword will be passed from right hand to right hand hilt first. The blade of the sword will be pointing away from the body and down the back of the forearm. The receiver will take the sword in his right hand, which is a cross grab receiving method. This is used because it gives the receiver better control if the giver has ill intentions.

To offer a sword to someone in an honorable manner and to give it to the receiver permanently then the giver will step forward with the right foot and go to a left knee. The giver will hold the sword palm down while extending the sword out in the right hand with the sword hilt to the left of the giver's body. The giver will also bow his head as he presents the blade. The receiver of the blade will take the sword palm down. The sword will be held above the head in the left hand by the center of the scabbard. The giver's head will be bent down.

C. BODY MANAGEMENT (TAISABARI)

Body Management is the yin of the yang of sword fighting. You are trying to persistently cut your opponent while maneuvering your body so as not to be cut. The sword fights on the vertical nine fighting angle while the body moves on the horizontal nine fighting angles. When two points on both planes line up blood is drawn. Sword fighting is only four steps involving nine angles with nine defensive angles involving four retreats. The blade will have four movements then you must redraw and reset for battle. The feet will have four movements before they must redraw and rest for battle. The ideal sword fight is (1) move in, (2 & 3) persist and damage, and (4) step away to safety.

Always seek to keep your center of gravity at all times. No matter how the feet are positioned the straddle should always be over the center of the imaginary line drawn between the big toes. The knees should always be bent, do not lock the hips keep the back straight, and do not slouch the shoulders forward. If the shoulders or hips un-line then the fight is lost. Stay on the balls of the feet because if you are flat-footed then you are slower and when fast drawing you can readjust the weight as the sword extends. If you ever have to cross step collapse the blade down the arm. Cross step only as a last resort.

D. PERSISTENCE (MA-AI)

The act of constantly cutting, beginning at the point of drawing and continuing to the satisfactory end of the sword dance. In essence it s constant pivoting, turning, and twisting of the edge "ken" of the sword in pursuit of cutting flesh.

E. SWORD WIND TRAINING (TAICHI-KAZI-JUTSU)

F. CHALLENGE MOVE (YOBI-DASU)

There are two ways to challenge someone. If the sword is sheathed then the challenger will only have to jerk the sword open without breaking the seal.

If the sword is already unsheathed then the challenging move is to stand in jusha kamae then roll the sword to the center of the body and perform a right slash to side.

G. SEATED FAST DRAW (SEIZA IAIDO)

From a kashia step slightly outward so that you always step into a good stance.

1. FAST DRAW WITH PIVOT CUT (KIRU IAIDO)
2. FAST DRAW WITH STEPPING PIVOT CUT (KIRU IAIDO NO DAN)
3. FAST DRAW WITH STEPPING PENETRATION (T'SUKU IAIDO NO DAN)
4. FAST DRAW WITH UPWARD SLASH (GYAKU KESA GIRI IAIDO)
5. HANDLE PENETRATION (T'SUKA SATORI)

H. DAI IAIDO

1. FAST DRAW WITH PIVOT CUT (KIRU IAIDO)
2. FAST DRAW WITH STEPPING PIVOT CUT (KIRU IAIDO NO DAN)
3. FAST DRAW WITH STEPPING PENETRATION (T'SUKU IAIDO NO DAN)
4. FAST DRAW WITH UPWARD SLASH CUT (GYAKU KESA GIRI IAIDO)

I. DAI UTSU

1. OVERHEAD THRUST WITH STEP (NOKORU SASU NO DAN)
2. RIGHT SLASH WITH STEP (MIGI UTSU NO DAN)
3. PIVOT WITH STEPPING THRUST (MAWASU NO DAN SASU)
4. THRUST, PENETRATION WITH STEP, REVERSE THRUST (SASU, SATORI NO DAN, URA SASU)

YOSU HACHI: STRIKE POINTS (UTSU TOKORO)

1. WAR FIST (KOBUSHI)

    A. XIPHOID PROCESS (SHITA MUNE NO HONE)

    B. STERNUM (MUNE NO HONE)

    C. TWO LOWER RIBS (NI SHITA ABARA-BONE)

    D. KIDNEYS (MURADO)

    E. LOWER BACK (SHITA SE-BONE)

    F. SIDE OF KNEE (YOKO HIZA)

    G. SHOULDER JOINT (KA'TA FUSHI)
    (WHEN ARM IS HELD)

    H. GROIN (MOMONE)

    I. PELVAS (MOMONE)

    J. SHINS (MAE ASHI)

    (HIT WITH THE AREA RIGHT UNDER THE NUCKLE LINE)

    NOTES: DO NOT HIT STOMACH NEVER HIT THE HEAD

2. HAMMER FIST (KANAD'ZUSHI-TE)

    A. TEMPLES (TERA)

    B. COLLARBONES (SAKOTSU)

    C. NOSE (HANA)

    D. GROIN (MOMONE)

    E. BASE OF SKULL (ATAMA)

    F. TWO LOWER RIBS (NI SHITA ABARA-BONE)

    G. XIPHOID PROCESS (SHITA MUNE NO HONE)

    H. ESOPHAGUS (MAE NODO)

    I. PELVAS (MOMONE)

    J. SHOULDER (KA'TA)

    K. INSIDE ELBOW JOINT (NAKA HIJI FUSHI)

    L. ANKLE (KURUBUSHI)

3. RIDGE HAND (MINE-TE)

   A. JAW LINE (AGO)
   B. VORTEX OF JAW (UDZU AGO)
   C. SIDE OF NECK (YOKO NODO)
   D. ESOPHAGUS (MAE NODO)
   E. OUTSIDE OF ELBOW JOINT (NOKA HIJI FUSHI)
   F. INSIDE OF ELBOW JOINT (NAKA HIJI FUSHI)
   G. GROIN (MOMONE)
   H. TWO LOWER RIBS (NI SHITA ABARA-BONE)

4. SPEAR HAND (YARI-TE)

   A. ESOPHAGUS (MAE NODO)
   B. SIDE OF NECK (YOKO NODO)
   C. SHOULDER JOINT (KA'TA FUSHI)
   D. ARM PIT (WAKI NO SHITA)

5. TIGER'S EYES (TORA-ME)

   A. EYE (ME)
   B. ESOPHAGUS (MAE NODO)

6. WHIP HAND (MUCHI-TE)

   A. NOSE (HANA)
   B. EAR (MIMI)
   C. ESOPHAGUS (MAE NODO)
   D. SIDE OF NECK (YOKO NODO)

7. CLUTCH FIST (NIGIRU)

   A. ESOPHAGUS (MAE NODO)
   B. SHOULDER JOINT (KA'TA FUSHI)
   C. STERNUM (MUNE NO HONE)

8. BACK FIST (URA-KEN)

A. BASE OF SKULL (ATAMA)
B. EARS (MIMI)
C. NOSE (HANA)
D. TEMPLE (TERA)
E. INSIDE ELBOW JOINT (NAKA HIJI FUSHI)
F. OUTSIDE ELBOW JOINT (HOKA HIJI FUSHI)
G. VORTEX OF JAW (UDZU AGO)
H. TWO LOWER RIBS (NI SHITA ABARA-BONE)
I. GROIN (MOMONE)

9. SWORD HAND (SHUTO)

A. WRIST (TEKUBI)
B. INSIDE ELBOW JOINT (NAKA HIJI FUSHI)
C. OUTSIDE ELBOW JOINT (HOKA HIJI FUSHI)
D. COLLARBONES (SAKOTSU)
E. SIDE OF NECK (YOKO NODO)
F. ESOPHAGUS (MAE NODO)
G. BRIDGE OF NOSE (HANA)
H. VORTEX OF JAW (UDZU AGO)
I. BASE OF SKULL (ATAMA)
J. TWO LOWER RIBS (NI SHITA ABARA-BONE)
K. HIP JOINT (KOSHI FUSHI)
L. GROIN (MOMONE)
M. INSIDE KNEE (NAKA HIZA)
N. OUTSIDE KNEE (HOKA HIZA)

10. <u>CLUTCH PALM (NIGIRU-TANAGOKOBORO)</u>

A. NOSE (HANA)
B. CHIN (AGO)
C. STERNUM (MUNE NO HONE)
D. XIPHOID PROCESS (SHITS MUNE NO HONE)
E. COLLARBONES (SAKOTSU)
F. EARS (MIMI)
G. ELBOWS (HIJI)
H. KNEE CAPS (HIZA)
I. TWO LOWER RIBS (NI SHITA ABARA-BONE)
J. BASE OF SKULL (ATAMA)
K. LOWER BACK (SHITA SE-BONE)
L. KIDNEYS (MURADO)

YOSU KU: ELBOW STRIKES (HIJI UTSU)

1. <u>FORWARD HORIZONTAL (MAE TAIRAKA NA)</u>

A. JAW (AGO)
B. NECK (NODO)
C. TWO LOWER RIBS (NI SHITA ABARA-BONE)
D. ARM PIT (WAKI NO SHITA)
E. LOWER BACK (SHITA SE-BONE)
F. XIPHOID PROCESS (SHITO MUNE NO HONE)

2. <u>REVERSE HORIZONTAL (URA TAIRAKA NA)</u>

A. JAW (AGO)
B. NECK (NODO)
C. TWO LOWER RIBS (NI SHITA ABARA-BONE)
D. ARM PIT (WAKI NO SHITA)
E. LOWER BACK (SHITA SE-BONE)
F. XIPHOID PROCESS (SHITA MUNE NO HONE)

3. UPWARD THRUST (AGERU SASU)

   A. JAW (AGO)
   B. SHOULDER JOINT (KA'TA FUSHI)
   C. XIPHOID PROCESS (SHITA MUNE NO HONE)
   D. GROIN (MOMONE)
   E. TWO LOWER RIBS (NI SHITA ABARA-BONE)
   F. ELBOW JOINT (HIJI FUSHI)

4. DOWNWARD THRUST (SHIMO SASU)

   A. TOP OF HEAD (KASHIRA ATAMA)
   B. COLLARBONES (SAKOTSU)
   C. KICKING KNEE JOINT (KERU HIZA FUSHI)
   D. ELBOWS (HIJI)
   E. KICKING HIP JOINT (KERU KOSHI FUSHI)

5. REVERSE PENETRATION (URA SATORI)

   A. RIBS (ABARA-BONE)
   B. THROAT (NODO)
   C. FACE (KAO)
   D. GROIN (MOMONE)

YOSU JU: FOREARM STRIKES (KO-UDE UTSU)

1. UPPER THRUST (AGERU SASU)

   A. FRONT THROAT (MAE NODO) {Overhead block}

2. PIVOTS (MAWASU)

   A. STERNUM (MUNE NO HONE) {Face black}
   B. SIDE OF THROAT (YOKO NODO) {Face block}

3. DOWNWARD SLASH (SHIMO KIRU)

   A. TWO LOWER RIBS (NI SHITA ABARA-BONE) {Kidney block}
   B. GROIN (MOMONE) {Kidney Block}

4. UPPER SLASH (AGERU KIRU)

   A. SIDE OF THROAT (YOKO NODO) {Neck and head block}

5. KNEELING PIVOTS (HIZAMADZUKU MAWASU)

   A. INSIDE KNEE JOINT (NAKA HIZA FUSHI)
   B. OUTSIDE KNEE JOINT (HOKA HIZA FUSHI)

YOSU JU-ICHI: STRIKE EVASION (UTSU NAGARERU)

1. BUTTERFLY STRIKE (CHO UTSU)

2. PIVOT STRIKE (MAWASU UTSU)

YOSU JU-NI: CHI KATA (DONE STANDING ON EARTH)

1. ENTRANCE FORM SALUTE
   (IRU KATA JIGI)

2. OUTSIDE FAN HANDS
   (HOKA OGI-TE)

3. DOWN STRIKING MASTER PALM HANDS
   (SHIMO UTSU SHUJIN TANAGOKOBORO -TE)

4. BACK TO CHEST
   (URA NI MUNE)

5. OUT STRIKING MASTER PALM HANDS
   (SOTO UTSU SHUJIN TANAGOKOBORO -TE)

6. BACK TO CHEST
   (URA NI MUNE)

7. SIDE STRIKING MASTER PALM HANDS
   (YOKO UTSU SHUJIN TANAGOKOBORO -TE)

8. LEFT MASTER SPEAR HAND TO FRONT
   (HADARI SHUJIN-YARI-TE NI MAE)

9. RIGHT MASTER SPEAR HAND TO FRONT
   (MIGI SHUJIN-YARI-TE NI MAE)

10. OUTSIDE FAN HANDS
    (HOKA OGI-TE)

11. DOUBLE KIDNEY KNIFE HAND
    (NISOBAI MURADO SHUTO)

12. LEFT DOWN BLOCK WITH RIGHT FRONT SNAP KICK TO LEFT SIDE
    (HADARI SHIMO KIRE NO MIGI MAE ORU KERU NI HADARI YOKO)

13. RIGHT DOWN BLOCK WITH LEFT FRONT SNAP KICK TO RIGHT SIDE
    (MIGI SHIMO KIRE NO HADARI MAE ORU KERU NI MIGI YOKO)

14. LEFT DOWN BLOCK WITH RIGHT FRONT SNAP KICK TO FRONT
    (HADARI SHIMO KIRE NO MGI MAE ORU KERU NI MAE)

15. STAY SALUTE (YAMU JIGI)
    [END BY PLACING KICKING LEG IN BOW POSITION.]

YOSHI

YOSU ICHI: QUEST (NEGAU)

1. NEGAI NI YORI O KUDASAI SENSAI

YOSU NI: GRAPPLING HOOK (KAGINAWA)

1. ENTANGLEMENT (MUTSURE)

   Sweeps, body wrap, wrist grapples (hold handle and grapple wrist with hooks)

2. THROW (NAGE-SUTERU)

   The grappling hook is thrown underhanded.

3. HOW TO TIE A ROPE TO THE GRAPPLING HOOK

   NOTE: In order to tie a rope to a grappling hook you will need to tie a noose in one end of the rope.

   A. Start out 30 inches from the end of the rope.
   B. Make a loop in the rope so that the center of the loop meets where you are holding the rope.
   C. Make another loop opposite the first loop.
   D. The two loops will make a figure eight in one end of the rope.
   E. Using the rest of your slack. Wrap the figure eight knot in a cascading wrap.
   F. Make sure that each wrap sits tightly on top of the previous wrap as you wrap the figure eight pattern.
   G. After you wrap 13 times around the figure eight pattern feed the end of the rope through the bottom loop.
   H. Pull the noose tight. This will tighten the bottom loop and secure the knot so it will not slip.

4. CLIMBING KNOTS

   NOTE: When climbing a rope attached to the grappling hook the rope will need to have figure eight knots tied through out the rope. The rope must be at least one inch thick to allow for uses such as lowering one's self from a tree or swinging from tree to tree while standing in the hook. The steps to tying a figure eight knot are listed below:

   A. Hold the rope in your hand.
   B. Fold the rope over itself so that the rope makes a loop.
   C. Take the lose end of the rope and run it under the rope so that it makes a figure " 8".
   D. Then feed the lose end through the top loop and pull tight.
   E. Once the knot is pulled tight it forms a flat shelf on one side and allows for you to put your foot on the rope and not slide off.

YOSU SAN: THROWING STAR (SHAKEN)

1. Throw vertical. This allows the weapon to cut through the air, and have the least wind resistance.

2. Never throw flat. When thrown flat the wind may cause the weapon to drift up or down.

3. When throwing always position yourself in a good stance.

4. <u>TYPES OF THROWS</u>.

   A. REVERSE ROLL (URA-KOROGARU)

      1. Hold the star point between the thumb and middle finger.
      2. Place the index finger on the edge of the next point.
      3. When thrown the star will roll off the index finger sending the star hurling through the air with a backward spin.

   B. POINT THROW (TEN-NAGURU)

   C. GUIDE THROW (MICHIBIKU NAGERU)

   D. BACK THROW (URA-NAGURU)
      (Thrown by popping the back of the hand.)

   E. THREE WAY THROW (NAGURU SAN-DO)
      (All three thrown at one time by popping the back of the hand.)

YOSU SHI: PRESSURE POINTS (OSU KOTO SAKI)

A. HEAD (KUBI)

1. TEMPLE (MIYA) - Right behind the eye socket.

2. BEHIND THE EAR (URA NI MIMI) - The dimple straight back from the ear lobe on the crest of the skull.

3. UNDER THE EAR (SHITA NI MIMI) - Where the jaw-line rounds directly under the ear.

B. NECK (KUBI)

1. SIDE (YOKO) - Located between the two muscles on either side of the neck.

2. FRONT (MAE /YOKO) - Located on either side of the Adam's apple.

2. UPPER JAW (AGERU AGO) - On the bottom side of the jaw.

3. THROAT DIMPLE (NODO YEKUBO) - Located at the base of the neck.

C. CHEST (MUNE)

1. SHOULDER DIMPLE (KA'TA YEKUBO) - Beside the neck on the backside of the base of the collarbone.

2. CHEST (MUNE) - Where the pecks meet the chest on the front and side of the abdomen.

3. ARM PIT (WAKI NO SHITA) - At the back of the joint between the muscles.

D. ARM (UDE)

1. INSIDE ELBOW (KANA HIJI) - On either side of the tendon.

2. OUTSIDE ELBOW (HOKA HIJI) - The dimple behind the elbow joint.

E. WRIST (TE KUBI)

1. TOP (ZETCHO) - Center of joint, roll wrist back over thumb or finger.

2. BOTTOM (SOKO) - Center of joint, roll wrist back over thumb or finger.

3. INSIDE (KANA) - Center of joint, roll wrist horizontally toward little finger to open joint then place thumb/fingers in joint and roll horizontally toward thumb. Hook thumb/finger on bottom of joint knuckle.

4. OUTSIDE (HOKA) - Center of joint, roll wrist horizontally toward thumb to open joint then place thumb/fingers in joint and roll horizontally toward little finger. Hook thumb/finger on top of joint knuckle

F. HAND (TE)

1. TOP - Center of the hand between the index and middle finger muscles. (ZETCHO)

2. BETWEEN KNUCKLE [At the base of the finger.] (AIDA NI GENKO)

3. FINGER NAIL (YUBI NO TSUME)

4. THUMB NAIL (OYAYUBI) - At the quick of the nail.

G. FOOT/LEG (ASHI)

1. BACK KNEE (URA HIZA) - On the inside between the tendon and ligament.

2. SIDE ANGLE (YOKO KADO) - On the underside of the ankle joint.

YOSU GO: SHINBO / SHABO
(A SMALL STAFF ABOUT TEN INCHES ATTACHED TO A RING)

A. SALUTES (JIGI): Held in closed grip and tips cross at waist level with the tips angled downward.

1. ENTRANCE SALUTE (IRU JIGI)
2. EXIT SALUTE (DE-GUCHI JIGI)
3. STAY SALUTE (YAMU JIGI)

B. STANCES (KAMAE)

** Note: Basic stances are made with closed hands and element stances are made with open hands.

1. ATTENTION STANCE (JUSHA KAMAE)
2. PRESENT STANCE (OKURU KAMAE)
3. ON GUARD STANCE (TO-BAN KAMAE
4. BASIC STANCE (BUDO KAMAE)
5. ADVANCE STANCE (AGERU KAMAE)
6. SADDLE STANCE (KURA KAMAE)
7. SHADOW STANCE (MIGI KAGE KAMAE)
8. MASTER STANCE (SHUJIN KAMAE)
9. DRAW STANCE (KAKU KAMAE)
10. EARTH STANCE (CHI KAMAE)
11. WIND STANCE (FU KAMAE)
12. FIRE STANCE (KA KAMAE)
13. WATER STANCE (SUI KAMAE)
14. VOID STANCE (KU KAMAE)

C. BLOCKS (KIRE)

1. DOUBLE PALM BLOCK (NISOBAI NIGIRU KIRE)
2. ADVANCE BLOCK (AGERU KIRE)
3. SIDE BLOCK (YOKO KIRE)
4. SUPPORT BLOCK (MIGI SHIMO MOTSU KIRE
   [Same as in Senpai Kata.]

D. COUNTERS (SOMUKU)

1. UPPER DOUBLE HAND ON ELBOW
   (AGERU NISOBAI TE NI HIJI)
2. ARM BREAK COMBINATION (UDE KOWASU CHOGO)
3. LOWER DOUBLE HAND ON ELBOW
   (SHITA NISOBAI TE NI HIJI)
4. BASIC GI GRAB (BUDO GI HITTAKURU)
5. THROAT PUNCH TAKE DOWN (NODO UTSU UKERA)
6. ELBOW TO CHEST COUNTER (HIJI NI MUNE HAPPO)
7. SHOULDER LOCK (KA'TA TOJIRU)

E. STRIKE (UTSU)

1. SLAP STRIKE (TATAKU)
2. BOTTOM HAND PENETRATION (SHIMO TE SATARI)
3. TOP HAND PENETRATION (KAMI TE SATORI)
4. BACK SLAP STRIKE (URA TATAKU)
5. SPLIT FINGER PENETRATION (WARU YUBI SATORI)

F. SPINS (MAWASU)

1. PALM SPIN (TANAGOKORU MAWASU)

YOSU ROKU: KNEE STRIKES (HIZA UTSU)

1. INSIDE KNEE STRIKE (NAKA HIZA UTSU) - No hand grab necessary, vertical or a 45-degree angle upward strike to target.

2. OUTSIDE KNEE STRIKE (HOKA HIZA UTSU) - Double hand grab, 90-degree/horizontal strike to target.

Primary Knee Targets

All knee strikes follow either the inside or outside strike patterns.

A. GROIN (MOMONE) - Vertical thrust strike.

B. UNDER ELBOW JOINT (SHITA HIJI FUSHI) - Vertical thrust strike.

C. STERNUM (MUNE NO HONE) - Vertical thrust strike.

D. DOUBLE GRAB LEAP INTO STERNUM - Vertical thrust strike. (NISOBAI HITTAKURU TOBU MUNE NO HONE)

E. STOMACH (ONAKA) - Vertical thrust strike.

F. UNDER CHIN (SHITA AGO) - Grab behind the head. Vertical thrust strike.

G. SHOULDER JOINT (KA'TA FUSHI) - Vertical thrust strike.

H. LOWER BACK (SHITA SE-BONE) - Vertical thrust or a 90-degree strike.

YOSU SHICHI: FOOT GRAPPLING (ASHI TSUKAMU)

1. INSIDE SINGLE FOOT ANKLE WRAP (NAKA ICHI ASHI TSUTSUMU)
2. OUTSIDE SINGLE FOOT ANGLE WRAP

   (HOKA ICHI ASHI TSUTSUMU)
3. SNAKE (HEBI) - Do not carry to the side. Carry the leg straight back on a 45-degree angle then set down on the leg joint. Used when a hip toss fails.

YOSU HACHI: SAI (THREE PRONG SWORD)

A. SALUTES (JIGI)

1. ENTRANCE SALUTE (IRU JIGI)

2. EXIT SALUTE (DE-GUCHI JIGI)

3. STAY SALUTE (YAMU JIGI)

B. STANCES (KAMAE)

1. ATTENTION STANCE (JUSHA KAMAE)
   [Both sai held in reverse inner section hold.]

2. PRESENT STANCE (OKURU KAMAE)
   [Both sai held in reverse inner section hold with sai in kidney block position.]

3. ON GUARD STANCE (TO-BAN KAMAE)
   [Both sai held in full handle hold with sai crossed in center of chest.]

4. BASIC STANCE (BUDO KAMAE)
   [Front sai held in inner section hold with back sai held in reverse inner section hold.]

5. ADVANCED STANCE (AGERU KAMAE)
   [Both sai held in full handle hold or inner section hold.]

6. SADDLE STANCE (KURA KAMAE)
   [Both sai held in reverse inner section hold.]

7. SHADOW STANCE (KAGE KAMAE)
   [Front sai held in reverse handle hold and back sai held in reverse inner section hold.]

8. MASTER STANCE (SHUJIN KAMAE)
   [Both sai can be held in inner section hold or full handle hold.]

9. DRAW STANCE (KAKU KAMAE)
   [Both sai held in reverse inner section hold.]

10. EARTH STANCE (CHI KAMAE)
    [Both sai held in reverse inner section hold.]

11. WIND STANCE (FU KAMAE)
    [Both sai held in reverse inner section old.]

12. FIRE STANCE (KA KAMAE)
[Both sai held in inner section hold.}

13. WATER STANCE (SUI KAMAE)
[Both sai held in inner section hold. Make sure the sai are held on 45-degree to body and the feet are in a saddle stance.]

14. VOID STANCE (KU KAMAE)
[Both sai held in reverse inner section hold with the feet in a basic stance.]

C. <u>SPINS, ROLLS, AND THROWS (MAWASU, KOROGARU, NO NAGERU)</u>

1. BOTTOM PRONG DOWN SPIN (SOKO MATA SHIMO MAWASU)
[Middle and ring finger spin.]

2. TOP PRONG DOWN SPIN (ZETCHO MATA SHIMO MAWASU)
[Middle and ring finger spin.]

3. BEHIND PRONG SPIN (URA MATA MAWASU)
[One finger spin.]

4. FLIP IN (MAWASU UCHI)

5. FLIP OUT (MAWASU SOTO)

6. IN BACK HAND ROLL (UCHI URA TE KOROGARU)
[Roll little finger to thumb.]

7. OUT BACK HAND ROLL (SOTO URA TE KOROGARU)
[Roll thumb to little finger.]

8. FORWARD ROTATION (MAE MAWASU)
[Rolls away from the body.]

9. BACK ROTATION (URA MAWASU)
[Rolls toward the body.]

10. SHOULDER DROP (KA'TA SHITATARU)

11. BARREL THROW (TARU NAGERU)

12. HANDLE THROW (T'SUKA NAGERU)

13. COMBINATION ROLL (CHOGO KOROGARU)
    A. Full handle hold
    B. Forward strike
    C. Forward rotation
    D. Split finger hold
    E. Counter clockwise rotation over back of hand
    F. Barrel hold
    G. One finger drop roll
    H. Forward inner section hold
    I. Flip back
    J. Reverse inner section hold
    K. Bottom palm roll out to inner section hold

14. "Z" SPIN (TSUMUGU)

15. OVERHEAD OPEN-HAND SPIN (SUGIRU KUBI TE TSUMUGU)

16. OVERHEAD FINGER SPIN (NOKORU YUBI TSUMUGU)

17. OVERHEAD HAND ROTATION (NOKORU TE MAWARU)
[Full section hold to a barrel hold.]

18. REVERSE OVERHEAD HAND ROTATION
(URA NOKORU TE MAWASU) [Barrel hold to a full section hold.]

19. SAI SPINS (SAI TSUMUGU)
[Spin the around each other by hooking the prongs.]

D. <u>GRAPPLES (TSUKAMU)</u>

1. BARREL HOLD (TARU MOTSU)

    A. TOP PRONG INWARD ROLL
    (ZETCHO MATA UCHI KOROGARU)

    B. BOTTOM PRONG INWARD ROLL
    (SOKO MATA UCHI KOROGARU)

    C. TOP PRONG OUTSIDE ROLL
    (ZETCHO MATA UWA KOROGARU)

    D. BOTTOM PRONG OUTSIDE ROLL
    (SOKO MATA UWA KOROGARU)

E. DOUBLE WRIST LOCK (NISOBAI TEKUBI YEYA)
[Side by side lock.]

F. DOUBLE WRIST PIN (NISOBAI TEKUBI TOMERU)
[Pins hand together in sai prongs with sai barrel pointing into chest.]

2. REVERSE INNER SECTION HOLD (URA NAKA SETSU MOTSU)
** Note: Shallow grapples are for pulling and deep grapples are for locks.

A. OUTSIDE BARREL GRAPPLE (UWA TARU TSUKAMU)
[Used on cross body punches.]

B. INSIDE BARREL GRAPPLE (NAKA TARU TSUKAMU)
[Used on same side body punches.]

E. <u>HAND HOLDS (TE MOTSU)</u>

1. FULL HANDLE HOLD (AKU T'SUKA MOTSU)
[Used against swords.]

2. REVERSE FULL HANDLE HOLD (URA AKU T'SUKA MOTSU)
[Used for ground fighting.]

3. INNER SECTION HOLD (NAKA SETSU MOTSU)
[Used for close quarters combat. Hold sai by placing middle and ring finger in bottom prong.]

4. REVERSE INNER SECTION HOLD (URA NAKA SETSU MOTSU)
[Used for hand to hand combat or grappling. Hold sai by placing thumb in top prong and fingers looped around bottom prong.]

5. BARREL HOLD (TARU MOTSU)
[Used for throwing and grappling. Hold sai by the barrel or long point.]

F. <u>STRIKE POINTS (UTSU SAKI)</u>

1. HANDLE (T'SUKA)

2. PRONG (MATA)

3. BARREL POINT (TARU SAKI)

4. BARREL SIDE (TARU YOKO)

5. PRONG CURVATURE (MATA KAGAMERU)

G. BLOCKS (KIRE)

** Note: When blocking with the sai always have the barrel extended out. Do not lay the barrel down the arm when blocking. Use that type of block, back-arm block, as a last resort because the sai can pinch the skin. The sai is only laid down the back of the arm when striking to the body or performing a penetration strike.

1. SLAP BLOCK (With Barrel)
2. KIDNEY BLOCK
3. NECK & HEAD BLOCK
4. FACE BLOCK
5. SIDE BLOCK
6. OVERHEAD BLOCK
7. UPPER CROSS BLOCK
8. MIDDLE CROSS BLOCK
9. LOWER CROSS BLOCK
10. PARALLEL BLOCK
11. HORIZONTAL BLOCK

YOSU KU: WIND KATA (KU KATA)

** Note: This kata is practiced while standing on top of a 6 inch diameter, five feet tall stump.

1. ENTRANCE FORM SALUTE
   (IRU KATA JIGI)

2. OUTSIDE FAN HANDS
   (HOKA OGI-TE)

3. DOWN STRIKING MASTER PALM HANDS
   (SHIMO UTSU SHUJIN TANAGOKOBORO -TE)

4. BACK TO CHEST
   (URA NI MUNE)

5. OUT STRIKING MASTER PALM HANDS
   (SOTO UTSU SHUJIN TANAGOKOBORO -TE)

6. BACK TO CHEST
   (URA NI MUNE)

7. SIDE STRIKING MASTER PALM HANDS
   (YOKO UTSU SHUJIN TANAGOKOBORO -TE)

8. LEFT MASTER SPEAR HAND TO FRONT
   (HADARI SHUJIN-YARI-TE NI MAE)

9. RIGHT MASTER SPEAR HAND TO FRONT
   (MIGI SHUJIN-YARI-TE NI MAE)

10. OUTSIDE FAN HANDS
    (HOKA OGI-TE)

11. DOUBLE KIDNEY KNIFE HAND
    (NISOBAI MURADO SHUTO)

12. LEFT DOWN BLOCK WITH RIGHT FRONT SNAP KICK TO LEFT SIDE
    (HADARI SHIMO KIRE NO MIGI MAE ORU KERU NI HADARI YOKO)

13. RIGHT DOWN BLOCK WITH LEFT FRONT SNAP KICK TO RIGHT SIDE
    (MIGI SHIMO KIRE NO HADARI MAE ORU KERU NI MIGI YOKO)

14. LEFT DOWN BLOCK WITH RIGHT FRONT SNAP KICK TO FRONT
    (HADARI SHIMO KIRE NO MGI MAE ORU KERU NI MAE)

15. STAY SALUTE (YAMU JIGI)
    [END BY PLACING KICKING LEG IN BOW POSITION.]

TAIBUSHI

YOSU ICHI: QUEST (NEGAU)

1. NEGAI NI YORI O KUDASAI SENSAI

YOSU NI: PROJECTILES (SHURIKENS)

A. SHARP METAL DISK OR FLAT STONE (TSUBUTE)

1. Throw vertical. This allows the weapon to cut through the air, and have the least wind resistance.

2. Never throw flat. When thrown flat the wind may cause the weapon to drift up or down.

3. When throwing always position yourself in a good stance.

4. TYPES OF THROWS:

    A. TOP HAND THROW (ZETCHO TE NAGERU)

    B. DISTANCE TOP HAND THROW (AIDA ZETCHO TE NAGERU)

    C. REVERSE SPIN THROW (URA MAWASU NAGERU)

    D. THREE POINT THROW (SAN TEN NAGERU)

    E. FOUR POINT THROW (SHI TEN NAGERU)

B. SPIKES (KUGI) AND DIRK (KUWAI-KEN)

1. Can be thrown vertically or horizontally.

2. Vertical throws are best for long distance and horizontal throws are best for short distance.

3. TYPES OF THROWS:

    A. ONE FINGER GLIDE (ICH YUBI NAGERU)

    B. RIDGE GLIDE (MINE NAGERU)

    C. FLIPPING POINT (MAWASU TEN)

C. THROWING KNIFE (MAMBA/ KOZUKA)

1. Can be thrown vertically or horizontally.

2. Vertical throws are best for long distance and horizontal throws are best for short distance.

3. Balancing the knife is important when judging distances and rotations. No one can teach you how to balance the knife. It is something that the thrower must learn on his own. A tool in helping to learn is flipping the knife through the fingers. This help in judging the weight of the blade and in calculating the number of rotations between the defender and the attacker.

4. TYPES OF THROWS:

   A. ONE FINGER GLIDE (ICHI YUBI NAGERU)

   B. RIDGE GLIDE (MINE NAGERU)

   C. FLIPPING POINT (MAWASU TEN)

D. BLADED DIRKS (AIKUCHI)

1. Can be thrown vertically or horizontally.

2. Vertical throws are best for long distance and horizontal throws are best for short distance

3. TYPES OF THROWS:

   A. ONE FINGER GLIDE (ICHI YUBI NAGERU)

   B. RIDGE GLIDE (MINE NAGERU)

   C. FLIPPING POINT (MAWASU TEN)

E. THROWING STANCES (NAGERU KAMAE)

1. RIGHT AND LEFT SIDE STANCE
   (MIGI NI HADARI YOKO KAMAE)

2. KNEELING CROSS BODY THROW (LEFT & RIGHT)
   (TAI NO NAGE-KOSU TO HIZAMADZUKU)

3. KNEELING SAME SIDE THROW (LEFT & RIGHT)
   (HIZAMADZUKU NAGE-YARU)

4. ALL ROLLS (KOROGARU)

5. TOP HAND (ZETCHO TE)

6. UNDER HAND (SHITA TE)

** HINTS AND TIPS:

1. If throwing from a kneeling position make sure to keep posture straight. If you have to slump over be sure to stabilize yourself before throwing.

2. Every weapon is to be thrown from four and nine paces, and must hit four out of four.

YOSU SAN: CALTROPS (METSUBUSHI)

1. UNDERSTANDING HOW TO THROW:

A. For hard surfaces caltrops should be thrown half the distance of the space that needs to be covered up into the air. Example: If a four-foot area needs to be covered with caltrops then throw the caltrops two feet high in the air. The height measurement is taken from the ground to assure that all the caltrops do not hit the ground and bounce into positions where they are useless.
B. For soft surfaces caltrops should be thrown the distance of the space that needs to be covered plus half that distances up into the air. Example: If a four-foot area needs to be covered with caltrops then throw the caltrops six feet into the air. (In steps A & B be sure to stand in the center of the area to be covered when throwing the caltrops.)
C. If a four-foot area needs to be covered and you are to the side of that position then the caltrops will need to be thrown double the distance of the area needed to be covered into the air. Example: If a four-foot area needs to be covered then throw the caltrops eight feet into the air.
D. If the distance that needs to be covered is larger than four or five feet the caltrops will have to be thrown using a horizontal fan motion.
E. Caltrops can be thrown into the face of an attacker with the same fan motion or with any other throwing movement. Caltrops can also be strung together with fishing line and dragged across roads to slow down attackers or assailant's vehicles.

2. UNDERSTANDING HOW TO DISPENSE:

When deciding how and where to dispense caltrops use common sense. Example: If your attackers are wearing thick soiled shoes and there is lose ground all around the caltrops then they will not do well as a good weapon. Other common tips in dispensing are to make sure that the caltrops blend in with where they have been thrown. If they can be seen then they are useless.

YOSU SHI: BLOW GUN (FUKIDíZUTSU)

1. No particular stance required when using the blowgun.
2. Load dart.
3. Place the mouthpiece in the curved portion of the hand between the thumb and index finger.
4. Close the hand around the blowgun. This helps to muffle the sound.
5. Before placing the blowgun to the mouth inhale deeply through the nose.
6. Place blowgun to mouth.
7. Sight in target.
8. Exhale and shoot. When exhaling be sure to exhale all at once. Do not drag the breath out because this makes unnecessary noise and reveal your location.

YOSU GO: MANRIKI-GUSARI JUTSU (WEIGHTED CHAIN WITH HANDLE TECHNIQUES)

1. <u>ARM WRAP (UDE TSUTSUMU)</u>

   A. Attacker throws right punch.
   B. Wrap punch with manriki-gusari. Make sure the manriki-gusari is on the outside of the elbow and the inside of the wrist.
   C. Push the wrist up and pull the elbow down while stepping through with the right leg. This will spin the attacker around and expose the back.
   ** Alternate ending- Pull the wrist out and push the elbow in while stepping directly to the side. This will dislocate the shoulder.

2. <u>ELBOW BREAK (HIJI KOWASU)</u>

   A. Attacker throws a right punch.
   B. Wrap punch with the manriki-gusari. Make sure the manriki-gusari is on the outside of the elbow and the inside of the wrist.
   C. Glide step on a 45-degree angle with the arm wrapping. This will lock the attacker's arm out and break it. The arm lock can be done by pushing it out or up with the manriki-gusari.

3. <u>INSIDE DOUBLE HAND TIE (NAKA NISOBAI TE MUSUBU)</u>

A. Attacker throws right punch.
B. Block the punch by sweeping the manriki-gusari outward. When the manriki-gusari makes contact with the punch bring the bottom (left) hand up in a circular motion.
C. Attacker throws left punch.
D. Wrap the punch by making a circle motion with the right hand.
E. This ties both hands together.
F. Glide step to the left on a 45-degree with the wrapping of the left arm.
G. Perform a right heel sweep and slam a left elbow into the opponent's right elbow.
H. Simultaneous with the slamming of the elbow squat to one knee. This will throw our opponent to the ground.

4. <u>BLOCK SWEEP (KIRE HAKU)</u>

A. Attacker throws punch.
B. Hold the manriki-gusari loosely in the hands.
C. When punch draws near strike up, down, left, or right in a sweeping motion with the belt.
D. When the manriki-gusari comes into contact with the arm pull the hands outward. This will pop the arm and send it out away from the body.

5. <u>SIDE TO SIDE ROLL (YOKO NO YOKO KOROGARU)</u>
** If you roll to early then you will miss the grapple.

A. Attacker throws left punch.
B. Hold the manriki-gusari loosely between the hands in a bo draw stance.
C. When punch draws near strike left in a sweeping motion with the manriki-qusari.
D. When the manriki-gusari comes into contact with the arm pull the left hand up and the right down in a returning motion to the bo draw stance. This will grapple the arm.
E. Slam your right elbow into your opponent's left elbow.
F. Break the attacker's left elbow with a right knee strike and right stomp the attacker's closest knee.

** Alternate- If attacker throws right punch and you are in a right bo draw stance with the rope then you will strike left in a sweeping motion the same way as step C and grapple the punch. Drop your left elbow into the back of the opponent's right elbow. Right reverse heel sweep and throw your opponent away from you.

6. LEG WRAP (ASHI TSUTSUMU)

A. Attacker throws a right kick
B. Make a sweeping block (left hand on bottom of block) to the outside.
C. Once the Manriki-gusari makes contact with the leg bring the bottom hand up in a circular motion. This will wrap the leg.
D. Pick up on the leg as fast as you can. This will force the attacker back ward.

7. ARM TO KNEE WRAP (UDI NI HIZA TSUTSUMU)

A. Attacker throws a right punch.
B. Make a sweeping block (left hand on bottom of block) to the outside of the body
C. When the Manriki-gusari strikes the arm make a circular motion with the bottom hand. This will wrap the arm.
D. Pull the Manriki-gusari down so that the attacker's arm twists and locks the elbow.
E. Strike the elbow with the outside knee.

8. ARM THROW (UDE NAGERU)

A. Attacker throws a right punch.
B. Perform a basic inside hand tie.
C. Step away from the attacker with the back leg while pulling the attacker off balance.
D. Jerk the attacker's arm toward the ground.
E. When the arm is 8 to10 inches from the ground jerk it straight up. This will cause the attacker to flip.

9. DOUBLE ARM WRAP AND BREAK (NISOBAI UDE TSUTSUMU NI KOWASU)

A. Perform a double hand tie.
B. Once the hands are tied them up over your shoulder while simultaneously twisting your back toward your attacker.
C. Pull the arms down onto your shoulders. This will break the elbows.

10. <u>OUTSIDE DOUBLE HAND TIE (URA NISOBAI TE MUSUBU)</u>

A. Attacker throws a right punch.
B. Block punch by sweeping the Manriki-gusari inward (right hand on top), across the body.
C. Wrap punch by bringing the top hand down.
D. The attacker throws a left punch.
E. Wrap the left punch by continuing the right hand on around.
F. This ties both hands together.
G. Glide step to the left on a 45-degree with the wrapping of the left arm.
H. Perform a right heel sweep and slam a left elbow into the opponent's right elbow.
I. Simultaneous with the slamming of the elbow squat to one knee. This will throw our opponent to the ground

YOSU ROKU: SHOGE (HOOK KNIFE WITH CHAIN AND RING)

Remember to hold low on the shoge handle when grappling so that the hand does not become entangled in the grapples. The shoge can also be thrown using either the cross-chest or " X " throw and the overhead throw.

1. CHAIN JUMP (KUSARI HANERU)
2. SOMMERSAULT SPIN (HIKKURI-KAQYERU TSUMUGU)
3. KNIFE WHIP (MAMBA MUSHI)
4. RING WHIP (NARASU MUCHI)
5. CENTER CHAIN WHIP (NAKABA KUSARI MUCHI)
6. NECK CHAIN LOOP (KUBI KUSARI WASA)
7. RING WRAP (NARASU TSUTSUMU)
8. RING HELD STRIKE (KORAYERU NARASU UTSU)
9. RING SWEEP (NARASU HAKU)
10. KNIFE SWEEP (MAMBA HAKU)
11. OVER HEAD CHAIN STRIKE (NOKORU KUSARI UTSU)
12. RINGED FIGURE EIGHT (NARASU KAKU HACHI)

13. KNIFE FIGURE EIGHT (MAMBA KAKU HACHI)

14. DOUBLE FIGURE EIGHT (NESOBAI KAKU HACHI)

15. CHAIN FIGURE EIGHT (KUSARI KAKU HACHI)

16. CHAIN BLOCK (KUSARI KIRE)

17. DOUBLE CHAIN BLOCK (NESOBAI KUSARI KIRE)

18. BASIC KI GRAB (BUDO KI HITTAKURU)

19. OVER THROW SWEEP (NOKORU NAGETSUKERU HAKU)

NOTE: The shoge maybe used to make many traps. Some of these traps are:

1. SNARE
   A. Tie the ring end around a tree and hook the shoge to another tree. When a person walks through the shoge will flip around and cut.
   B. Stick the point into a tree so that the sickle can cut passer buyers.

2. DRAG
3. PIT
4. SPRING
5. FREEFALL

YOSU SHICHI: SHOGE STANCES (SHOGE KAMAES)

1. BASIC STANCE (BUDO KAMAE)
   - Ring held in back hand & shoge held pointing up in front hand.

2. ADVANCED STANCE (AGERU KAMAE)
   - Ring held in front hand & shoge held pointing up in back hand.

3. MASTER STANCE (SHUJIN KAMAE)
   - Ring held in hand by knee & shoge held pointing up by hand at head.

4. SHADOW STANCE (KAGE KAMAE)
   - Ring held in hand by knee & shoge held horizontal, sickle pointing down, by hand at chest.

5. DRAW STANCE (KAKU KAMAE)
   - Ring held by bottom hand & shogee held horizontal, sickle pointing out, by top hand.

6. SADDLE STANCE (KURA KAMAE)

YOSU HACHI: GROUND FIGHTING (MOTODZUKU KUMITE)

1. STICKY CLUTCH HANDS (NEBARI NIGIRU-TE)

2. STICKY BACK HANDS (NEBARI URA-TE)

3. STICKY ARMS (NEBARI-UDE)

YOSU KU: NINJA- TO STANCE (NINJA-TO KAMAES)

1. <u>EARTH STANCE (JIMEN KAMAE)</u>

   A. Get into a right basic stance.
   B. Hold the blade in a reverse grip with the right hand.
   C. Hold the right hand at shoulder height.
   D. Angle the blade across the front of the body.
   E. The left hand is in a kidney block position with hand kept open.
   F. The back of the sword blade will rest on the back of the left hand.

2. <u>WIND STANCE (FU KAMAE)</u>

   A. Get into a right basic stance.
   B. The right hand will hold the sword.
   C. Place the right hand above the head so that the blade runs down the side of the face.
   D. The left hand is in a basic stance position with the tip of the blade running down the back of the hand. The blade will be held one to two inches away from the back or the hand.

3. <u>FIRE STANCE (KA KAMAE)</u>

   A. Get into a right fire stance.
   B. Hold the sword in your right hand in a reverse grip.
   C. The blade goes from the center of the chest to the top of the shoulder.

4. <u>WATER STANCE (SUI KAMAE)</u>

   A. Get in to a saddle stance.
   B. Hold the sword point down in your left hand. Make sure that the blade is facing outward.
   C. Place the right hand on the hilt of the sword palm out and upside down.

5. MIND STANCE (SHIN KAMAE)

A. Get in to a right basic stance.
B. Hold the sword in the right hand and point is at the ground behind you. The sword and arm will be at a 45-degree angle to the body.

6. BODY STANCE (TAI KAMAE)

A. Get in to a right basic stance.
B. The right hand will hold the blade in a reverse grip.
C. Hold the right hand at shoulder height and keep the left in a kidney block.

7. SOUL STANCE (KI KAMAE)

A. Place feet in to a bow-in-position.
B. Hold hands out in front of the body shoulder width apart.
C. The handle of the sword will be in the left hand while the blade rests in the right. The sword can be sheathed or unsheathed. This is traditionally only practiced inside Konigun because it could be viewed as an insult by others.

8. ENERGY (POWER) STANCE (CHI KAMAE)

A. Get into a right basic stance.
B. Hold the sword in the left hand and point it at the ground in front of you.
C. The arm and blade will be at a 45-degree angle to the ground.

9. VOID STANCE (KU KAMAE)

A. Get into a right basic stance.
B. Hold the sword in the right hand in a reverse grip. Make sure that the blade runs up the arm.
C. Hold the right hand behind you so that your body shadows the weapon.

YOSU JU: FAN BLOCK AND STRIKE (OGI KIRE NI UTSU)

1. DOUBLE PALM STRIKE (NISOBAI TENOHIRA UTSU)

   A. Opponent throws a right punch.
   B. Block the opponent's punch to the outside of the body with a left outside fan and a right inside fan block.
   C. Strike the opponent in the left peck with a left palm hand while striking the opponent in the right lower ribs with a right palm hand strike.

YOSU JU-ICHI: BOUND HAND FIGHTING (MUSUBU TE NO JUTSU)

* Note: The counters are preformed with the hands tied in front of the body.

1. <u>ELBOW STRIKE COMBINATION (HIJI UTSU CHOGO)</u>

   * Note: There is no set pattern to the elbow combinations.

   A. Opponent throws a right punch.
   B. Block the punch with an outward left elbow strike.
   C. Opponent throws a left punch.
   D. Block the punch with an outward right elbow strike.
   E. Grapple the opponent's left arm then left elbow strike the face.
   F. Spin under the opponent's left arm and right elbow strike the opponent's left kidney.
   G. Right knee strike the opponent's knee.
   H. Right elbow strike the back of the opponent's head.

2. <u>SPEAR TO SHOULDER (YARI NO KA'TA)</u>

   A. Opponent throws a right punch.
   B. Block the punch to the left with the side of the bound hands. If you block to the left be sure to step with the left leg and if you block to the right be sure to step to the right.
   C. Double spear hand strike the side of the opponent's neck. Keep the thumbs turned in toward the opponent so that if the double spear misses then the thumbs can follow up as a strike.
   D. Double knife hand strike the floater ribs.

3. <u>LEFT ELBOW BLOCK (HADARI HIJI KIRE)</u>

A. Opponent throws a left punch.
B. Block the left punch to the left side with the side of the bound hands.
C. Right elbow strike the opponent's left jaw. While performing the strike make sure that you place your right foot behind the opponent's left foot.
D. Left elbow strike the back of the opponent's neck as you spin around.
E. Double knife hand strike the side of the opponent's throat.

4. <u>CENTER GRAPPLE (NAKABA HASUKAAMU)</u>

A. Holds your hands above your head.
B. Opponent throws a right punch to the chest.
C. Capture the punch between the tied hands.
D. Twist your arms as you step to the left. This will lock out the opponent's arm.

5. <u>SIDE ELBOW STRIKE (YOKO HIJI UTSU)</u>

A. Hold hands down at waist level.
B. Opponent throws a right punch.
C. Capture the punch between the left arm and the left rib cage.
D. Bring the bound hands up to lock in the grapple.
E. Right forward elbow strike to the opponent's left jaw.
F. Right reverse elbow strike to the back of the opponent's neck.
G. Spin around and rip shoulder out of joint.

6. <u>SIDE LOCK (YOKO YEYA)</u>

A. Hold hands down at waist level.
B. Opponent throws right punch.
C. Capture the punch between the left arm and the left rib cage.
D. Slide up the arm to the shoulder and lock out with the hands.
E. Right leg sweep the opponent's feet.
F. As the opponent falls to the ground barrel roll off of them.

7. <u>UPPER CROSS BLOCK (AGERU JIRERU KIRE)</u>

A. Hold the tied hands down at waist level.
B. Opponent throws a right punch to the face.
C. Upper cross block the opponent's punch.
D. Double palm strike the opponent's chest.

8. SIDE WRIST LOCK (YOKO TE0KUBI YEYA)

A. Opponent throws a left punch.
B. Catch the punch between the left arm and the left rib cage.
C. Rotate the hands under the captured arm and lock out the opponent's elbow.

9. HEAD STOMP (KUBI TSUKU)

A. The opponent is standing to your right side while you are lying on the ground.
B. The opponent performs a right stomp kick to the head.
C. Block the kick to the left side of the body with a double knife hand strike to the opponent's ankle.
D. Double spear hand the opponent's groins.

10. FRONT SNAP (MAE ORU)

A. The opponent is standing to your right side while you are lying on the ground.
B. The opponent kicks with a left front snap to the head.
C. Roll into the kick in order to block it with the body before it reaches full power.
D. Double knife hand strike the opponent's right ankle.
E. Double ox hand strike the back of the opponent's left knee.
F. Double knife hand strike the opponent's groins.

** Note: The last three techniques bend the opponent over and off balance so that you can perform the next technique.

G. Grab the opponent's left ankle and roll into the opponent.
H. Elbow strike the opponent's ribs once he is on the ground.

11. FAN BLOCK (OGI KIRE)

A. The opponent is standing to your right side while you are lying on the ground.
B. Opponent kicks with a right stomp kick to the stomach.
C. Perform a clockwise fan motion from the stomach toward the left shoulder and collapse the knee while grappling it between the forearms and the chest.
D. As soon as the knee is captured roll into the opponent. This will drive him down to the ground.

YOSU JU-NI: SUI KATA

** Note: This kata is practiced while in the main current of a river or stream.

1. ENTRANCE FORM SALUTE
   (IRU KATA JIGI)

2. OUTSIDE FAN HANDS
   (HOKA OGI-TE)

3. DOWN STRIKING MASTER PALM HANDS
   (SHIMO UTSU SHUJIN TANAGOKOBORO -TE)

4. BACK TO CHEST
   (URA NI MUNE)

5. OUT STRIKING MASTER PALM HANDS
   (SOTO UTSU SHUJIN TANAGOKOBORO -TE)

6. BACK TO CHEST
   (URA NI MUNE)

7. SIDE STRIKING MASTER PALM HANDS
   (YOKO UTSU SHUJIN TANAGOKOBORO -TE)

8. LEFT MASTER SPEAR HAND TO FRONT
   (HADARI SHUJIN-YARI-TE NI MAE)

9. RIGHT MASTER SPEAR HAND TO FRONT
   (MIGI SHUJIN-YARI-TE NI MAE)

10. OUTSIDE FAN HANDS
    (HOKA OGI-TE)

11. DOUBLE KIDNEY KNIFE HAND
    (NISOBAI MURADO SHUTO)

12. LEFT DOWN BLOCK WITH RIGHT FRONT SNAP KICK TO LEFT SIDE
    (HADARI SHIMO KIRE NO MIGI MAE ORU KERU NI HADARI YOKO)

13. RIGHT DOWN BLOCK WITH LEFT FRONT SNAP KICK TO RIGHT SIDE
    (MIGI SHIMO KIRE NO HADARI MAE ORU KERU NI MIGI YOKO)

14. LEFT DOWN BLOCK WITH RIGHT FRONT SNAP KICK TO FRONT
    (HADARI SHIMO KIRE NO MGI MAE ORU KERU NI MAE)

15. STAY SALUTE (YAMU JIGI)
    [END BY PLACING KICKING LEG IN BOW POSITION.]

Types of Class Drills

1. Block Drill
2. Sticky Palm
3. Sticky Backhand
4. Sticky Arm
5. Sticky Wrist
6. Speed Punch
7. Grapple Drills
8. Kick Drills
9. Walking Kick Drills
10. Stance Hops
11. Target Practice Drill
12. Tiger Crawl
13. Crab Walk
14. Bear Crawl
15. Duck Walk
16. Frog Hop
17. Three Step Sparring
18. Balance Drills
    - Look up and grab one ankle
    - Look up and hold hands out to side while standing on one foot
    - Airplane
    - Bend over on one leg and touch floor with fingertips
    - Toad stool- place hands on floor then place your knees on the back of the elbows. Do this while balancing entire weight on the palms.

BUSHIDO CODE
(IN NO PARTICULAR ORDER)

"ACHIEVING AN HONORABLE JUSTICE"

A man's honor is what makes him a man. A man is only worth his honor. The man, who is a true shadow warrior, guards honor and what he views honorable, honor and self-pride should not be confused or mixed. Self-pride is not honorable, to assure justice, is to be humble and understanding, and never taking advantage of others.

A man of honor must judge what is honorable and just, by what is right in the inner self. Therefore an honorable man must seek wisdom through experience and knowledge so to make a better judgment.

After making this judgment, then he/she must seek to achieve an honorable justice.

1. Live each day prepared to face death tomorrow.
2. Honor
3. Humility
4. Loyalty of obligations-all warriors are born to six

Obligations:

A. Obligation to God.
B. Obligation to self.
C. Obligation to family.
D. Obligation to style.
E. Obligation to sensei.
F. Obligation to community.

5. Respect all living things.
6. Maintain the skills of your art to your best ability.
7. Never strike an unjust blow.
8. Never show fear.
9. Never show pain.
10. Never lose composure.
11. Never draw a weapon until the decision has been made to use it.
12. Never accept failure.

MEDALLION RANKING SYSTEM

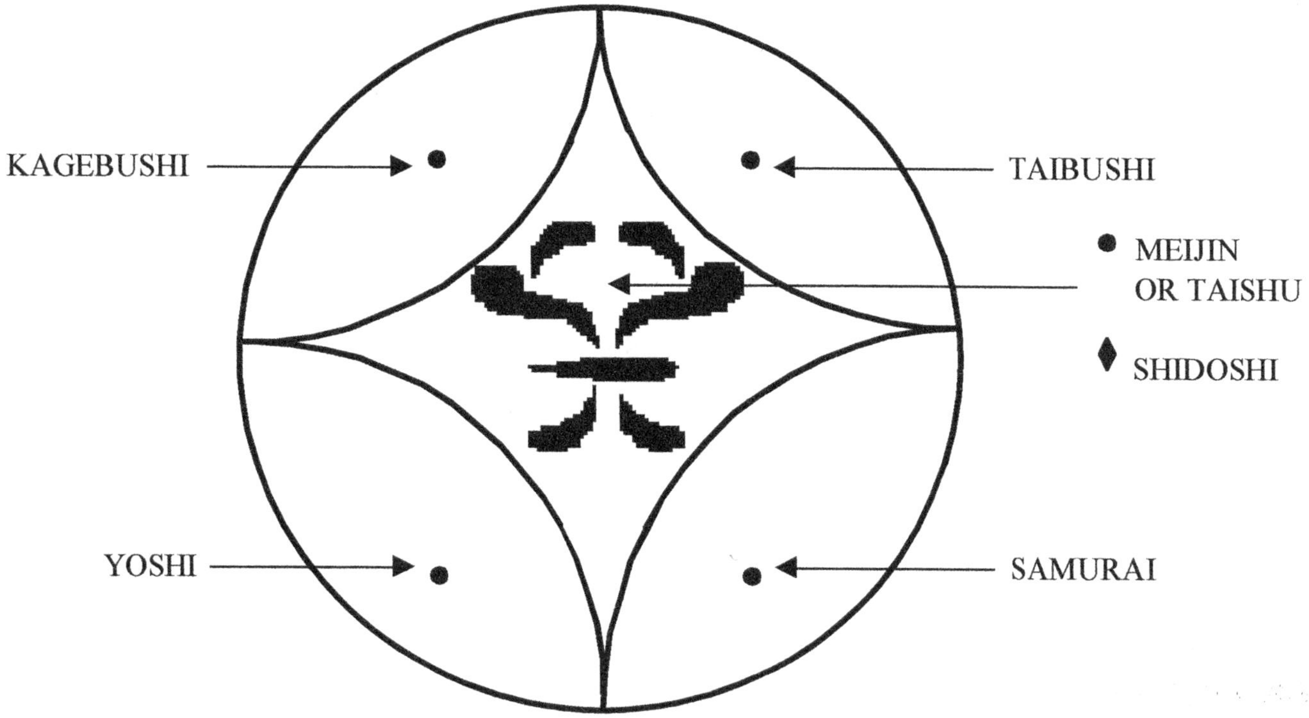

*** BUSHI IS THE MEDALLION WITHOUT ANY POINTS ***

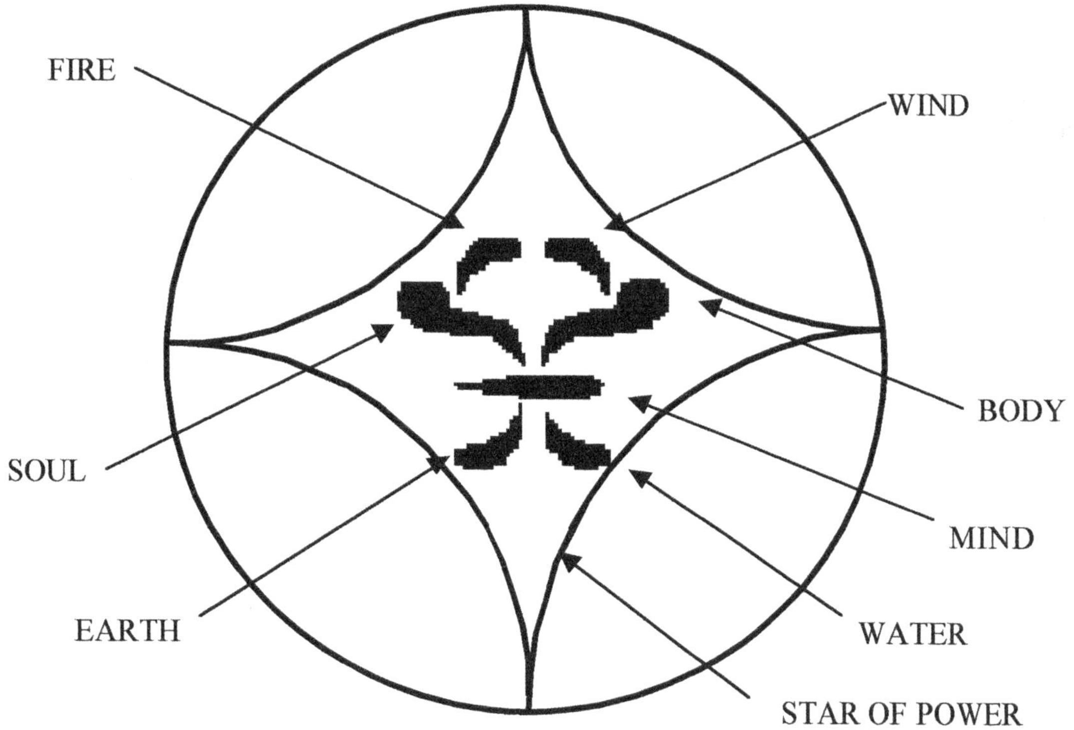

<u>CIRCLE OF LIFE</u>

KAGE-TORA

QUALIFICATION:

To become a kage-tora, one must be a member of the style for a period of three months or be voted into the group by final decision of the acting director of that group. A minimal ranking of gold belt is required.

PHYSICAL TRAINING REQUIREMENTS:

12 BASIC KICKS PERFORMED WITHOUT SETTING FOOT DOWN

50 PUSH-UPS IN 2 AND 1/2 MINUTES/FEMALES IN 3 MINUTES

60 SIT-UPS IN 2 AND 1/2 MINUTES/ FEMALES IN 3 MINUTES

FULFILL A QUEST OF DIRECTOR'S CHOICE

RULES AND HONOR:

A kage-tora is allowed to learn black sash material and hold such privileges while active. He/she must always give as much respect as he/she wishes to receive and must never disgrace their person or style. They must act not only as a black sash, but also as an adult.

PURPOSE:

All kage-tora will perform and promote the dojo through demonstrations and handing out flyers as well as by setting example.

Members of the kage-tora should be aware that on out of class nights or weekends they will be asked to hand out flyers. Or perform demonstrations or promote the style.

BENEFITS:

The Kage-Tora is permitted to learn from the black sash ranks as the director approves it. Further benefits and extra training time is permitted.

OFFICERS:

Each Kage-Tora chapter will have only 5 members per dojo. The Kage-Tora will have one student Jonin (chapter assistant-leader), one student Chunin (chapter leader), and Shunin (director) as head instructor of the dojo.

Each chapter is a part of the Kageshu pledge with exception of the Shunin. The Kage-Tora must obey the Kageshu members when acting in official functions

SPECIAL NOTE:

The Kage-Tora replaces the elite knights and elite guards as well as abolishes the elite chapters.

THE KONIGUN TIGER

THERE IS A SAYING IN KONIGUN:

"WHEN YOU BECOME A MEMBER OF KONIGUN, A TIGER IS BORN."

HININ: *YOUR TIGER HAS LEARNED TO WALK.*

SHIROTO: *YOUR TIGER HAS LEARNED TO LEARN.*

DESHI: *YOUR TIGER HAS OPENED ITS EYES.*

MONJIN: *YOUR TIGER HAS CLAWS.*

SENPAI: *YOUR TIGER HAS TEETH.*

BUSHI: *YOUR TIGER HAS WINGS.*

SAMURAI: *YOUR TIGER HAS GREAT HONOR.*

YOSHI: *YOUR TIGER MOVES WITH THE SHADOWS.*

TAIBUSHI: *YOUR TIGER HAS FOUND ITS COURAGE.*

KAGEBUSHI: *YOUR TIGER HAS MASTERED NATURE AND BECOME AS ONE.*

MEIJIN: *YOUR TIGER HAS THE ABITITY TO KNOW WITHOUT KNOWING.*

POEM

(AUTHOR UNKNOWN)

IRO WA NIEDO CHIRINURR O

WAGA YO TARE ZO TSUNE NARAN

U YO OKUYANA KYO KOETE

ASAKI YUME MIJI EI MO YO

TRANSLATION

COLORS ARE FREQUENT, BUT THEY FADE AWAY.

IN THIS WORLD OF OURS, NONE LAST FOREVER.

TODAY CROSS THE MOUNTAINS OF LIFE'S ILLUSION.

AND THERE WILL BE NO MORE SHALLOW DREAMING……

…..NO MORE DRUNKENESS.

WEAPONS ETIQUETTE

When standing up from a kashia with weapons do not spring up in to a kamae. The right knee will step forward then the left foot will follow suit into the proper stance.

A. PRESENT

1) TWO WEAPONS-

The weapons are placed at a 45-degree angle on the floor and the weapons split your side and front areas. The short sword is the first one in and the last one out.
When going to a ka-shia the right hand will pull the fabric of the hakama on the right leg outward to allow the person to kneel without becoming entangled in the fabric.
Remember as with all ka-shia stances the right leg moves first and last when getting up or sitting down.

2) SINGLE WEAPON-

The weapon is placed on the ground directly in front of you.

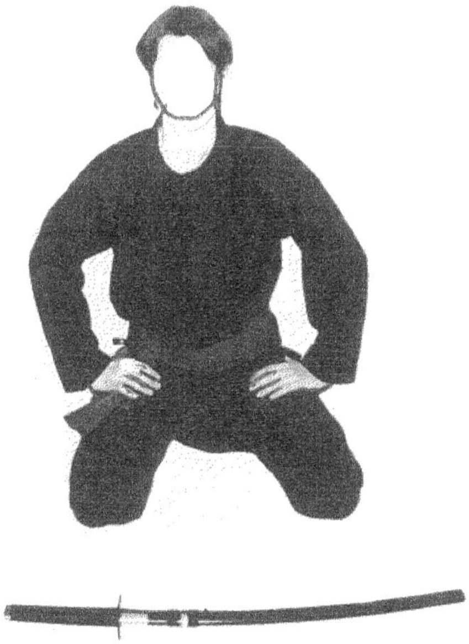

B. CEREMONY

1. TWO WEAPONS-

The weapons are placed directly at your sides.

2. SINGLE WEAPON-

The weapon is placed at your right side because you have to put it in your left hand in order to draw your weapon for combat.

General Weapons Etiquette

When passing a weapon from one to another it is customary to follow these procedures to assure proper respect, control, and safety to both parties.

When passing the staff, sword, three-sectional staff, shinbo, shabo, belt, bow and arrows use the following bow.

- If the weapon has a handle make sure that it is always to the right of the passer's body.
-
- The passer of the weapon will have his palms face up with the hands in one-third two-thirds position on the weapon. If the passer is handling a belt, shinbo or shabo then the passer is to grasp the ends of the weapon to assure safety.
- The receiver will reach between the passer's hands and retrieve the weapon palms up. Only a master may receive a weapon palms down
- The receiver will say "Domo", thanks, to tell the passer that he has hold of the weapon and the passer will say "Yoi", welcome, to tell the receiver that he is letting go of the weapon.

When passing a single han-bo, tonfa, kama, sai, unsheathed knife or sword use the following bow.

- If the weapon has a handle make sure it is passed first. Never pass a weapon point first.
- The feet will be together in the bow-in-position.
- Pass the weapon with the right hand and pass it to the receiver's right hand.
- The blade or barrel of the weapon will be running down the back of the passer's arm and if it has a blade then it will be pointed away from the passer's body.
- The receiver will take the sword in his right hand, in a cross-grab exchange, because it gives the receiver better control if the passer has ill intentions.
- The receiver will say "Domo", thanks, to tell the passer that he has hold of the weapon and the passer will say "Yoi", welcome, to tell the receiver that he is letting go of the weapon.

When passing double han-bo, tonfa, kama, sai, manji-sai or any other double weapon use the following bow.

- The feet will be together in the bow-in-position.
- The weapon will be palms down with the barrel or handle extended forward.
- The receiver will reach and take both weapons simultaneously.
- The receiver will say "Domo", thanks, to tell the passer that he has hold of the weapon and the passer will say "Yoi", welcome, to tell the receiver that he is letting go of the weapon.

When passing the grappling hook:

- The feet will be together in the bow-in-position.
- The rope will be in the left hand.
- Hold the hook by the top two prongs so that the shaft is extending toward the receiver.
- The receiver will reach and take hold of the shaft and rope simultaneously.
- The receiver will say "Domo", thanks, to tell the passer that he has hold of the weapon and the passer will say "Yoi", welcome, to tell the receiver that he is letting go of the weapon.

When passing the shoge:

- The feet will be together in the bow-in-position.
- The ring and chain are held in the left hand.
- The shoge is held in the right hand so that the knife points to the right side and the sickle points toward the passer.
- The receiver will grab between the sickle and the passer's hand with the left hand as he grabs the ring and chain with the right hand.

BASIC TESTING OUTLINE

I. Test begins by the man judge or test narrator calling "Gorupu" or formation.

II. Roll is called for testing candidates.
Judge or narrator will stand in from of the testing candidate and say "O-namae" and the testing candidate will reply "(Rank & Name) To-moshimasu"

III. The judge or narrator will give a brief statement as to what is expected during the test. The length that the test may take and any other pertinent information.

At this point the main judge or testing narrator will take over and dictate the test.

IV. The testing candidates will then bow in by first bowing to the audience, second the panel of judges, and thirdly the testing narrator.

V. The test begins. If at any point in time a testing candidate can not perform a technique due to lack of skill and training he will be asked to sit down and his/ her test stops at that moment. Under no circumstances is a testing candidate failed due to a physical disability.

VI. If the test is going to take several days then the judge or testing narrator will stop the test at the end of that days test by calling "goropu", formation, and bow the testing candidates out and place their test on hold until the following testing time.

VII. At the end of the entire test the judge or narrator will call "goropu", formation. The testing candidates are call to the front of the formation one by one and officially awarded or declined their sash. When called to the front of a formation use the ryu jigi, sect salute, exit bow and turn to the right. Fall out of the line you are in by turning to the right and walking briskfully or jog down the line and lock out in "jusha kamae", attention stance, at the left side of the instructing Black Sash. The Black Sash wil the award or decline the sash. Once the sash has been awarded then the testing candidate will salute the formation and the formation will return salute.

VIII. After all sashes are awarded and declined then formation is recalled and the formation is dismissed.

PROTOCOL CLASSIFICATION AND PUNISHMENTS

THE FOLLOWING PROTOCOLS AND REGULATIONS WILL BE PUT INTO CLASSES.

THESE CLASSES ARE A, B, AND C.

VIOLATION OF CLASS-A MAY RESULT IN ONE OF THE FOLLOWING:

OPTION 1: VERBAL WARNING

OPTION 2: THE PERSON MAY BE DISCIPLINED WITH ONLY CLASSROOM TYPE PHYSICAL EXERCISE. (INSTRUCTOR MAY RECEIVE THE SAME UP TO EXTREME DISCIPLINE IF NEGLIGENT OR ABUSIVE.)

VIOLATION OF CLASS-B MAY RESULT IN ONE OF THE FOLLOWING:

OPTION 1: REDUCTION OF RANK

OPTION 2: MAY USE CLASS-A- RESOLUTION

VIOLATION OF CLASS-C MAY RESULT IN ONE OF THE FOLLOWING:

OPTION 1: EXCOMMUNICATION FROM STYLE.

**ALL PUNISHMENTS MAY BE USED IN CONJUNCTION WITH ANY OTHERS REGARDLESS OF CLASSIFICATION.

**REMEMBER, TEACHING AND RECEIVING KNOWLEDGE FROM KONIGUN NINJUTSU IS A PRIVILEGE, NOT A RIGHT! ALL DISCIPLINE IS A PUNISHMENT OF YOUR PRIVILEGES, NOT AN INFRINGEMENT UPON YOUR RIGHTS.

RATING AND BANNING SYSTEM

BAN
The Shidoshi maintains the right to ban or un-ban anyone. If another black sash wishes to ban someone he/she must submit a signed document stating the reasons behind their request.

ACTIVE
Individual maintains all rights and privileges accustomed to their rank and title.

CLASS A PROTOCOLS:

1. Unsupervised sparing and acrobatics are prohibited due to possible injuries caused by high impact techniques.
2. Return equipment to its place of storage when finished using it.
3. No horseplay (i.e. running play fighting, annoying others, etc.)
4. Leave all equipment in designated areas.
5. When called forward, or to the sparing line jog briskly (quickly) to position. Do not walk.
6. No sparing in dojo unless under direct black sash supervision.
7. Safety is first always.
8. If you dirty it, you clean it.
9. Any damaged or unsafe items are to be reported immediately.
10. No bad attitude.
11. Always use rank title when in class or uniform, outside of class titles can be used or Mr. and Mrs..
12. Always conduct yourself in a professional manner.
13. Always stay centered and in control.
14. No student may touch another student's sash without permission.
15. A member must salute when passing through a martial arts arch.
16. No dishonoring other styles, their sensei, or students.
17. Only a red sash or kageshu may wear red unless otherwise noted.
18. Spar only in control of yourself.
19. No misleading or lying to a black sash.
20. A Kageshu is over his equal regular ranks all ranks below.
21. Only a black sash may award ranks.
22. "Time in grade" does not give seniority all belts are equal in that rank.

CLASS B PROTOCOLS:

1. Do not touch any equipment on walls shelves, floor, or in boxes unless otherwise told to do so (especially weapons).
2. Only an instructor or assistant instructor is allowed to have keys to the dojo.
3. No student is to dishonor another member of konigun.
4. All black sash test are given at the gathering.
5. Only the Shidoshi may give family names.
6. There will be two shidoshi meetings a year in which all black sash must attend.
7. Only Shidoshi can give out medallions.
8. Only a black sash can have a dojo, temple, shrine, or rai after approval from shidoshi.
9. Medallions are for members only.
10. An order must not be defied on an assignment.
11. "Decree" is the same as "order".

CLASS C PROTOCOLS:

1. No one is to be taught past his or her current rank without written authorization by Shidoshi.
2. No black sash may start their own style.
3. All but Kagebushi or above rank must re-certify yearly.
4. No representation of any type of gang or occult in class.

STUDENTS IN CHARGE: (Class-B)

1. Only a black sash can leave a student in charge.
2. Any student in charge may give up to 50 pushups for rule violations.
3. Students under the lead student have the authority to object to the lead students orders, but only to a black sash.
4. The lead student is in charge of the safety and training of the student placed under him/her.
5. The lead student will lead by example.
6. A student has the right to turn down the role of being left in charge.

RIGHTS:

1. For Shidoshi to retire there must be a meeting in which all black belts are present. They must receive a written notice two months in advance stating when and where the meeting will take place.
2. Any black sash may ban a student.
3. Shidoshi may over ride the ban list.
4. Superior ranks may only punish to classification code when the oath is broken.
5. You have a right to ask any question, but not the right to have them all answered.

MARTIAL ARTS GUEST PROTOCOLS: (Class-A)

1. Students from other systems are asked not to demonstrate techniques to other students. This causes difficulty in learning similar skills in class, although Konigun implores students to experiment with other styles once they have grasped the fundamentals of ninjutsu.

ETIQUETTE: (Class-A)

1. When you approach an instructor, stand within his/her view until your presence is acknowledged, then speak.
2. If you drop it, pick it up; if it breaks, fix it; if you can't fix it report it; if the instructor can't fix it, you bought it.
3. What happens in class stays in class.
4. Do not test the edge of another black sash, student, or visitor's sword. It is very disrespectful and dishonorable.

SPARRING RULES: (Class-A)

1. Master hands are to be used only on black sashes within Konigun, or in defense of black sashes from other styles, or in public when defending against a better opponent.
2. Master stances can be used at any time once they have been learned.
3. Element bow is only used when sparring others with element knowledge.
4. Warrior bow is only used between black sashes.

WEAPONS PROTOCOLS: (Class-A)

1. No person (unless a black sash or staff personal) is to remove any weapon from the wall.
2. No one is to touch another student's weapons without permission.
3. No weapons on the floor without black sash supervision.
5. Never draw or unlock anyone else's sword without permission.

BLACK SASH:

DATING:

1. No black sash is to date a student of their dojo, shrine, temple, or rai. (B-class)
2. A black sash may not date a former mate of another black sash without the former black sash's permission and/or with shidoshi. (C-class)
3. This style will not interfere with another black sash's relationship with spouse. (A-class)

WAIVERS

1. Unless having a doctor's waiver on file, the prospective black sash must successfully complete every category from white to black. Any person not up holding this protocal will commit a class – C - violation.

VIOLENT FELONY

1. A black sash will not commit violent felonious acts. Unless in self-defense of family, loved ones, or another person. (Class –C-)

CONDUCT

1. A black sash must sign a black sash agreement. (Class –C-)
2. A black sash must follow rules of agreement. (Class –C-)
3. Do not threaten punishment as a joke, no cruel or unusual punishment. (Class –A-)

ACCULT

1. A black sash may not be a member of a(n) accult- system claiming use or knowledge of powers from the deceased, occult- a system claiming use or knowledge of secret or supernatural powers or agencies from the devil, or black witchcraft- a system, art, or practice of a witch, sorcery, or magic. (Class –C-)

ATTITUDE

1. A black sash must maintain a positive attitude about the Style, functions or its members while in the accompaniment of students. (Class –A-)
2. Aggressive slander prohibited (I.E. I'll cut your head off, or I'll kill him). (Class –A-)

MEDIA

1. No black sash may make an appearance on TV, news, or other such media events that pertain to the style without permission of Shidoshi. (Class –B-)

CROSSING TRAINING

1. Shidoshi must clear any appearance in an outside style martial arts function. (Class –B-)

UNDERSTANDING & AGREEMENT

1. Teaching certificate will only be valid for one year, and then it must be renewed. The black sash may be asked at anytime to re-certify by the Shidoshi. (Not Classed)
2. It is understood that before accepting the black sash and certificate that it has been presented as a gift and at anytime may be requested to be returned. Black sash and certificate will remain property of Konigun Ninjutsu. (Class-C)
3. A black sash may not teach without a teaching certificate. (Class –C-)

BLACK SASH RIGHTS

1. A black sash has the right to have a training ground of their own.
2. A black sash has the right to wear white over black.
3. A black sash has the right to teach immediate family without teachers certificate, but cannot rank them.
4. A black sash has the right to be a member of any Christian religion he/she deems fit.
5. A black sash may attend any martial art function the style holds or any function in konigun ninjutsu, via class, cookout, meetings, dojo activity, and/or camp, (no matter what style family or function). Kageshu are the only waiver in this right, whereas the shidoshi invites the attendance.

DUTY

1. The duty of a black sash is to be a leader to his peers, and the students around him.
2. The black sash must report all rule violations of class –b- or –c- to Shidoshi in writing within 5 days.
3. The black sash is to set a good community example.

RESPONSIBILITY

1. It's a black sash responsibility to try to solve any conflict in the style whether it concerns them or not. (Class-A &B)
2. A black sash is responsible to report all infraction of the style to the Shidoshi. (Class-B)
3. A black sash is responsible to keep up their training to the point of their certification level and attend all re-certification meetings. (Class-B)

UNIFORM DRESS CODE

SASH (CLASS-A RULES)

1. Sash may touch walking surface when tied on waist, but may not touch walking surface any other time or condition.
2. When used as a weapon, the sash may touch walking surface as long as it has never been worn around the waist.
3. Student knot will be the common knot with the warrior knot being worn by a green sash or above.
4. Sash knot is worn on the right side at the ties of the uniform top.
5. The sash is between three to four inches wide and wraps at least two times around the waist.
6. The end of the sash is not to go below the knee of the person wearing the sash.
7. The ends of the sash once tied should not be different in length or more than the index finger of the person wearing the sash long.
8. The seam is up when being worn around the waist. The seam is noted as also being a pocket.
9. All markings or writings must be approved in writing from the Shidoshi before placement on the sash.
10. The only time a sash may be worn is with the uniform top and bottom or with just the bottom. The top must be solid black: tank tops, t-shirt, gi top, muscle shirt or bare skin. (The top may be with or without symbols.) Black sash may wear white tops as already mentioned in the same manner.
11. A sash once worn is always a sash, however until a sash is worn on the waist for the first time it is just a piece of cloth.
12. Sashes should always be hung or folded when not being worn.
13. Keep sash flat and not rolled up on waist.
14. The student knot will be worn by white and gold sashes.

15. The warrior knot may be worn by green sash or higher.
16. The sash knot is always worn on the person's right.

**Note: There is not set way to fold hakamas or a standard gi but the sash is roll and not folded.

GI (CLASS-A RULES)

1. When wearing gi top, it must be tied or tucked.
2. When wearing a tied gi top, the sash must be worn.
3. No sleeveless gi tops.
4. Gi sleeves may be rolled up if desired.
5. Gi tops may not have short sleeves.
6. Gi colors may only be white, black, moonlight camouflage, or camouflage.
7. A white bottom can never be worn under a colored top.
8. Extra gi trim or symbols must be approved in writing by shidoshi.
9. Gi pants may be worn by themselves.
10. Tabis and gauntlets may be worn if they match the gi color. Black tabis may be worn with any gi.
11. Gi pants may not be rolled up.
12. Gi pants must be properly worn around the waist.
13. Any camp or event style shirt may be worn as a gi top.
14. Any type of shoes may be worn with a gi to and from style events.
15. No public possession of alcoholic beverages while in a gi.
16. No smoking while in a gi.
17. Your uniform should be worn clean and neat to class. It does not have to be pressed but shouldn't be covered with wrinkles. Two uniforms are suggested)
18. Unless you have not received your uniform, the only type of t-shirt to be worn to class is the style (ryu) t-shirts with traditional pants and sash.
19. Only the tabi may be worn on the main floor

OTHER UNIFORM APPAREL (CLASS-A RULES)

1. Shidoshi must approve capes, hoods, and other attachments.
2. No chain mail armor for students.
3. Hip and backpacks are allowed for woodland or camp events.

DRUGS: (CLASS-C RULES)

1. No possession of illegal recreational drugs. (IE any laboratory or plant drug.)

CAMP RULES

CLASS-A RULES

1. Students may smoke in designated areas only.
2. Black sash must assign an attendant to watch the fire with the shift not to exceed two hours.
3. Fire must be attended at all times.
4. You dirty it you clean it.
5. No pets without permission.
6. No one is to sleep in his or her vehicles during camp.
7. Coaching whistle is the same as gurupu.
8. No glass containers outside.
9. Chewing tobacco complies with the smoking rules.
10. Men may not go bare-chested without permission from a black sash.
11. Conduct yourself at camp in the same manner that you would at home.
12. Only fire tenders or black sashes may put wood on the fire.
13. No clothing with profanity, alcohol companies, or pro drug logos.
14. No jewelry may be worn during camp except by black sashes.
15. All drivers must turn in their keys into camp director.
16. No one in kitchen area without permission.
17. No extra food without permission.
18. Everyone should be in bed ten minutes before lights go out.

CLASS-B RULES

1. Gurupu:
   A. Everyone at camp must assemble at gurupu immediately!
      Visitors will assemble to the teacher's right of the formation.
   B. Only a black sash may call gurupu; unless a student is given permission, or a student deems an emergency.
2. Guests and students are to check in and out of camp with the camp director.
3. Only a black sash may go into the woods alone.
4. Shidoshi's quarters are off limits unless invited.
5. All damaged or unsafe items must be immediately reported to a black sash.
6. No firearms at camp without permission from Shidoshi.
7. All cameras and camcorders must be signed in.
8. The office is off limits unless a staff member is present.
9. No off-the-ground training equipment is to be used without another person present.
10. No sparring without a black sash present.
11. Never throw any containers onto the fire.
12. No horse playing around the fire or training area.
13. Always close the gate after leaving camp.
14. Propelled objects are to be used on the propelled object range only.
15. Archery is allowed on the archery ran[illegible].

CAMP PROTOCOLS

1. All guests must follow camp rules.
2. Tents are allowed at camp.
3. Cooking crew eats first, followed by ladies, then the white sash to the highest rank at camp; black sash and instructors eat last always.
4. No children under twelve years old without permission.
5. All videos shown at camp must be pre-approved.
6. No video cameras or still cameras may be used at camp without Shidoshi's permission.
7. No visitors at camp without pre-approved permission from camp director or Shidoshi.

PRONUNCIATIONS

A AH	I EE	U UU	E EH	O OH
KA KAH	KI KEE	KU KUU	KE KAY	KO KOE
SA SAH	SHI SHE	SU SUE	SE SAY	SO SOE
TA TAH	GHI GHEE	TSU TSUE	TE TAY	TO TOE
NI NEE	NU NUU	NE NAY	NO NO	HA HAH
HU WHO	HE HAY	HO HOE	MA MAH	MI ME
MU MOO	ME MAY	MO MOE	YA YAH	YO YOE
RA RAH	RI REE	RU RUE	RE RAY	RO ROE
GI GEE	GU GOO	GE GAY	GO GOH	ZA ZAH
JI JEE	ZU ZOO	ZE ZAY	ZO ZOE	DA DAH
DE DAY	DO DOE	BA BAH	BI BEE	BU BOO
BE BAY	BO BOO	PA PAH	PI PEE	RYA RE-YAH
NA NAH	HI HE	GA GAH	NYU NE-YUU	HYA HE-YAH
HYU HE-YUU	HYO HE-YOE	GHA GHAH	GHU GHUU	GHOE GHOE

BODY
(MI)

1.	ARMS	UDE	30. INSTEP	ASHI NO KO
2.	ARM PIT	AKI NO SHITA	31. JAW	AGO
3.	ANKLE	KURUBUSHI	32. JOINT	FUSHI
4.	BACK	SENAKE	33. KNEE	HIZA
5.	BACK OF BODY	SENAKE	34. KNUCKLE	GENKO
6.	BACK BONE	SE-HONE	35. KIDNEY	JINZO
7.	BALL OF FOOT	MARI	36. LEG (S)	ASHI
8.	BONE	HONE	37. LIPS	KUCHIBIRU
9.	BUST	BAASTO	38. LITTLE FINGER	KOYUBI
10.	CHEST	MUNE	39. LUNG (S)	HAI
11.	CHIN	AGO	40. MOUTH	KUCHI
12.	COLLAR BONE	SAKOTSU	41. MUSCLE	KIN-NIKU
13.	EAR	MIMI	42. NECK	KUBI
14.	EYE	ME	43. NOSE	HANA
15.	EYE BROWS	MAYUGE	44. REAR	O'SHIRI
16.	ELBOW	HIJI	45. RING FINGER	KUSURI YUBI
17.	FINGER (S)	YUBI	46. RIB	ABARA-HONE
18.	FINGER NAIL (S)	YUBI NO TSUME	47. SHOULDER	KA'TA
19.	FIST	GENKOTSU	48. SKULL	DOKURO
20.	FOOT (FEET)	ASHI	49. STOMACH	I
21.	FOREFINGER	HITOSASHIYUBI	50. STOMACH	ONAKA
22.	FOREHEAD	ODEKO	51. TOOTH	HA
23.	GROIN/PENIS	MOMONE	52. THROAT	NODO
24.	HAND	TE	53. TOP OF FOOT	ZETCHO
25.	HEAD	ATAMA	54. THUMB	OYAYUBI
26.	HEAD & NECK	KUBI	55. TOE	ASHI NO YUBI
27.	HEEL OF FOOT	KAGATO	56. WAIST	KOSHI
28.	HEART	SHINZO	57. WRIST	TE KUBI
29.	HIP	KOSHI		

THE KONIGUN RANKING SYSTEM

When the first Shidoshi of Konigun Ninjutsu started training men he trained Samurai that were ronin for the Community Guard. Warriors that were known as Bushi were specialized solders. The Samurai were good in all weapons, bow, yari, as well as the sword. The ronins were divided into four levels of leadership and experience. They were, Bushi, Samurai, Yoshi, and Taibushi. The common foot solders were known as Senpai, and the common person were known as Hinins. The officers of the Samurai were divided into two classes known as Yoshi and Taibushi. Basically your NCOs and your officers. When all of these had learned up to Shidoshi Saija's standards they were known as Kagebushi or Shadow Warrior, Ninja. If they learned the priestly ways they were known as Yamabushi. When this Yamabushi taught a student up to the rank of Yamabushi the teacher became a master. And so when the student taught someone to Yamabushi the student became a Master and the Master became a Grandmaster. The original ranking system was, Hinin, Senpai, Yamabushi, Mejin, and Shidoshi. The rank of Shidoshi was passed down from farther to son, until the 37th Shidoshi was adopted by the 36th and became the first American to become Shidoshi in the Konigun Ryu. When you had learned up to the fifth level or Yamabushi, you were then a priest of nature, harmony and void. Nothing in nature is square everything is round. Is not a square corner withered down by the wind? The color of the ranks were, white, gold, black, and red, the simplest way. They wore plain red belts or obis during work out. The red tiger belts were red belts with a black tiger on the belt were worn only during ceremonies. The color of the belt signified, student, monk, teacher, and master. The black belt tigers were colored for each upper rank. Gold for Yamabushi, red for master, and silver for Shidoshi. The word Shidoshi comes from the words, Shido, meaning leader and Shi meaning master. Therefore you have the title of Shidoshi meaning leader master or master leader. The word Shidosha means director and Shidoshu means vice-director. The words for master or senior teacher use a suffix or prefix such as Shujin, Mejin. Shihun, Hunshi, Shidoshi, Shidoshu and Taishu. Tai is a prefix for grand. When ninjas are set up in detachments they go though a chain of command. The Shunin meaning headperson or head master is in charge. Then there is the Chunin ninja leader or ninja co-leader; the Jonin is sometimes referred to as the co-leader or ninja leader. The manin is the ninja associate and the genin is the ninja agent. At a ninja camp the Shunin would be the master of ceremony, the Chunin the coordinator, Jonin, the teacher, the manin the assonate to the teacher, the Jonin and genin would be the cooks.

KONIGUN NINJUTSU HISTORY

As far back as the mid-4500's B.C., the Japanese islands were inhabited. This early culture was known as the Jomon era. The people are thought to be a Caucasian race known as the Ainu. The Japanese who inhabit the islands today are believed to have lived on the island since about 200 B.C. and are known as Yayoi. The Caucasian race of Japan is mostly found on the northern islands of Hokkaido.

In 660 B.C., legend has it as a person known as Jimmu Tenno brought about a confederation of clans on the island of Kyushu. Tenno also conquered the people of Kinki later giving birth to the Yamato state and dynasty. He would become known as "the divine warrior."

The era of 1192 to 1333 was named after the Kamakura Shogunate that was ruled by militaristic bushi (samurai) class. This era also saw the birth of zen buddisim.

The Japanese imperial government allotted control over the countryside estates and provinces to different daimyo(s). The daimyo were given a retainer from the emperor to own or control a measure of land, as well as to employee bands of warriors to protect their estates and the peasants working the estates. These warriors were known as samurai. In exchange for these estates, the emperor would get a small percentage of the crop and a self-contained "national guard army" that he could call on as part of the retainer agreement. The peasant farmer had title to his crop only through his overlord.

During this era, there were two imperial families, the Minamoto and the Taira. Yoritomo, lead the Minamoto family to victory when the two families clashed openly in Kyoto, in what is known as the Hogan war of July 1156. Later, the Minamoto were defeated in 1159 in the Heiji war. Twenty-one years later, Yoritomo ('s) brothers, Noriyoro and Yoshitsune, created the samurai-dokoro or board of retainers in eastern Japan. This board imposed disciplinary control on their military vassals.

In 1185, the destruction of the Taira family came with Yoritomo regaining power and then appointing military governors (shugo) in all the provinces and military stewards (jito) in both private and government land estates. These shugos and jitos were responsible for law enforcement and tax collecting. The need for funds to pay war cost, which included samurai(s) for protecting estates and for performing other duties, was brutally imposed on the villagers. If a person could not pay his taxes, the samurai would take the children, wife or even the farmer himself for slaves. Those that protested were put to death.

As legend has it, a horde of samurai(s) descended upon a tiny village made up mostly of farmers existing in the foothills northwest of Kagoshima, Japan. The samurai demanded taxes and reminded the villagers of their obligations and consequences while marking their day of return for the tax payment. The people of the tiny village knew they were too poor to raise the money. It was agreed that some would flee to the mountains while others would stay behind to make the town appear regularly populated, so that the samurai(s) would not follow the others that fled to the mountains.

When the samurai(s) returned, the taxes could not be met and the villagers were either killed or enslaved during the burning and destruction of the village. The members of the village who fled to the mountains stayed hidden for years. The leader of these people was known as Saija. Saija left the group and went to find ways to protect his people and to bring back a better way of life. He went to the Yamabushi priests. There, he studied and mastered their ways. Then he brought the technique back to the people of the village.

Priests, sickened by their own imperial order's pursuit of wealth and power, left the order and moved to the mountains. Once in the mountains, these priests built several shrines in order to seek a better way of life and enlightenment through the understanding of nature. The mountain priest would become known as the yamabushi. These yamabushi(s) would seek this enlightenment by observing nature and testing themselves against nature. The yamabushi would sit under ice cold crushing waterfalls, hang from cliffs upside down, sit in snow naked and run through woods in the dark and much more in their pursuit of wisdom.

Travelers, woodcutters, sportsmen, and other people often saw the unusual habits of study. All who saw those unusual acts would go back to the estates and tell of the things they witness, which made the lowlanders of the estates look up to the priests and the yamabushi order. As time went by, the yamabushi developed higher skills with nature. Some of these skills seemed magical such as walking on water and flying. The walking on water technique was no more than standing in two small foot tubs and using poles to keep balance and to propel forward. Flying was by a fall glider, which was somewhat similar to the hang glider of today. Although easy to explain, stories grew with each telling with yamabushi becoming more like gods. The stories and the fame of the yamabushi made imperial priests jealous. With little needed effort, the imperial priests had the yamabushi priests declared outlaws and their practiced priesthood outlawed.

Around the 1600's, the ways of the yamabushi would become known as ninjutsu. All who mastered ninjutsu would become the ninja. Some say the word ninja means "in stealth". Others say it means "he who studies nature".

The clan era of history details hundreds of scattered peasant revolts. These revolts were against both feudal lords and wealthy power seeking priests. The daimyo ruled the Amakusa area raised taxes in 1637. The taxes were collected very severely and without bounds from the farmers and business people. Already under tension, Tokugawa Jemitsu decided to prohibit Christianity in an attempt to regain control, giving birth to the rebellion. When the daimyo could not suppress the revolt, he called on the shogunate. The shogunate army quickly ended the revolt and put to death the rebels and their families.

According to *THE BOOK OF THE ASSASSINS (1982 PUBLICATION)* 1,000 konigun ninja(s) were attacked by 10,000 samurai(s) and fought a battle, in which the ninja(s) were almost totally annihilated. Many historians state that after this battle the code language used was undecipherable outside the realm of the konigun ninja. In fact, konigun still has it's own colloquialisms remaining today. The word "konigun" is actually two words. "Koni" means friendly and "Gun" means forces.

The ninja got his name from the feudal samurai (s). Often the feudal samurai (s) hired the ninja to scout and spy because of their special abilities. The ninja were at an era where samurai(s) retained them to destroy samurai, often the very ones who hunted them. What they once did for survival now was a paycheck. The era gave the ninja time to grow and sharpen their skills. Although it had its drawbacks, the ninja found that their samurai ('s) enemies had also hired ninja clans to do as they were doing. In time, this brought ninja clans to war with each other. Currently, the Konigun clan (ryu) is in its 39th generation. The ninja grandmaster (Shidoshi) is of the 37th generation, from the yamabushi priest saija. The word shidoshi comes from the word shidosha, which translates to director. The word shido translates to leader.

The ryu still holds its secrets. One held secret is the name of all retired ninja(s) to assure a peaceful retirement. A ninja ryu is a group of ninja(s). To be a ninja ryu, the ryu has to study ninjutsu and follow a form of the bushido code. To this code every clansman must give an oath of loyalty. The things make a ninja clan and the style of ninjutsu. If a style has no ninja(s) left, then it is no longer a style of ninjutsu. The style of ninjutsu is what makes the clans different. Since ninjutsu has developed over hundreds of years in different areas of Japan, the techniques of fighting and thinking, as well as, codes are different. Hardships caused by wars, treatment from locals, and encountering foreign people with different fighting techniques, had a big impact on each ninjutsu style. Enlightenments adopted from these occurrences make up the mindset of the system.

The families in the style consist of a master and all of his black sashes, students, and his black sash's students. New families are born with the coming of new meijin, (or master's). Only one master will head a family. History reminds us of how the ninja(s) were able to adapt and survive throughout time.

The fall of the t'sang dynasty in china brought many refugees to Japan. The yamabushi welcomed refugees. With them came the knowledge of gunpowder, which was later used to make ninja smoke bombs. Other weapons such as the san-setsu-kon, bladed shuriken as well as hand and foot techniques, were adopted form these Chinese refugees. History shows that these refugees from china had some influence in creating and developing the yamabushi priesthood order and may have been part of its founding fathers.

As the daimyo began to fight each other more and more, the ninja began to grow famous. Often when the samurai were beaten in combat by the ninja and lived, they would make up stories in order to retain their honor. When they reported to their lords, the myth of the tengu was born from these tales in order to save face and life. The samurai often said the ninja were demons that could change from human form to a bird like beast. The stories were supported by the way the ninja was said to be able to disappear, fly, walk on water, make fire come from the ground (via flash bombs) and many other things.

This is a brief history of konigun ninjutsu handed down from generation to generation and now on to you. "A konigun ninja is one with himself and nature, as well as being the possessor of great abilities to help mankind. Nature is the path, honor is our duty, and to seek and honorable justice with all our action is the code.

"My honor is my life."

End

WEAPONS AND EQUIPMENT
(DOGU/ TEATE)

1. "P-34" (TONFA)
2. SAMURAI SWORD (KATANA)

3. 3' STAFF (HAN-BO)

4. 30" - 60" SWORD (KODACHI)
5. 6' STAFF (ROKUSHAKU-BO)

6. 7'-8' STAFF (SAO)
7. 8"-10" BO (YUBI-BO)
8. 9' STAFF (KU-BO)

9. 9"-11 "BLADE WITH FINGER RING (SHINBO)

10. 9"-11 "ROD WITH RING (SHABO)

11. A PAIL INTO WHICH TO THRUST (KAN-SHU)

12. ARROW (YA)

13. AXE (ONO)

14. BAMBOO POLE (SAODAKE)

15. BAMBOO PRACTICE SPEAR (KEIKO-NAGINATA)

16. BAMBOO SWORD (SHINAI)

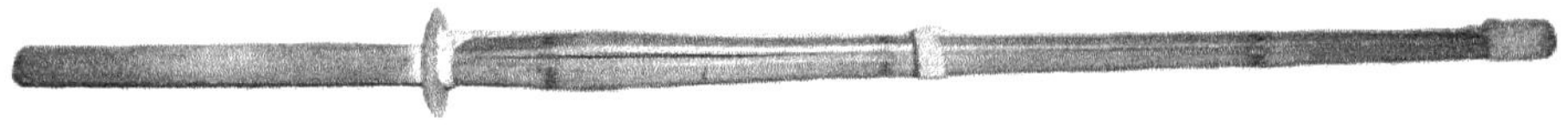

17. BELT (OBI)

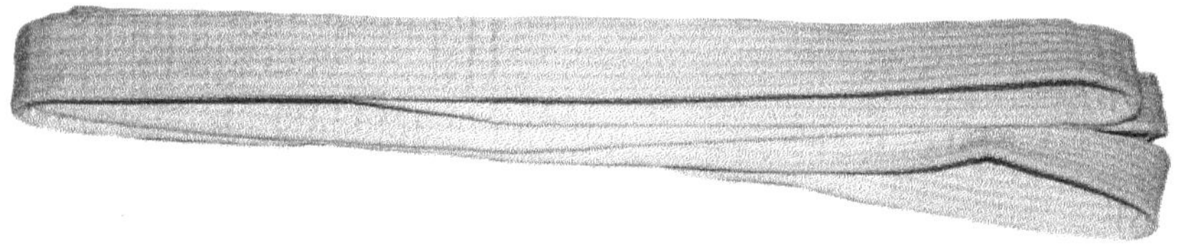

18. BLADE WITH A CHAIN (SHOGE)

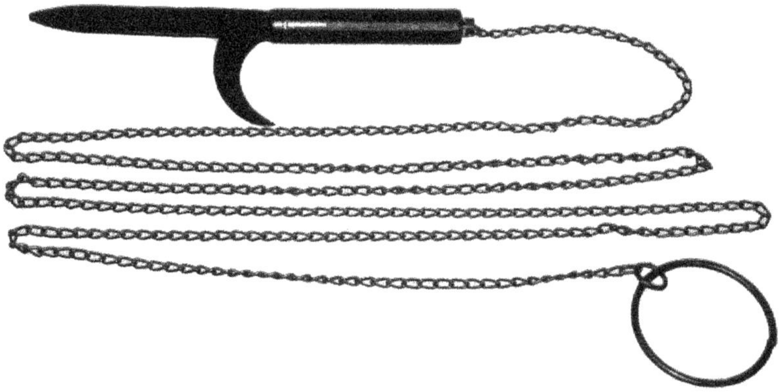

19. BLADED DIRK (AIKUCHI)

20. BLADED HAIR PIN (KANZASHI)

21. BLINDING POWDER (METSUBUSHI)

22. BLOW GUN (FUKI D'ZUTSU)

23. BOOBY TRAP (BAKA-WANA)

24. BOW (YUMI)

25. CALTROPS (MIT'SUBUSHI)

26. CANDLES ON IRON SPIKED HOLDERS (NINSHOKUDAI)

27. CHAIN WITH WEIGHT AT ONE END & STAFF AT THE OTHER (CHIGIRIKI)

28. CHEST PROTECTOR USED IN KENDO (MUNE-ATE)

29. CHINESE BUTTERFLY KNIFE (BADIK)

30. CROSSING WATER TUBE (KAMEIKADA SAYA NO JUTSU)

31. DECORATIVE BINDING ON SWORD (TSUKA ITO)

32. BLADED DIRK (KUWAI-KEN)

33. DOUBLE ENDED SAI (MANJI)

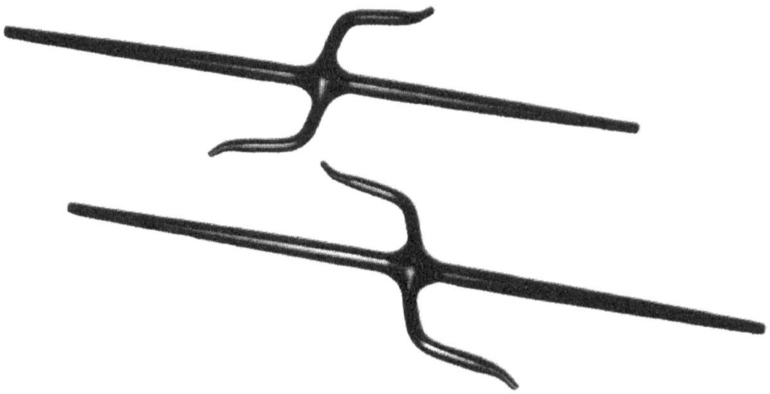

34. EXTRA SWORD (NODACHI)

35. FACE MASK USED IN KENDO (MEN)

36. FIRE CRACKERS SHAPED LIKE EGGS (TORINOKO)

37. FLASH BOMB (HARETSU-DAMA NO

38. FORK HEADED SPEAR (FUTAMATA-YARI)

39. GRAPPLING HOOK (KAGERU-KAGI)

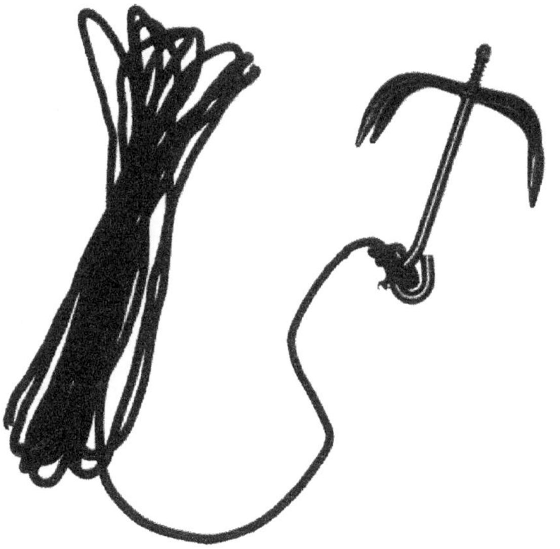

40. GUN (TEPPO)

41. HANDLE OF THE SAMURAI SWORD (TSUKA)

42. HARD WOOD STAFF REINFORCED (KONSAIBO)

43. HOOKS WORN ON THE HAND WITH METAL BAN (TEKAGI)

44. IRON BRACELET (TEKKEN)

45. IRON STAFF (TETSUBO)

46. IRON STAFF (TETSUBO)

47. JACKET WORN IN KENDO (KEIKOGI)

48. JAPANESE BOW	(YUMI)
49. JAPANESE KNUCKLEDUSTER	(TEKO)
50. JAPANESE SPEAR CLASSIFIED UNDER STRAIGHT SPEAR CATEGORY	(SU-YARI)
51. JAPANESE SPEAR WITH A CROSSED	(TSUKUBO)
52. JAPANESE SPEAR WITH BARBED HOOKS	(SODEGARAMI)
53. JAPANESE SPEAR WITH FORKED HEAD	(SASUMAATA)
54. JAPANESE SPEAR	(OMI-GARI)
55. JAVELIN WITH A SHORT SICKEL-LIKE	(NAGE-GAMA)
56. JUDO SLIPPERS	(ZORI)
57. JUDO TROUSERS	(ZUBON)
58. KNIFE FITTED INTO ONE SIDE OF	(KOGATANA)
59. LARGE BRONZE SPEAR HEAD	(TSUKUSHI-BOKO)
60. LONG SAMURAI SWORD	(DAITO)
61. LONG STICK WITH BLADE AT END	(BISENTO)
62. LONG SWORD	(DACHI)
63. NARROW BLADED STAFF	(KAMA)

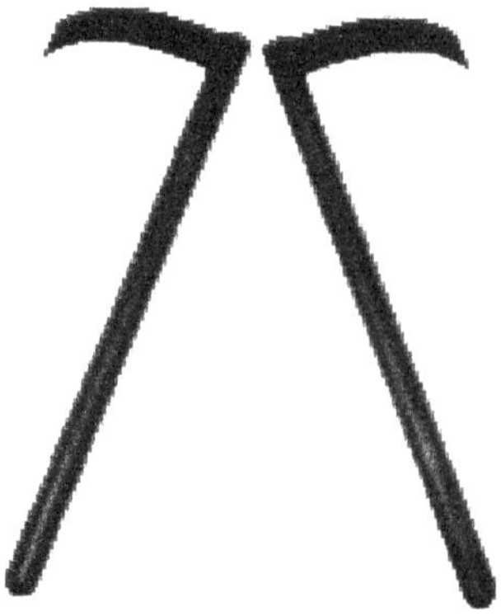

64. NINJA BOOT (TABI)

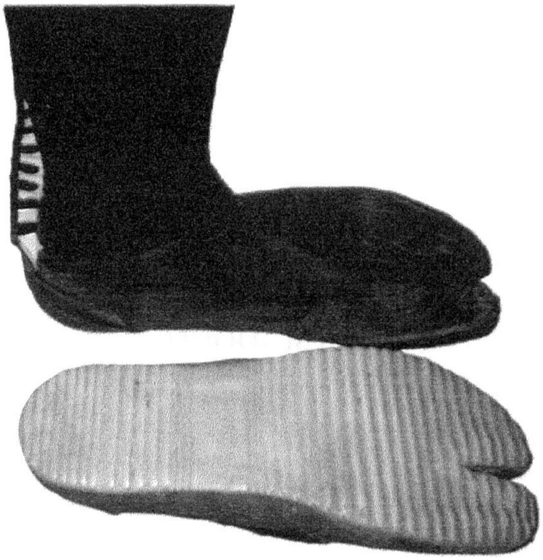

65. NINJA SWORD (NINJA-TO)

66. NINJA UNIFORM (SHINOBU SHOZOKU)

67. NUN-CHUCKS (NUN-CHAKU)

68. OLDEST JAPANESE SPEAR (HOKO)

69. ONE MAN RAFT USED BY THE NINJA (KAMEIKADA)

70. POISON PINS OR DART SHOT FROM BLOW GUN (FUKIYA)

71. POISON (DOKU)

72. THREE CLASSICAL WEAPONS USED IN UNISON FOR RESTRAINING A SAMURAI SWORDSMAN (MITSU-DOGO)

73. SAFETY EQUIPMENT HANDS AND FEET (CHIGIRIKI)

74. SAMURAI SWORD (SHOTO)

75. SCABBARD OF THE JAPANESE SWORD (SAYA)

76. SCIMITAR LIKE BLADE, 3' IN LENGTH (NAGINATA)

77. SERIES PLUM STUMPS (MEI-HWA-CHUANG)

78. SHAFT OF A JAPANESE SPEAR (NAKAE)

79. SHARP METAL DISK OR FLAT STONE (TSUBUTE)

80. SHOOTING GLOVE (YUGAKE)

81. SHORT STRAIGHT BLADE SWORD (TANTO)

82. SHORT SWORD 16"-20" LONG (WAKIZASHI)

83. SMALL DIRKS CONCEALED IN MOUTH (FUKUMI-BARI)

84. SMALL METAL THROWING WEAPONS (TONKI)

85. SINGLE PRONG SAI (JUI)

86. SMOKE BOMB (HARETSU-DAMA NO KEMURI)

87. SPEAR WITH A SICKLE-SHAPED BLADE (KAMA-YARI)

88. SPEAR (YARI)

89. SPECIAL SWORD (SHIKOMI-ZUE)

90. SPIKE (KUGI)

91. SPIKED FINGER RING (KAKUDE)

92. SPITTING NEEDLES (RUKI-BARIOR FUKUMIBAI)

93. STAFF WEAPON WITH HIDDEN CHAIN (SHINOBI-ZUE)

94. STATUES OF KARATE STANCES (NIO BODISATTVAS)

95. STRIKING POST IN THE GROUND WITH (TANSHIKI)

96. STRIKING POST IN THE GROUND (FUKUSHIKI)

97. STRAIGHT SPEARHEAD CLASSIFICATION (SU-YARI)

98. STRIKING POST (MAKIWARA)

99. TANTO WITH 1/2 HAND GUARD (HAMIDASHI)

100. TANTO WITH NO HAND GUARD (AIKUCHI)

101. THREE PRONGED SPEAR (MAGARI-YARI)

102. THREE PRONGED SWORD (SAI)

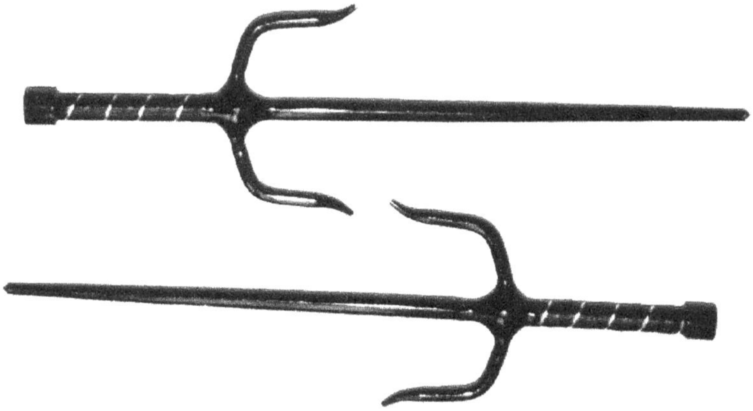

103. THREE SECTIONAL STAFF (SAN-SETSU-KON)

104. THROWING BLADE (SHIRIKEN)

105. THROWING KNIFE (KOZUKA)

106.	THROWING STAR	(SHAKEN)

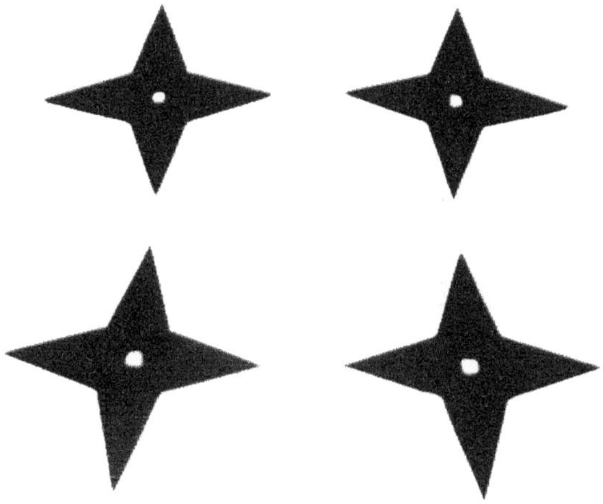

107.	TWO PRONGED SAI	(JUTTE)
108.	TYPE OF LONG SWORD	(NAGEMAKI)
109.	TYPE OF THROWING KNIFE	(MAMBA)

110.	WALKING KNUCKLEDUSTER	(TEKKEN)
111.	WATER CROSSING DEVICE	(UKIDARU)
112.	WEIGHTED CHAIN WITH HANDLES	(MANRIKI-GUSARI)

113. WEIGHTED CHAIN (MANRIKI)

114. WHITE GI (DOBOK)

115. WOODEN DUMMY (MOOK JONG)

116. WOODEN FLOATS (MIZUGUMO)

117. WOODEN NINJA CLOGS (GETA)

118. WOODEN SAMURAI SWORD (BOKUDO)

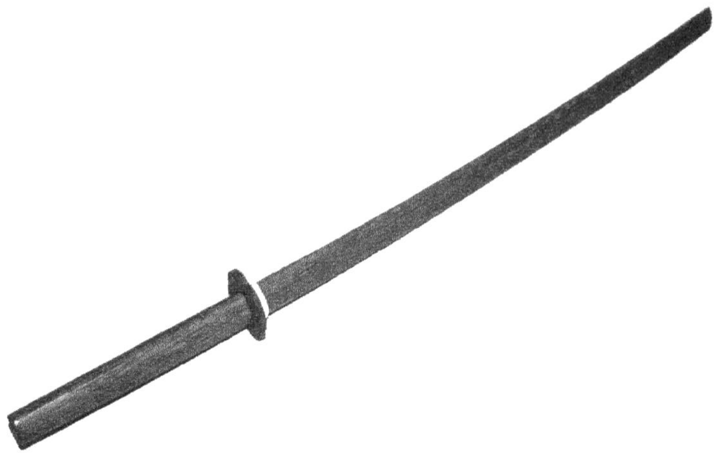

119. WOODEN SHABO (KOBO)

120. WOODEN SPEAR (HASSAKU-BO)

121. WOODEN STAFF (TOYA)

122. ICE FOOT CLAWS (SHIKOS)

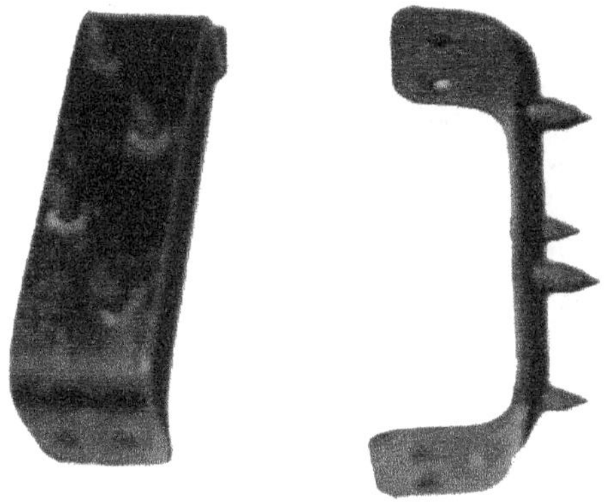

123. ICE HAND CLAWS (SHUKOS)

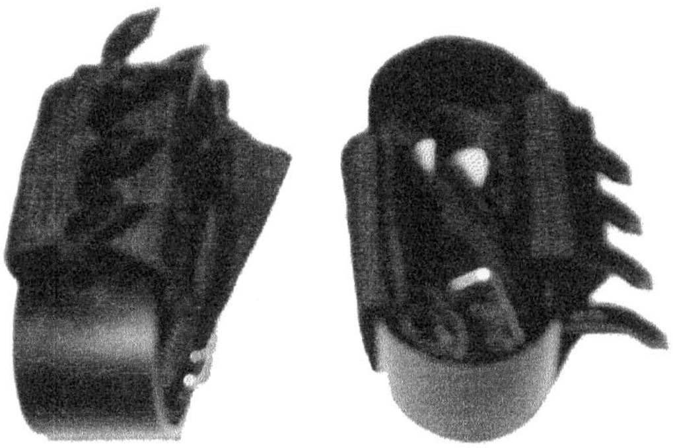

124. STEEL FAN (OGI)

125. KAMA WITH CHAIN (KAMA-GUSARI)

GLOSSARY

A

Ai: harmony

Aikido: A discipline of hand-to-hand martial arts employing pivoting movements to neutralize an attack.

Aikuchi: bladed dirk

Akai: Ninjutsu use for good.

Aku: disengage

Akuma: An evil spirit, Devil

Arerugi: Allergy

Atemi: Percussive Aikido strike

Ayumi ashi: Normal walking

Ayuryo: also see Mempo: Facemask shaped like a demon

B

Badik: Chinese butterfly knife

Baka: Fool

Baka-wana: Booby trap

Bane: spring

Batsugun: Instantaneous promotion

Battojutsu: Drawing the sword

Bempi: Constipation

Bifuteki: Beefsteak

Bisento: Spear-like weapon with a blade resembling a scimitar fixed to its end; much favored by the ninja.

Bo: 6 ft (1.8m) wooden staff, around which is built a complete fighting system, and which can be likened to the old English quarterstaff.

Bogyo: Defense

Boken: Wooden ninja sword

Bokudo: Wooden samurai sword

Buddhism: Religious doctrine founded in India by the philosopher Gautama (Buddha). In ancient times it was closely connected to the practice of Kung-fu, through the Buddhist monks who helped develop the art

Budo: Martial arts or Warrior way

Bujinkan: Ninja training hall or club dojo. Also the name for Masaaki Hatsumi's organization

Bujutsu: Generic heading for all Japanese martial arts.

Bushido: Samurai's strict and unforgiving code of honor

C

Caltrops: Sharp metal spiked weapon for throwing in the pathway of pursuers. Often the tips were poisoned. Natural caltrops used were the spiked shells of the water chestnut fruit. Also known as tetsubishi.

-chan: informal suffix to name indicating love and a certain special closeness

Chano-yu: Tea ceremony

.

Chiba prefecture: Home of Dr. Masaaki Hatsumi, the present grandmaster of the Tokagure ninjutsu system.

Chikara-no-kyujaku: Timing in the use of force and strength

Cho: districts within a city's wards

Chodo: Just right

Chome: Sub-districts within a city's cho.

Chui: warning

Chunin: Literally means, "middle person". The second of the three military ranks in the ninja hierarchy. The chunin set the mission for the field ninja to carry out, and was ultimately responsible for its success.

D

Dachi: Long sword or stance

Daigaku: University

Dai-katana: The longest of the samurai's katana, or long swords

Daikon: Giant Japanese white radish, which grows abundantly and has great food value.

Daimyo: Japanese feudal lords

Daito: Long samurai sword

Dan: Actually means step; But is often applied to the level of a Black Belt.

De ashi harai: Advancing foot sweep

Demasu: Leave

Denka no hoto: Bureaucratic phraseology for the katana, the samurai sword

Dento: light

Denwa: Telephone

De wa mata: Again

Do: Way of life or use

Dobok: White uniform (gi) top

Do gakure: throwing copper coins to injure and distract pursuers.
Also see **Goton-no-jutsu**

Dohyo: A sumo ring, where the wrestling is performed

Dojo: The "place of the way" a training hall or gymnasium for martial arts practice.

Doku: poison

Dokuen gakure: this is the use of poison smoke screen to cover a retreat. Also see **Goton-no-jutsu**

Dokukeshi: Antidote

Dora: Gong

Doton: using ground, walls and stone for hiding. Also see **Goton-no-jutsu**

Doyobi: Saturday

E

Eboshi: Ninja hood

En-no-Gyoja: Yamabushi or mountain warrior ascetic who tried to restore order in Japan in the 6th century by propagating a new way of Buddhism which was called Shugendo.

Eri: Uniform lapel

Erika: Spot below arm pit portion

F

Feng shui: He who reads in the elements of life such as Earth, Wind, Fire, and Water.

Fu: Ninja method of acting like the "wind". Fu is a method of fighting in the ninja body art of taijutsu and is characterized by harmonious interaction with other elements. It gives the user of the fu approach the appearance of being everywhere at same time.

Fudo ken: Ninja clenched fist used for punching and striking body targets

Fuki D'zutsu: Blowgun

Fukiya: Pins and poisoned darts shot through a blow- gun at an unsuspecting enemy. Greatly used by many of the ninja clans during stealth activities.

Fukumi-bari: Small dirks concealed in mouth

Fukushiki: Striking post in the ground

Fun: minute

Fusegi: Escape

Futamata-yari: Fork headed spear

G

Gakkai: school

Gakkusei: student

Gata: wooden ninja clogs

Gatame: Lock or hold

Genin: A genin was a ninja of the lowest rank and the one responsible for actually carrying out the mission.

Getsuyobi: Monday

Globefish: Known also as the blowfish or fugu. Its deadly poison was used by the ninja to tip darts and spikes for a faster and more effective kill.

Goton-po: Ninja's five principles of evasion, involving camouflage techniques and concealment tricks by blending in with the natural surroundings of the environment.

Goton-no-jutsu: "Five methods of escape"

1. Mokuton (using trees and grasses)

   A. Kusa gakure: Being traced and facing capture, the ninja hides behind bushes or in tall grass.

   B. Tanuki gakure: The ninja climbs a tree and blends with limbs and foliage without motion to avoid detection.

2. Katon (using fire)

   A. Hitsuke: At the enemy's residence, the ninja lights a fire on the opposite side to where he will enter or search.

   B. Hidama: The ninja uses bombs or smoke screens to cover his escape and frighten the enemy.

   C. Raikadama: The ninja puts fireworks around the area of infiltration, set to go off by trip wires to warn him of enemy approach.

   D. Dokuen gakure: This is the use of poison smoke screen to cover a retreat.

3. Doton (using ground, walls and stone for hiding)

   A. Imori gakure: The ninja clings to walls, stones, and other objects like a newt to blend with background.

   B. Kagashi gakure: The ninja stands in a field like a scarecrow to avoid detection.

   C. Uzura gakure: In the darkness the ninja rolls his body into a ball giving the appearance of a stone and remains motionless on the landscape.

4. Katon (using metal objects for distraction)

   A. Kama gakure: Throwing metal objects for distraction.

   B. Do gakure: Throwing copper coins to injure and distract pursuers.

5. Suiton (water escapes)

   A. Kame gakure: Breathing underwater through special instruments while remaining motionless.

   B. Ukigusa gakure: Preparation for escape by throwing a large quantity of duckweed on the surface of water so that on escape it is possible to hide among its leaves and stalks and move with the floating mass to safety.

Gotto no kamae: Specific opening for Manri ki gusari

Gun: force

Gunsen: An iron war fan

H

Hakike: Nausea

Hamidashi: Tanto with _ hand guard

Hanashimasu: speak

Han: half

Han-bo: 3' staff or stick, han meaning half, and bo meaning staff. This weapon is used prolifically in modern ninjutsu training.

Hanzo Hattori: Clan chief of the Iga ninja in feudal Japan. Was responsible for the early founding of the Japanese secret service.

Happo no kuzushi: Forms of off balancing

Hara: inner strength

Haragei: A martial artist's sixth sense

Haretsu- dama no: Flash bomb

Haretsu- dama no kemuri: Smoke bomb

Hashi: Chopstick

Hassaku-bo: Wooden spear

Hatsumi: Dr. Masaaki Hatsumi, the present leader and 34th grandmaster of the Tokagure ninja.

Hayai: fast

Heiho: Study of military strategy; one of the training skills a ninja had to master.

Hia: Yes

Hidama: the ninja uses bombs or smoke screens to cover his escape and frighten the enemy. Also see **Goton-no-jutsu**

Hidari-yoko-erj: Left side collar of the Judo gi.

Hiji: Secret

Hito washi: Ninja glider

Hitsuke: At the enemy's residence, the ninja lights a fire on the opposite side to where he will enter or search. See also **Goton-no-jutsu**

Hiza geti: Jumping knee kick

Hombu: Headquarters. This term can be used to define any headquarters for a martial arts school. It is the head or main training place of a martial arts system.

Ho Jutsu: Firearms

Hoko: Oldest Japanese spear

Hon: Basic

Hotai: Bandage

I

Iai: The art of sword drawing

Ichi: one, using the voice to influence the enemy's thought or action

Ichiji: 1 O'clock

Ichizoku: clan

Ido Gekko: transfer training

Iga: Remote area in feudal Japan where the ninja lived and trained. It is situated on the main island of Honshu.

Iia: No

Iki: Breath

Ikioi: Force/Power/Energy

Ima: now

Imori gakure: the ninja clings to walls, stones, and other objects like a newt to blend with background. Also see **Goton-no-jutsu**

Itachi: Hard blow or severe wound

Itameru: Hurt or injure

Itami: Bruise, pain or sore

Itapaku: to receive

J

Jaho: magic

Ji: Clock

Jibiki: Lexicon

Jigi: Salute

Jigo: defensive

Jikoku hyo: schedule or timetable

Jinja: Shrine

Jisen: actual competition

Jitsu: Fullness in breathing

Jonin: Ninja leader who negotiated with the feudal lords over ninja missions and fees exacted.

Ju: gentle or giving way

Jui: Small short sword used like a utility knife

Jugyo: Lesson

Juka: Part of body just under ear

Juku: Elite private study group

Junbi: Preparation

Jutsu: Technique of, art of, or state of

Jutte: Two pronged sai

K

Ka: Ninja fire posture.

Kafu: Tradition

Kagashi gakure: the ninja stands in a field like a scarecrow to avoid detection. Also see **Goton-no-jutsu**

Kagemusha: Person who pull strings or exerts influence behind the scenes

Kageru-kagi: Grappling hook

Kaginawa: Ninja weapon consisting of a rope with a huge hook on the end for scaling walls and also for entangling a sword wielding enemy.

Kaitoh: Ulcers

Kaiwa: conversation

Kakude: Spiked finger ring

Kakuma'u: to protect

Kakushibuki: Secret weapon

Kakusu: Conceal/to hide

Kama: narrow bladed staff

Kama gakure: throwing metal objects for distraction. Also see **Goton-no-jutsu**

Kamar: General term for a fighting posture

Kama-yari: Spear with sickle-shaped blade

Kame gakure: breathing underwater through special instruments while remaining motionless. Also see **Goton-no-jutsu**

Kameikada: One-man raft used by the ninja for crossing water

Kamen: Mask

Kamiza: A sitting place of honor in dojo

Kan-aku-na-ninjutsu: Evil Ninjutsu

Kani: Grab

Kanrei: Deputy General

Kanryodo: Martial art's purely of mind

Kan-shu: A pail into which to thrust

Kantokusha: Male commander of kunoichi (female ninja)

Kanzashi: Long bladed hairpins

Karen Da: Calendar

Karma: ones destiny

Kata: Form

Katana: Samurai Sword

Katon: using fire for escape & using metal objects for distraction
See also **Goton-no-jutsu**

Katteguchi: Side entrance

Kayobi: Tuesday

Kazoku: family

Keibo: staff the length of a small sword

Keiko: practice or swordplay

Keikogi: Jacket worn in kendo

Keiko-naginata: Bamboo practice spear

Kekko: Fine

Keri: Block

Keru: Kick

Ki: Inner energy

Kiai: spirit yell

Ki masu: come

Kinyobi: Friday

Kire: Block

Kiyosute: attention

Ko ashi: little step

Kobo: Wooden shabo

Kobujutsu: finger weapons

Kobushi: War fist

Kodachi: 30"-60" Sword

Koga: Province in Japan that supported many ninja clans.

Kogatana: knife fitted into one side of sword

Koho ukemi: back falls

Koitsu: "you rat"

Komi: pull

Koni: Friendly

Konigun: friendly force

Konsaibo: hard wood staff reinforced

Koppo: Bone- breaking techniques of ninjutsu.

Kozuka: Throwing knife

Kugi: Spike

Kuji-kiri: Mystical finger-knitting patterns of the ninja. Kuji means the number nine. The ninja used this method to channel energy to conjure up their intrinsic powers. Also known as kuji-in.

Kumi kata: forms of gripping

Kumitachi: kata

Kunoichi: Female ninja agent

Kusa gakure: being traced and facing capture, the ninja hides behind bushes or in tall grass. See also **Goton-no-jutsu**

Kusaritundo: Short weighted chain - a ninja ensnarement weapon.

Kusarigama: Chain and sickle weapon of the ninja.

Kuwai-ken: Dirk

Kuzure: modified

Kyoketsu shoge: Early ninja weapon consisting of a length of cord with a metal ring attached to one end and a pointed implement such as a knife attached to the other.

Kyukyu bako: First aid kit

M

Magari-yari: three-pronged spear

Makiwara: Striking post

Mamba: Type of throwing knife

Manji: Double ended sai

Manriki: weighted chain

Manriki-gusairi: weighted chain with handles

Mata: Thigh

Matte: wait

Mawasu: To rotate/ role/ turn

Me gusuri: Eye drops

Meibo: Roster or class roll

Mei-hwa-chuang: Series plum stumps

Meirei: order or command

Mempo: Facemask shaped like a demon.

Men: Facemask used in kendo

Metsubushi: Blinding powder

Mikkyo: Secret doctrines of Shegendo Buddhism. These teachings are said to have originated in Tibet.

Mini goitai: Ear ache

Mit'subushi: Caltrops

Mitsu-dogo: Three classical weapons used in unison for restraining a samurai swordsman

Mizugumo: wooden float

Mokuton: using trees and grasses for escape in **Goton-no-jutsu**

Mokuyobi: Thursday

Momochi: Sandayu Momochi, ninja clan leader and teacher of Goemon Ishikawa, the famous bandit hero of Japan

Mook jong: wooden dummy

Mundansha: holder of any rank below black

Mune-ate: chest protector used in kendo

Mutodori: Empty hand sword defense.

N

Nagamono: Staff the length of a long sword.

Nage: throw

Nage-gama: Javelin with a short sickle-like

Nagemaki: Type of long sword

Naginata: Spear-like weapon with a curved blade. First used by infantrymen on the battlefield and later favored in a shortened staff version by the wives of the samurai warriors.

Nakae: Shaft of a Japanese spear

Nichiyobi: Sunday

Niku: meat

Nin: Duty, responsibility, task, office, and post

-Nin: people, suffix

Ninja: Collective term for the three levels of genin, chunin, and jonin. Also known As shinobi. One who practices the art of ninjutsu.

Ninja-to: Ninja sword

Ninjutsu: study of nature

Ninpo: inner circle of ninjutsu group officers.

Ninshokuda: Candles on iron spiked holders

Nio Bodisattvas: Statues of karate stances

Nodachi: Extra sword

Nuki ashi: stealthy steps

Nun-chaku: nun-chucks

O

Obi: belt

Oda: Order

Oda Nobunaga: Japanese shogun who was the avowed enemy of all ninja. His troops lost the battle of Tensho Iga no Ran in 1579 against the massed ninja clans.

Ogi: a folding fan

Okuri: To slide

Okuri ashi harai: Sliding foot sweep

Omae: the "you" meaning men

Omi-gari: Japanese spear

Omyodo: Ancient science thought to be of Chinese origin, which includes the arts of divination and astrology.

Onaka gaitai: Stomach ache

Onibi gakure: this refers to the wearing a mask to frighten an enemy while blowing from a tube.

Ono: Axe

Onshinjutsu: Ninja art of invisibility.

Osoi: slow

Otera: temple

Otoshi: Drop

R

Raikadama: the ninja puts fireworks around the area of infiltration, set to go off by trip wires to warn him of enemy approach. Also see **Goton-no-jutsu**

Randori: free practice

Rei-suru: bow

Referii: referee

Reime: Bow

Renraku waza: Combination techniques

Ripopa: excellent

Ritsurei: standing bow

Rokushaku-bo: 6’ Staff

Ruki-barior fukumibai: Spitting needles

Ryu: Japanese for school of style.

S

Sai: Three-pronged sword

Saija: knowing one

Saiminjutsu: Ninja’s art of hypnotism.

Samurai: “One who serves” The knightly warriors of feudal Japan. Second Dan of Konigun Ninjutsu

San-setsu-kon: Three sectional staff

Saodrake: Bamboo pole

Sasae tsuri komi ashi: feet stop throw

Sasumaata: Japanese with forked head

Saya: Scabbard of the Japanese sword

Seiken: forefist

Seki gyu deru: cough

Seiten: fair

Sen-jutsu : The study of tactic and stragety

Senpo: one's destination

Senpuku: Concealment

Sensei: Teacher

Seoi gatame: shoulder hold

Seoi nage: shoulder throw

Shabo: 9" to 13" Rod

Shadows of Iga: Ninja appreciation and training society founded by American ninja practitioner Stephen Hayes.

Shaken: Throwing stars

Shiai: tournament or contest of skill

Shidai: order of things

Shido: Guidance or leader

Shigo: After death

Shiho: corners

Shikomi: Training

Shikomi-zue: Special sword

Shime ashi: Tight step

Shimiru: Penetration

Shimpan: referee

Shinai: Bamboo sword

Shinbo: 9" to 13" blade with finger ring

Shinobi: Original name and training by which the ninja were known.

Shinobishozuki: Ninja uniform. The ninja outfit was usually reversible and had many concealed pockets.

Shinobi-zue: Ninja staff that held a length of a chain inside with a heavy weighted end.

Shinobu Shozoku: Ninja uniform. Usually reversible with many concealed pockets.

Shino mahi: Heart attack

Shintai: body movement

Shinto: Indigenous animistic religion of Japan. The word means "divine spirit way".

Shisei: posture

Shiriken: Throwing blade

Shiro: Castle or Fortress

Shizen: natural

Shizen hontai: natural posture

Shoge: hook knife on chain

Shogun: Japanese military dictator

Shoto: Samurai sword

Shuko: Metal band that slipped over the hand, concealing four sharp spikes on the palm side. They were used in pairs for scaling castle walls and other difficult heights. Used as a defense and attack weapon against the sword, the metal spikes would rake the face of an attacker.

Shumatsu undo: cool off exercise

Shuriken: Multi-pointed throwing stars used as weapon by ninja agents. These stars, which came in all sizes, often had the ends tipped in poison. They were carried concealed in a ninja's uniform. Also known as shaken

Soa: 7'-8' Staff

Sode: uniform sleeve

Sodegarami: Japanese spear with barbed hooks

Sogo-budo: total martial arts

Sojutsu: Ninja spear art.

Son-go: Honorary title

Sono mama: don't move

Suburi: over head strike

Suiton: water escapes. Also see **Goton-no-jutsu**

Suiyobi: Wednesday

Sun Tsu: Chinese military genius who wrote a treatise on warfare called "The Art of War". The ninja clans are said to have arisen from the teaching of this book. Even today it is widely read.

Suri ashi: Rub step

Su-yari: Japanese spear classified under straight spear category

T

Tabi: Ninja boot

Tadashi: Correct

Tai: Body

Taijutsu: Grappling or body part of ninjutsu. All ninjutsu practiced today consists of 90 per cent taijutsu and is the mainstay of the style.

Tai otoshi: Body drop

Tai sabaki: Pivot

Taiya: Tire

Tanto: Short straight blade sword

Tanshiki: Striking post in the ground with

Tanuki gakure: The ninja climbs a tree and blends with limbs and foliage without motion to avoid detection. See also **Goton-no-jutsu**

Tatakau: Fight

Tatami: Straw mat

Tekagi: Similar the shuko but only worn on legs. Used in pairs this instrument was useful as an aid for climbing walls, trees, etc.

Tekken: walking knuckle-duster

Teko: Japanese knuckle-duster

Teppo: Gun

Tetsubishi: See **Caltrops**.

Tetsubo: Iron staff

Tobu ashi: Flying step

Tofu: Soft beancurd made from soybeans. Standard ration for the field ninja when out on a mission.

Tokoro-gaki: Directory

Tokugawa Ieyasu: Founder of the Tokugawa shogunate in 1603. His family ruled Japan for 250 years.

Tonfa: "P-34"

Tonki: Small metal throwing weapons

Tonyoboy: Diabetes

Tori: Attacker

Torii: Martial arts or Shinto gate

Torinoko: Firecrackers shaped like eggs

Toya: Wooden staff

Tsubami gaeshi: Swallow flight counter

Tsubute: Sharp metal disk or flat stone

Tsugi ashi: Sliding foot walking

Tsuka: Handle of the samurai sword

Tsukaito: Decorative binding around

Tsuki: Punch (karate)

Tsukubo: Japanese spear with a crossed

Tsukushi-boko: Large bronze spearhead

Tsuri: Lift

Tsuri komi goshi: Lifting pulling hip throw

U

Uchi mata: Inner thigh throw

Uchiotosu: To strike down/ knock down

Uchikomu: To drive in

Uchiwa: Private or inner circle.

Ugoki: Motion/ movement

Uke: defender

Ukemi: Falling methods

Uki: to float

Ukidaru: Water crossing device

Ukigusa gakure: preparation for escape by throwing a large quantity of duckweed on the surface of water so that on escape it is possible to hide among its leaves and stalks and move with the floating mass to safety.

Ura-ken: Back fist

Uwagi: Jacket

Uzura gakure: in the darkness the ninja rolls his body into a ball giving the appearance of a stone and remains motionless on the landscape. Also see **Goton-no-jutsu**

W

Wakarimasu: Repeat

Waza-no-kankyu: The tempo of the technique

Wazikashi: Short sword 16" to 20" long

Y

Ya: Arrow

Yamabushi: Mountain warrior hermit priests

Yari: Spear of the Japanese foot soldier

Yoko Aruki: Special ninja method of walking for stealth. The word means 'sideways walking.

Yoko shiho gatame: Side hold

Yubi: Grace

Yubi-bo: 8"-10" Bo

Yudansha: Holder of any black sash rank

Yugake: Shooting glove

Yumi: Japanese Bow

Z

Zarei: Kneeling bow

Zenkusu: Dachi forward leaning stance

Zempo kaiten ukemi: Font rolling falls

Zempo ukemi: Forward falls

Zensoku: Asthma

Zori: Judo slippers

Zubon: Judo trousers

This book is written by Shidoshi Bryce Dallas, who has dedicated his entire live to the study of Konigun Ninjutsu. Shidoshi Bryce Dallas brought Konigun Ninjutsu to the United States after receiving his mastership in 1985 from Shidoshi Saija. The techniques contained within this book are the set criteria for obtaining titles and ranks within Konigun Ninjutsu. Please do not attempt to perform these techniques or teach these techniques without the proper instruction from a licensed instructor.